# A PROSPEROUS PEOPLE:
# THE GROWTH
# OF THE
# AMERICAN ECONOMY

# A PROSPEROUS PEOPLE: THE GROWTH OF THE AMERICAN ECONOMY

**EDWIN J. PERKINS**
*University of Southern California*

**GARY M. WALTON**
*University of California, Davis*

Prentice-Hall, Inc., Englewood Cliffs, New Jersey 07632

*Library of Congress Cataloging in Publication Data*

Perkins, Edwin J.
   A prosperous people.

   Includes index.
   1. United States—Economic conditions. I. Walton,
Gary M.   II. Title.
HC103.P42    1984      330.973      84-23719
ISBN 0-13-731399-3

Printed in the United States of America

10  9  8  7  6  5  4  3  2  1

Editorial/production supervision and
   interior design: Virginia Cavanagh Neri
Cover design: Lundgren Graphics, Ltd.
Manufacturing buyer: Barbara Kelly Kittle

ISBN 0-13-731399-3    01

Prentice-Hall International, Inc., *London*
Prentice-Hall of Australia Pty. Limited, *Sydney*
Editora Prentice-Hall do Brasil, Ltda., *Rio de Janeiro*
Prentice-Hall Canada Inc., *Toronto*
Prentice-Hall Hispanoamericana, S.A., *Mexico*
Prentice-Hall of India Private Limited, *New Delhi*
Prentice-Hall of Japan, Inc., *Tokyo*
Prentice-Hall of Southeast Asia Pte. Ltd., *Singapore*
Whitehall Books Limited, *Wellington, New Zealand*

For Braxton, Julie, and Lloyd

E.J.P.

For Linda, Surrey, Devon, Rhodes, Heath, and Ashley

G.M.W.

# CONTENTS

# TWENTY

# TWENTY-ONE

# PREFACE

We titled this book *A Prosperous People* because we believe this statement represents an accurate description of the economic accomplishments and general well-being of the citizens of the United States. Several decades ago the historian David Potter studied the effect of abundance on the United States national character and entitled his book, *People of Plenty*. Our effort is in that same spirit.

We do not claim that the record of our republican, capitalist society has been perfect. It has had its flaws and some are still among us. The existence of slavery over a period of two centuries remains the most serious blot. Racism before and after slavery is another. So too are sexism and other forms of deep-seated prejudice against individuals. In addition, there were major wars such as the Civil War plus recessions and depressions that brought deprivation, dislocation, and ruin to millions of American families. Not every group or individual has had equal opportunity to participate in our economic system and to use his or her talents to their fullest potential. The free market has not always been open to every person who wished to enter it on whatever level.

Yet despite its blemishes, the United States economy has still outperformed every other national economy in the world by several standards of measurement. Following are some important factors that have reinforced our generally positive assessment:

1. The ownership of farmland and individual homes has been more widespread among private citizens, and for a longer period of time, than in any other society in any previous historical era. The opportunity to acquire fertile land relatively cheaply (or even free) was the primary factor leading to the migration of thousands of Europeans to the thirteen colonies in the seventeenth and eighteenth centuries.

2. By the mid-eighteenth century, and earlier in some regions, white income per capita—or living standards—were near to, or higher than, any other country in Europe or anywhere around the globe.

3. American living standards have risen steadily for over three hundred and fifty years, and in 1980 were roughly ten times greater than in the colonial era. It has only been in the last quarter of the twentieth century that the United States relinquished its leadership position in income per capita to a few European nations (Sweden, Switzerland) and some small states in the oil-rich Middle East (United Emirates, Kuwait).

4. Since the 1850s, when the United States bypassed Britain and China, the nation's output of goods and services has remained the largest in the world. Throughout the twentieth century, this nation alone has accounted for over one-quarter of gross world product. In the mid-1980s the United States economy was twice as large as the economies of its major rivals, the Soviet Union and Japan.

5. No other nation has had a more productive agricultural sector than the United States. American diets have met minimum nutritional standards for over three centuries. Moreover, this high output of foodstuffs occurred despite the shift in farm employment from 85 percent of the total workforce in the colonial era to a mere 3 percent in the 1980s. Since the last quarter of the nineteenth century, the United States has consistently been the largest exporter of food in the international market. The cost of food as a percentage of American personal income at 15 to 17 percent was the lowest in the capitalist world in the 1980s.

6. Since its settlement this nation has always had high energy consumption relative to other nations. For the first two hundred and fifty years, large timber lands were the major energy resource; thereafter, coal fueled much of the nation's industrialization. In the twentieth century, petroleum and natural gas became widely available at low prices. American homes are warmly heated in the winter and cooled in the summer, and they are filled with a myriad of electrical appliances. The ownership of automobiles and the consumption of gasoline has been the highest in the world for decades. In 1975 total energy usage per capita was over twice the rate for any other nation.

7. The United States has been a leader in the adoption of new technology in manufacturing. In the early twentieth century United States firms set the pace in steel and automobiles. After World War II, the nation became a pioneer in aerospace, computers, and other "high-tech" fields.

8. Despite a long history of discrimination, the United States now has more women in lower and middle management positions than any other society. Even during the colonial era, it was generally easier for women to own and manage property than elsewhere. The rise of the service sector and greater access to higher education in the twentieth century have contributed greatly to the increased power of women within the corporate world. In most of the nation's leading MBA programs, women comprised at least one-quarter of

the student body in the early 1980s and their numbers were continuing to climb. Minorities of both sexes were also receiving more professional and technical training.

9.  United States business firms have been in the forefront of making direct investments in other countries. These multinational firms were involved in a range of activities including agriculture, mining, oil exploration, manufacturing, and banking. By the early 1980s American direct investments overseas totalled over $200 billion compared to about one-half that amount for foreign investments in the United States.

How these accomplishments were achieved is revealed in the following twenty-one chapters.

We have tested much of this material in university classrooms, and it has received an enthusiastic response from students. We hope others will find this book equally stimulating. Meanwhile, we encourage readers to write to us in the event that they discover any errors of fact or interpretation in these pages, and we are always open to suggestions for improvement. Finally, we thank Sharon Mather and Martha Rothermel for expert typing of the text.

# A PROSPEROUS PEOPLE: THE GROWTH OF THE AMERICAN ECONOMY

# CHAPTER ONE
# INTRODUCTION
# TO EARLY AMERICA

## MOTIVATION FOR EUROPEAN EXPANSION

Beginning with the arrival of Christopher Columbus in the New World in 1492 and accelerating over the next two centuries, Europeans steadily penetrated the Western Hemisphere. The main motive for European expansion into this region was the prospect of enhanced wealth for both nations and individuals. For nations and their political leaders, the prevailing system of thought guiding economic policy was mercantilism, which placed great emphasis on increasing the volume of *specie* (gold and silver) flowing into a country. In an era without organized banks, checking accounts, or paper currency, specie was the major component of the money supply. Nations measured the success or failure of economic policies largely on the basis of whether they promoted an inflow or outflow of precious metals. Huge stocks of specie were viewed as a clear sign of a successful economy. Today, it is worth noting, we have a different and more sophisticated approach to measuring a nation's economic strength; now we determine success on the basis of the volume of goods and services produced by a nation's citizens, or its gross national product (GNP), not the size of money stocks. But five hundred years ago, increasing the inflow of gold and silver was the primary economic goal of European leaders.

Colonies in the New World aided in the accumulation of specie in two ways. In the most direct manner, gold and silver were simply obtained from the native

American inhabitants and shipped back to Europe. Precious metals were either seized under the threat of military force or gained in exchange for goods of comparably small value in Europe, such as mirrors, hardware items, and various novelties. Often the European conquerors enslaved natives to mine more gold and silver for transport across the Atlantic. During the first century of discovery and exploration, the Spanish pursued this strategy with greater success than other nations.

A second, indirect method of stimulating an inflow of specie was through the achievement of a favorable balance of trade with rival European states. This outcome was accomplished when exports, or overseas sales, exceeded imports, and the balance due in payment was collected in gold or silver. The American colonies were potentially very useful in promoting a favorable trade balance for their mother country. Certain agricultural products such as sugar and tobacco were highly valued by European consumers, yet they could be grown easily and relatively inexpensively in the Western Hemisphere. By gaining access to large quantities of these American crops and then selling them to buyers in other countries, one European country could accumulate precious metals by draining them from its rivals. Indeed, mercantilist policies were designed to promote a favorable balance of trade because they had the dual advantage of strengthening the economy of one nation while simultaneously weakening the economies of its trading partners—or so policy makers in the sixteenth century believed. In the long run, it was the agricultural output of the colonies and the sale of staple products on international markets that made them such valuable assets in the overseas empires of the European powers, especially England.

## MOTIVATION FOR EARLY IMMIGRATION

Individual Europeans also crossed the Atlantic in search of wealth. In the sixteenth century, Spanish adventurers came with the hope of extracting gold and silver from native Americans and thus obtaining sudden riches with little effort. But by the seventeenth century, most were immigrants with the more modest goal of acquiring their own farmland and becoming independent citizens. The vast majority of English settlers in North America were in this category. Their goals were to grow sufficient foodstuffs to provide their families with a healthful and abundant diet and to produce an agricultural surplus for sale in the marketplace. Owning a sizable farm and possibly one day a vast estate was the aspiration of most of the immigrants who arrived in the territories that later formed the United States.

Land was the primary source of wealth and income in all preindustrial societies, and agriculture was the main occupation of people everywhere around the globe. In England and other parts of Europe, the bulk of the land was held by a small group of aristocrats who collected rents, in money or produce, from a multitude of tenant farmers. Social and economic mobility was severely limited, since opportunities for the typical landless farmer to move up into the property-owning class were negligible. Immigration to the Western Hemisphere, which was inhabited by a native population without a tradition of legally documented land ownership, promised a wonderful opportunity for enterprising Englishmen to seize land for themselves and improve quickly their standard of living and status in society. Land-less tenants could obtain farms cheaply, or even free, while others who had already accumulated some property in England aspired to becoming rich men in the New World. For the daring and adventuresome who were willing to risk the dangers of an overseas voyage of two to three months and the uncertainties of making a fresh start in an unfamiliar environment, the North American continent was a region with greater opportunities for advancement in the economic and social order than tradi-tion-bound and class-rigid England.

Beginning early in the seventeenth century, thousands of English men and women voluntarily met the challenge of starting a new life in a distant territory where farmland was readily available. Despite fluctuations from decade to decade, migration from Great Britain, and later continental Europe, continued for over 150 years—up until the War of Independence in the 1770s. After 1670 the white popu-lation was augmented by the involuntary arrival of thousands of enslaved Africans forcibly transported to the colonies. Following a brief period of acclimation and the emergence of a fairly even sex ratio between men and women, natural popula-tion growth was very rapid for both races.

## POPULATION GROWTH

Although improvements in the productivity of farmers and other workers contrib-uted to the development of the economy during the colonial era, the rapid rate of population growth was the critical factor in propelling the economy forward. Be-tween 1650 and 1775 the colonial economy grew at a rate of around 3.5 percent annually and doubled in size every twenty years or so. The population became fifty times larger during this 125 year period, while the productivity of individual workers rose about 50 percent. New additions to the labor force produced more foodstuffs, more tobacco, more handicrafts, more ships, and more goods and ser-vices in general.

Population grew steadily but in spurts during the first half of the seventeenth century. In 1650, around 50,000 English settlers were located in coastal regions. By the end of the century, population had risen above 250,000, but settlement still had not moved very far inland and went no farther south than Virginia. During the eighteenth century, population growth was spectacular and the colonies passed the one million mark around 1740. The number of free citizens and slaves had climbed to over 2.5 million in 1775, with 80 percent of European background and 20 per-cent black.

Population expanded as a result of two factors—immigration and natural in-crease. New arrivals made the largest impact during the seventeenth century when the population base was still small. English adventurers arrived in Virginia as early as 1607, but the pace of migration was erratic until the 1620s, when the emergence of tobacco as a valuable crop for export drew a new round of permanent settlers. For the next half century, the Chesapeake colonies of Virginia and Maryland attracted a steady flow of English immigrants. Over one half arrived as indentured servants, a form of quasi slavery which enabled people to pay for their passage across the ocean by selling voluntarily a claim on their labor services for a period normally ranging from four to seven years. Following the shift from white servitude to black slavery in the Chesapeake, Africans were brought to the colonies in large numbers during the first half of the eighteenth century.

From ten to fifteen thousand Puritans sailed to Massachusetts in the 1630s and early 1640s. They came in part to escape religious persecution and in part to pursue economic goals. The Puritans arrived largely in family units, and over the ensuing decades their descendants populated the adjoining colonies in the region. The New England colonies were different in this respect: immigration played a very small role in their demography after the middle of the seventeenth century.

In the first half of the eighteenth century, a substantial number of immigrants settled in the middle and southern colonies. Many came from locations other than England. Scotch, Irish, and Germans in numbers up to 200,000 poured into the colonies after 1700. The Germans concentrated in Pennsylvania, and they eventually accounted for about one third of the population in the colony. A fair percentage of the arrivals from the continent came as redemptioners. They had sufficient funds to pay for a portion of the transportation costs to the colonies and went into temporary servitude, often in entire family units, to pay off the balance due to shippers. Scotch and Irish settlers moved not only into the middle colonies but also into unpopulated areas of the south—the Shenandoah Valley in western Virginia, the two Carolinas, and later Georgia.

## NATURAL GROWTH OF POPULATION

Despite the continued role of immigration in stimulating population growth, by the end of the colonial era the vast majority of Americans, black and white, were native born. Natural increase was the primary force fueling the population boom in the eighteenth century. Birth rates were very high for both races—very near the biological maximum for the human species. For every one thousand women, between 45 and 50 births occurred every year in the colonies, compared to only 35 births annually in Europe. In addition, infant mortality rates were lower in the colonies, which meant that more children reached puberty. Fewer babies died in their first year of life, because their mothers, who breast-fed them, consumed more varied and healthful diets and because both mothers and infants lived in houses more warmly heated in the colder months since wood fuel was more readily available and less expensive than in Europe.

A unique blend of economic factors—a scarcity of labor combined with the availability of cheap land—encouraged a fast pace of household formation. The typical colonial couple married when the man was 24 and the woman was 21, or several years younger than couples in Europe. Earlier marriages produced more children per household. The typical European marriage yielded 4 to 5 children, but colonial marriages normally produced 7 children, and a higher percentage lived to adulthood. Few colonial couples made any effort to practice contraception or limit fertility in any way, because in a land with so many opportunities for economic advancement and plentiful food, children were rarely considered potential burdens on their parents.

Not only was the infant mortality rate low, but the general death rate for adults was substantially below the figure for Europe. Whereas 35 to 40 persons per thousand died in Europe each year, only 20 to 25 died in the colonies. The population was scattered widely throughout the countryside so that plagues and other infectious diseases were prevented from spreading rapidly, as happened so often in Europe. Although there were local outbreaks of disease, the colonial population as a whole was never subjected to a devastating epidemic. Famine was likewise not a serious threat, for the production and consumption of foodstuffs was among the highest per capita around the globe. Nutritious diets led to a healthier and long-lived populace. Once past adolescence, males typically lived beyond 60, while the average for women was lower because of the constant threat of death during and immediately after childbirth.

The very rapid increase in population was the predictable outcome of a high birth rate and a low death rate. Since economic resources (primarily in the form of undeveloped but fertile land) were abundant, the increase in population did not lead to any general decrease in personal incomes. In most other societies around the world, where access to new farmland was more restricted, quickened population growth usually translated into poorer diets and lower living standards. In the colonies, in contrast, new mouths to feed put little pressure on the productive capacity of natural resources. Indeed, living standards climbed slowly but steadily despite a population boom. This achievement was unprecedented in the economic history of humanity.

## ECONOMIC ADVANCEMENT

Even after a century of steady development, colonial output in 1700 was still trifling in comparison with England. By 1775, however, conditions had changed drastically. On the eve of the American War of Independence, aggregate output was approximately $2.5 billion (in 1982 prices). The American economy was nearly 40 percent as large as England's and the gap was closing at an accelerating pace. In the first seventy-five years of the eighteenth century, the colonial economy had been growing at a faster rate than any other contemporary society, and that growth continued after the war. Within seventy-five years of the drafting of the Declaration of Independence, the new United States had passed Great Britain and populous China to become the country with the largest gross national product in the world.

## SELECTED REFERENCES

ANDERSON, TERRY, and ROBERT PAUL THOMAS. "The Growth of Population and Labor Force in the 17th-Century Chesapeake," *Explorations in Economic History* (1978), 290–312.
_____. White Population, Labor Force, and Extensive Growth of the New England Economy in the Seventeenth Century," *Journal of Economic History* (1973), 634–667.
CURTIN, PHILIP. *The Atlantic Slave Trade: A Census.* Madison: University of Wisconsin Press, 1969.
FRANKLIN, BENJAMIN. "Observations Concerning the Increase of Mankind." Philadelphia, 1751.
KULIKOFF, ALLAN. "A 'Prolifick' People: Black Population Growth in the Chesapeake Colonies, 1700–1790," *Southern Studies* (1977), 391–428.
NASH, GARY. *Red, White, and Black: The Peoples of Early America.* Englewood Cliffs, N.J.: Prentice-Hall, 1974.
SMITH, DANIEL SCOTT. "The Demographic History of Colonial New England," *Journal of Economic History* (1972), 165–183.
_____. "The Estimates of Early American Historical Demographers: Two Steps Forward, One Step Back, What Steps in the Future," *Historical Methods* (1979), 24–38.
WELLS, ROBERT V. *The Population of the British Colonies in America before 1776: A Survey of Census Data.* Princeton: Princeton University Press, 1975.

# CHAPTER TWO
# EARLY AGRICULTURE
# AND FARM WORKERS

Agriculture accounted for over 80 percent of colonial economic output. Today that percentage is under 3 percent, which points out how dramatically our economy has changed over the last two hundred years. With the application of new technology and increased capital, modern farmers are more than twenty-five times more productive than their colonial forefathers. In terms of soil and climate, American farmland has always been among the most productive in the world. In the colonial era farmers easily grew enough food to provide their families with a generous diet, and in addition they frequently had a surplus of foodstuffs, tobacco, or indigo (dye) for overseas export. They used the earnings from foreign trade to import tropical products, mainly sugar, from the Caribbean and finished goods, primarily textiles and hardware, from England. This pattern of exporting surplus agricultural output has persisted over the centuries and explains, in part, the growth and success of the American economy. At present, the United States is one of a very few nations regularly exporting food, and it is normally the source of over one-half of all agricultural goods entering the international market.

## FARM OWNERSHIP AND SIZE

Most colonial farmers owned their own farms, and they reaped all the benefits of productivity and subsequent appreciation in market value. In North America, farmers have always been not merely cultivators of the soil, but small businessmen and real estate speculators as well. The distribution of property among white colonists was much wider than in Europe and other heavily populated areas. As a result, property-holding qualifications failed to eliminate most white males from participation in political activities, including voting for local and provincial offices. In other societies, a very small minority of rich landowners exercised a monopoly on political power, with their tenant farmers excluded. The American colonies, in contrast, were a territory of economic independence and genuine citizenship for white inhabitants.

Farms in the colonies were generally much larger than elsewhere. Whereas in Europe most cultivators tilled plots of less than twenty acres, colonial farmers typically owned around 100 acres. About one-third of the farm was planted in crops, with the remainder in pasture and forest. Over the years farmers rotated their pattern of land usage in order to maintain soil fertility. The clearing of forests provided an inexpensive source of wood energy for heating and cooking, while the existence of pasturage enabled farmers to keep a fair number of cows and other livestock. Farm work was performed by the male head-of-household, his wife, and their children, with the assistance of servants and slaves in some regions. The occupational skills of men and women, adults and children, and members of the black and white races were less differentiated in this earlier era, when over four fifths of the total population engaged in agriculture.

## AGRICULTURAL PRODUCTION

The main activities of farmers in all climates were growing foodstuffs and maintaining livestock. At least one half of the harvest was consumed by the farmer and his immediate family, plus any servants and slaves held in bondage. A substantial portion of excess grain was fed to livestock to increase their numbers and fatten them for human consumption. The colonists consumed an extraordinarily varied and healthful diet, including up to 200 pounds of meat per person annually—about the same quantity eaten by Americans today. One piece of evidence indicating the high nutritional value of colonial diets was the recent discovery that the population had already reached modern stature in terms of average height. Americans were taller by several inches than the English, which testifies to the large amount of protein, minerals, vitamins, and calories in their diet.

Corn, wheat, and rye were the main food crops. Even in the Chesapeake colonies, more land was planted in grain than in tobacco. Southern farms and plantations were normally self-sufficient in food, with increasing amounts available for export over the course of the eighteenth century. Corn was a mainstay in colonial diets, particularly in New England and the South. An indigenous crop widely cultivated by Indian tribes, corn was a reliable food source because it thrived in a variety of soils and climates and was resistant to disease and insects. One farm worker was capable of caring for six to eight acres, which yielded sufficient corn to feed five to seven persons annually. The North American continent is ideally suited to corn production, and it has remained the country's largest food crop (accounting for over 40 percent of world output in 1980), although most corn now enters the food chain indirectly through livestock consumption.

In the middle colonies farmers concentrated on wheat. This grain was the major source of food in the home and also the region's principal export. Wheat had a shorter harvest season than corn, because once the grain began to ripen, the farmer and his family had to work quickly to avoid spoilage in the field. Indeed, farmers in the colonies could usually grow more wheat than they could harvest by hand. Huge increases in the productivity of wheat farming came later in the nineteenth century with the introduction of harvesting machinery pulled by horses.

Rye was an important crop in New England. In the seventeenth century farmers in this region had favored wheat but frequent outbreaks of disease discouraged its planting. As a substitute, farmers shifted to rye, which was a hardy plant but less tasty to most palates. Nutritionally an excellent replacement for wheat, rye was a poor economic substitute because overseas demand was limited.

Most farms maintained several varieties of livestock. Hogs were more common than cattle because, without refrigeration, pork was more safely preserved by salting and smoking than beef. Hogs were also more efficient at converting feed grain into edible meat, since 10 pounds of grain yielded around 2.5 pounds of pork but only 1.5 pounds of beef. Cows provided milk, sheep were prized for their wool, chickens were useful for both eggs and meat, and horses pulled plows and wagons.

The production of food crops and livestock deserves special emphasis in this era because the largest component of personal income went for food. Most of the harvest was eaten on the farm and never entered the marketplace, either in local towns or abroad. Since the colonists consumed a more varied and nutritious diet than any other large population group in the eighteenth century, we can state with a fair degree of certainty that they enjoyed the highest per capita living standards anywhere on the face of the earth. In this preindustrial era, when income levels around the world were still relatively low and varied less than at present from country to country, living well generally meant eating well. Indeed, the diet of colonial Americans was vastly superior to the twentieth-century diets of at least one quarter of humanity—the one billion undernourished people now living in the poorest nations of Asia and Africa.

## AGRICULTURAL EXPORTS

In addition to the production of foodstuffs for their own consumption, the colonists also engaged in agriculture in order to raise crops for sale in overseas markets. The colonies possessed what economists call a "comparative advantage" in the production of certain agricultural goods. Put simply, this term means that it was cheaper for the colonists to specialize somewhat on growing certain valuable crops for sale in other countries and then to use the sales proceeds to import manufactured goods than it would have cost them to manufacture those same goods in the domestic market. In other words, the colonists maximized their net incomes by foregoing complete self-sufficiency and exchanging surplus crops for foreign manufactured goods. The comparative advantage of the colonies in agriculture was the primary reason that manufacturing developed at a slower pace than in England. Moreover, in the twenty-five years before the War of Independence, world prices for agricultural goods rose in relation to prices for English manufactured products, thus encouraging the colonists to devote even more of their economic resources to the development of farmland.

### Tobacco: The Leading Crop

Some of these agricultural exports were edible, and others were not. The most important crop in the second category was tobacco. The use of tobacco became increasingly common in England during the sixteenth century, although King James I condemned it as a "vile and stinking custom." Supplies were imported largely from Spanish territory, and prices were high, which had a negative impact on England's balance of trade. Thus the English were relieved when the Jamestown settlers discovered in the early 1620s that tobacco grew exceptionally well in the Virginia climate. The cultivation of this plant guaranteed the permanence of the colony and simultaneously provided a steady source of tobacco within the British empire for consumption at home and export to the European continent. As a result, the Chesapeake colonies were highly valued because they evolved in a manner consistent with mercantilist precepts. They raised a crop which did not compete with agriculture in England and one which could generate an inflow of specie from rival powers. Moreover, with the proceeds of tobacco sales, the colonists purchased English finished goods, thereby aiding the mother country's balance of trade in yet another way.

Shiploads of new immigrants sailed to Virginia in the early 1620s with the hope of reaping huge profits from tobacco cultivation. But increased supplies in Europe soon led to declining prices, and by 1630 profits had fallen significantly. Despite annual fluctuations, prices remained high enough, however, to justify a steady increase in production for the next century and a half. Chesapeake tobacco quickly captured the lion's share of the European market because of its flavor, texture, and relatively low cost. Tobacco was the most valuable American export, and it was one of the main reasons why the average (mean) wealth of whites was 50 percent greater in the southern than the northern colonies.

Tobacco was grown on both small farms and large plantations, and by family farmers, indentured servants, and slaves. The typical farmer, with only family members as a source of labor, planted around three acres in tobacco (plus ten to fifteen acres in corn, wheat, and other food crops). He produced about 2,500 pounds of saleable tobacco, and based on price levels in the eighteenth century, family income was normally increased from 10 to 25 percent. Most farms were large enough so that by moving the location of the tobacco plots every few years, the overall fertility of the land was preserved. The argument, prevalent at one time, that tobacco farming wore out the Chesapeake farmland is untrue. Some fields were temporarily exhausted, but after a fallow period they regained their productivity.

## LABOR SHORTAGES: INDENTURED SERVANTS

Because tobacco cultivation continued to return profits higher than those available in alternative activities, Chesapeake landowners sought ways of increasing output. New land was inexpensive but farm labor for hire, plentiful and cheap in England, was scarce or nonexistent in the colonies. The solution to this labor shortage was the acquisition of bonded workers. White indentured servants recruited from England were the primary source of new labor until the 1680s.

Indentured servants signed formal documents committing themselves to perform any reasonable work demanded by the owners of their contracts for a specified period of time, usually four to seven years. What induced free English men and women to enter into contractual obligations which invariably made them slaves temporarily to unknown and distant masters? The motive was economic advancement—in the long run. The lure was the opportunity to obtain free transportation to a new country where land was reportedly cheap and wages high and where upward mobility was a realistic expectation.

Most servants were young people, between the ages of 15 and 30, predominantly male, who were adventuresome and ambitious enough to sacrifice a few years of freedom for the opportunity of becoming independent farmers or artisans. They sold a claim on their labor but did not waive all civil rights. Under English law, servants who were mistreated or were the victims of contractual violations could sue their owners for redress, usually requesting a shortened term of service or larger freedom dues.

In England, prospective servants bargained with a host of merchant contractors in a competitive market atmosphere. Both parties tried to make the best possible deal. All servants received free passage to the destination of *their* choice (either the Caribbean sugar islands or the Chesapeake Bay in the seventeenth century), plus clothing, a steady diet (with meat normally specified), and an allowance of beer or spirits for males. The tough negotiations were over the length of the indenture and the amount of freedom dues, the lump sum paid to servants on the expiration of their contracts. Skilled laborers, who were in the greatest demand overseas, generally were able to bargain for the most attractive terms. All negotiations took place while the prospective servant was still in England. After the contract was signed, the merchant shipper paid for the servant's passage to the New World and all the attendant costs. When servants died enroute, the merchant absorbed the loss. Upon arrival in the Chesapeake colonies, the English entrepreneur sold the contracts of his surviving servants to the highest bidder.

The indentured servant system was a method of financing transatlantic migration in which the claim on labor services acted as a form of collateral. The operation of this market benefited all the parties involved. Servants received transportation across the ocean and a few years later enough freedom dues to acquire land on the frontier. Colonial tobacco farmers obtained the labor to expand production and increase profits. Finally, English merchant contractors were usually able to sell their indentures in the New World for sums greater than the cost of passage and incidental outlays.

## LABOR SHORTAGES: SLAVERY

Beginning in the 1670s and accelerating in the 1690s, Chesapeake planters began to substitute African slaves for indentured servants. Why? Relative prices between slaves and servant contracts dictated that decision. The cost of attracting indentures to the colonies rose for two reasons: economic conditions in the mother country improved, and potential migrants saw that opportunities for advancement overseas were less inviting than before. Together they encouraged more English servants to remain at home. Those who were still willing to emigrate insisted on better contracts—shorter terms, higher freedom dues, more meat and alcohol in their diets, and even the payment of modest wages. And because of a chronic labor shortage, they could get it.

Meanwhile, the cost of acquiring black slaves remained steady or fell. Bigger and faster sailing vessels lowered the cost of transporting human cargoes to the Western Hemisphere, in part because the death rate fell. Since their migration was involuntary, slaves had no opportunity to compare the benefits of remaining in Africa versus transferring to a new land, nor had they any chance to bargain with their captors for better conditions. They sacrificed a claim on their labor permanently, not temporarily, and it included the labor of future generations as well. Slaves lost not only their economic freedom but their civil rights as well. Slavery in the thirteen colonies was an inhuman system because it robbed its victims of their independence, their dignity, and, worst of all, their dreams of a better life for their children. (The actual living standards of slaves will be discussed in Chapter Eleven.)

The substitution of slaves for servants occurred in two stages. First, Africans were purchased to replace servants in the fields since slaves had become a cheaper source of unskilled labor. Few Africans possessed craft skills demanded by the colonists, however, and indentured servants with artisan skills or low-level supervisory experience in the mother country were still actively recruited in the early eighteenth century. Eventually, however, planters discovered that it was less costly to train native-born slaves for skilled work than to buy the short-term contracts of English servants. In 1650 all of labor on large Chesapeake tobacco plantations had been performed by whites; by 1750 blacks did almost all the skilled and unskilled work except the supervisory tasks of overseers and the entrepreneurial activities of the landowner.

## SLAVERY IN THE LOWER SOUTH

Slave labor was also used extensively in the production of two other agricultural crops grown primarily for export—rice and indigo. Rice was shipped to markets in Europe and the Caribbean, while indigo went, by law, strictly to England. A single colony, South Carolina, grew most of the rice and indigo. By the late colonial period they had emerged as the most profitable plantation crops, and whites in South Carolina on an individual basis held the largest wealth and earned the highest incomes on the mainland.

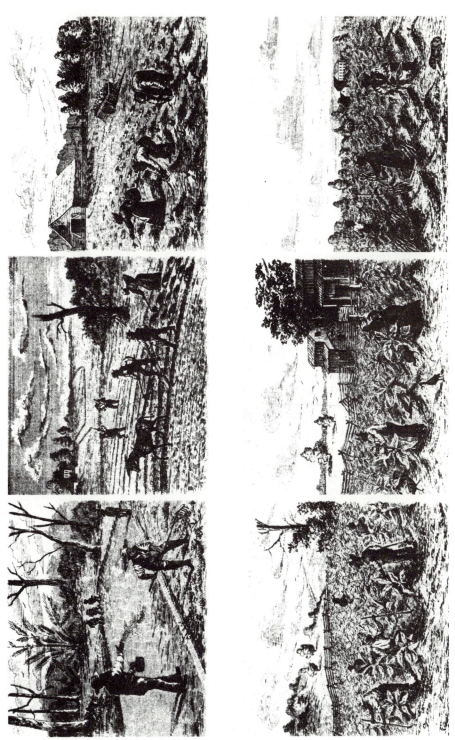

FIGURE 1  Tobacco Cultivation (Source: New York Public Library Picture Collection)

13

This colony was settled after slavery was already an established institution in the Chesapeake region. Thus, Africans were the source of new labor supplies from the outset. By the outbreak of the War of Independence, the population of South Carolina was 70 percent black, and it became the only colony where whites were a minority.

Rice was grown in lowland areas where flooding of the fields could be controlled. Many slaves from West Africa were already familiar with the techniques of rice cultivation; thus some historians suspect that many blacks were more knowledgeable than their masters about techniques of dike building, flooding, weeding, and harvesting. The so-called task system was frequently used in rice agriculture; slaves were assigned specific tasks on a daily basis and once completed, a worker could rest for the remainder of the afternoon. In other regions slaves generally worked in the fields from sunrise to sunset.

Work in the rice fields was more arduous than in tobacco plots. The climate was more dangerous for the health of laborers as well. Many whites were so frightened of "swamp" fevers that they lived in Charleston most of the year and hired

PEOPLE WHO MATTERED—*Eliza Lucas*

During the colonial era, many European consumers loved cloth dyed with the deep blue or purple colors boiled out of leaves from the indigo plant. In the seventeenth century these plants were cultivated only on islands in the Caribbean Sea, and the English imported most of their indigo dyes from Spanish possessions in the region. Such imports had a negative impact on England's balance of trade. Some attempts were made to grow the indigo plant on the North American mainland, but none succeeded until the 1740s. The person who made the breakthrough was Eliza Lucas.

Born in 1722 on the island of Antigua (300 miles east of Puerto Rico) into the family of a high-ranking local British official, she came to South Carolina at the age of sixteen after her father inherited three plantations in the colony. Despite her youth and inexperience, she was placed in charge of the business activities of these estates. Lucas had an interest in botany as well as plantation management, and she decided to make another attempt at cultivating the indigo plant. Within three years she had succeeded. In the following decades indigo production expanded rapidly in South Carolina. The plant was a good complement to rice because it grew on a plantation's high ground. Parliament was so anxious to stimulate output that it authorized payment of a regular subsidy to colonial growers. By 1770 indigo had become the fifth most valuable export of the thirteen mainland colonies.

Eliza Lucas married Charles Pinckney, a prominent Charleston lawyer, in 1744. She traveled with him to London in 1753 when he was appointed colonial agent for South Carolina. After her spouse's death in 1758, she assumed managerial responsibilities over his plantation holdings until their two sons came of age. When her own health began to fail in 1793, she sailed to Philadelphia in hope of obtaining surgical relief, but Lucas died soon after arrival. President George Washington served as one of the pallbearers at her funeral.

overseers to manage their plantations. Planters observed over the years that some blacks seemed more immune to disease in the rice-growing regions, but they had no explanation for the superior health record of certain (but not all) black workers. Modern science has revealed the secret. Many blacks have blood cells that exhibit the sickle-cell trait, and carriers of this genetic trait are unusually resistant to malaria and similar diseases common in swampy, rice-growing regions. (On the negative side, the children of two people carrying the trait are likely to be born with sickle-cell anemia, a serious and often deadly genetic disease.)

Large plantations were more common in South Carolina than in the Chesapeake colonies. While the majority of tobacco growers in Virginia and Maryland were actually family farmers who owned no slaves at all, the typical planter in the lower south had bonded labor, and many agricultural units were huge with hundreds of slaves. This outcome suggests to economists that there were greater economies of scale in rice and indigo production than in tobacco cultivation. In nontechnical language, large estates could produce rice and indigo at a significantly lower cost per pound than small family farms. In later chapters we will learn how some types of manufacturing became subject to very large economies of scale, which led to lower prices for consumers and a greater concentration of economic power in the hands of a few producers.

## WHEAT PRODUCTION

The last major crop grown for export was wheat, the premier grain in international trade—then and now. Wheat went to markets in southern Europe, mainly the Madeira Islands and the Mediterranean coast of Spain, and the Caribbean islands, where planters concentrated almost exclusively on sugar production and imported foodstuffs from the mainland. Some of the wheat was converted into flour or bread before shipment overseas.

The middle colonies were the principal wheat exporters, with Pennsylvania the leader. The family farm was the predominant agricultural unit. Farmers grew wheat for their own consumption and sold the excess in the marketplace. In southeastern Pennsylvania up to one half of the total harvest was excess production and potentially available for sale (some farmers fed grain to animals instead to boost livestock herds). The fact that this region's main crop for export was also its main source of sustenance has tended to obscure the market orientation of the farm community.

Few northern farmers held slaves, but not because of moral conviction—since that issue was rarely considered—but rather because slavery was not a very profitable enterprise in areas which concentrated on the production of wheat. Wheat production required intensive labor only at planting and harvesting, which meant that there were too many idle days during the year when slaves could not be worked to full capacity. By the late colonial period, planters in the Chesapeake discovered that tobacco and wheat in combination were crops well suited to slavery since periods of intense labor came at different seasons. But in areas where wheat was the major crop for the outside market, slavery was unprofitable and thus avoided. The type of agricultural unit which evolved in the middle colonies was the prototype of the family farm which later became typical in the great food belts of the Midwest.

## OTHER EXPORTS

New England was the only region where field crops were not the most valuable export. This region had a comparative advantage in fishing, for its main ports lay close to the habitat of great schools of cod. Huge catches of fish were regularly shipped to the Caribbean and southern Europe. The only significant agricultural surplus came from the production of livestock. Many live animals, horses and cattle, were transported from Connecticut and Rhode Island to the Caribbean sugar islands. Some livestock was slaughtered first, and then shipped out as beef and pork—salted, dried, or smoked.

## IMPORTANCE OF AGRICULTURE

The colonial economy was based overwhelmingly on agriculture, with commerce and other activities of secondary importance. The role of farmers cannot be over-emphasized. Over 80 percent of the population was engaged in some form of agricultural production. Their society was more homogeneous than our own because most people were engaged in a common occupation. Even slaves performed tasks very similar to white farmers, and the skill levels between the two races were not very different by the middle of the eighteenth century. The main cause of economic uncertainty on a year-to-year basis was the same for almost everyone—the weather and its effect on crops.

At least one half of the income realized by the colonists came from the production of food that they consumed on their own farms. Compared to societies elsewhere, they ate extremely well. Meat and dairy products were a large source of calories and protein. Slaves did not consume as balanced a diet as whites, but quantities were abundant and the overall level of nutrition was probably not deficient by modern standards. Not only did the local population eat well, but there was substantial agricultural production available for overseas trade.

One pattern of economic performance has remained consistent over the last 350 years. Given the existing level of technology, this country has invariably enjoyed the fruits of a prodigious agricultural sector. Food production has been more than adequate to provide a healthful and relatively inexpensive diet for the population. Moreover, agriculture has normally yielded a surplus for export. In the colonial era, Americans used their earnings from the overseas sale of crops to purchase tropical products like sugar and finished goods from England. Even today, when the size of the agricultural sector has been dwarfed by the rise of manufacturing, this country still provides up to three quarters of all the grain entering the international market and earns enough from agricultural exports to pay most of the bill for imported petroleum.

## SELECTED REFERENCES

BERLIN, IRA. "Time, Space, and the Evolution of Afro-American Society on British Mainland North America," *American Historical Review* (1980), 44–78.

COON, DAVID. "Eliza Lucas Pinckney and the Reintroduction of Indigo Culture in South Carolina," *Journal of Southern History* (1976), 61–76.

EARLE, CARVILLE. *The Evolution of a Tidewater Settlement System: All Hallow's Parish, 1650–1783.* Chicago: University of Chicago Press, 1975.

GALENSON, DAVID. *White Servitude in Colonial America.* London and New York: Cambridge University Press, 1981.

GRAY, LEWIS C. *History of Agriculture in the Southern United States to 1860.* Washington, D.C.: Carnegie Institute, 1933.

KLINGAMAN, DAVID. "The Significance of Grain in the Development of the Tobacco Colonies," *Journal of Economic History* (1969), 267–78.

LEMON, JAMES. *The Best Poor Man's Country: A Geographical Study of Early Southeastern Pennsylvania.* Baltimore: Johns Hopkins University Press, 1972.

MENARD, RUSSELL. "From Servants to Slaves: The Transformation of the Chesapeake Labor System," *Southern Studies* (1977), 355–90.

MORGAN, EDMUND S. *American Slavery–American Freedom: The Ordeal of Colonial Virginia.* New York: Norton, 1975.

THOMAS, ROBERT PAUL, and RICHARD BEAN. "The Adoption of Slave Labor in British America," in H. Genery and J. Hogendorn, eds., *The Uncommon Market: Essays in the Economic History of the Atlantic Slave Trade.* New York: Academic Press, 1978.

# CHAPTER THREE
# NATURAL RESOURCES
# AND OCCUPATIONAL
# GROUPS

Although agriculture dominated the colonial economy, 10 to 15 percent of the population earned a living from other pursuits. Most found employment in four general types of activities: gathering resources from the forest or ocean, fabricating handicrafts and hardware, constructing ships, and buying and selling merchandise.

## LABOR CONDITIONS

Labor was scarce in the colonies, which meant that wages were generally high—reportedly one third or more above wage rates for comparable work in Europe. Since work was almost always readily available, unemployment was not a serious social problem. Only a small number of people were engaged in activities which we would now label as manufacturing, and much of that was done in the home. There were no real factories and thus no throngs of unskilled industrial workers; a blue-collar working class had not yet emerged. A few transient day laborers were located in the largest towns and cities, but they were on the periphery of the labor force.

Employment patterns were very different in this earlier era since a high percentage of all workers, irrespective of occupation, were self-employed. In their economic relations with others, the vast majority of workers viewed themselves as independent citizens. Most nonagricultural male workers held sufficient property to qualify as voters and to enjoy the full rights of citizenship. They generally set their own working hours, which were never rigid, and did not punch a time clock or any similar device. Even when workers became hired hands, the relationship was normally only temporary—seasonal or an apprenticeship for youth. For example, Benjamin Franklin began his career as an apprentice to a Philadelphia printer; later he opened his own shop. Most Americans expected to become self-employed eventually or at least never to become excessively dependent for their livelihood on any other individual. The thought of assuming the status of a permanent employee in someone else's business enterprise was an abhorrent idea to most colonists.

## FOREST RESOURCES: THE FUR TRADE

Some colonists made their livings by tapping the resources of the vast American forest. The forest yielded a variety of valuable products including furs, lumber, ship masts, and naval stores. During the early years of settlement in Massachusetts, the Pilgrims and Puritans became heavily involved in hunting beaver for their soft, warm, and water-resistant fur. The colonists acquired beaver pelts by setting traps in nearby waterways and by trading with numerous Indian tribes. The net result was an ecological disaster, for by the end of the seventeenth century, beaver were nearly extinct in New England. (After receiving government protection following the passage of environmental legislation in the 1970s, beaver made a strong comeback in this region—after an absence of over 250 years.)

In the eighteenth century the center of the fur trade moved westward, bringing the British colonies in competition with French Canadians. Their rivalry over furs was one of the causes of the French and Indian War, which ended formally in 1763 with the British and their colonial allies victorious. In addition to beaver, the colonists trapped other animals such as fox and mink, which also had furs highly valued by European buyers. In the southern colonies deerskins were the main object of hunters. Indian tribes did most of the hunting and skinning, and the colonists acquired the deerskins through trade.

## WOOD PRODUCTS

The trees in the forest were a more valuable natural resource than the animal inhabitants. The colonists still lived in an age of wood, not metals and fossil fuels. Wood was the basic material for making furniture and constructing homes, wagons, and ships; it was also used for everything from plates, bowls, and eating utensils to plows and crude machinery. In addition, wood was the primary source of fuel for cooking, heating, and iron smelting.

Since most of North America was heavily forested when settlers arrived, wood was generally plentiful. In rural areas the cost of acquisition was merely the labor expended in cutting and chopping, while in cities like Philadelphia craftsmen normally spent up to 10 percent of yearly income for wood supplies. In England, by comparison, much of the countryside was already nearly treeless because of overcutting and the absence of any systematic program of forest management. In the mother country, wood was relatively expensive, which meant that the cost of ship construction was high.

During the seventeenth century, the English identified the colonial white pine, which sometimes reached a height of 120 feet, as an extremely valuable source of ship masts. At the time, most ship masts were imported from Scandinavia and were therefore another negative item in England's balance of trade with the European continent. In an effort to secure a supply within the British Empire, Parliament declared all white pines of the required height the sole property of the king and ordered them marked by cutting an identifying arrow in their bark. Government contracts to supply the royal navy with ship masts were political plums vied for by various political factions in New England.

The forest yielded other products valuable in overseas markets. In the process of clearing land for agriculture, the colonists felled several million trees. Often the timber was burned and the ashes were then leached with water to produce potash or the more highly refined pearlash. These two wood derivatives were used to make soap and glass. Potash became the second leading export from the New England and middle colonies in direct trade with England. Pine trees were a source of naval stores—pitch, tar, and resins—used to protect the surfaces and caulk the seams of wooden ships. North Carolina produced large quantities of naval stores, with many slaves trained to gather these products from living trees.

## IRON PRODUCTION

The largest colonial industry was iron production, and it too was linked closely to the forest. The technology of iron smelting had not changed significantly since the Middle Ages, although the size of furnaces had increased. Iron smelting was feasible only in locations where three critical requirements converged. The ore, water power to operate the machinery, and huge stands of timber, which could be converted into charcoal for use in the furnace, were all needed at the same site. The cost of overland transportation was too high to permit either the ore or the timber to be moved any distance. Iron production was therefore a rural enterprise performed at what were called "iron plantations."

The colonies became substantial producers of iron in the eighteenth century. Output was large enough to meet local demand and provide a healthy surplus for export to England. Indeed, the number of furnaces and forges in the colonies in 1770 probably exceeded those operating in the mother country. By that date American output was around 30,000 tons and accounted for about 15 percent of total world production.

In comparison with other colonial enterprises, iron production was a large-scale operation. Substantial funds were necessary to acquire the mineral rights and timber stands, to construct the furnace and other machinery, and to build housing for the workers recruited to an isolated site. Some iron plantations employed up to 100 laborers, with about one half of them engaged in gathering wood. In an era when owners invariably managed their own businesses, iron smelting was different because it usually required one or two salaried managers. When the Brown family firm (which later founded Brown University in Providence, Rhode Island) opened an iron plantation in the 1760s, it hired both a general business superintendent and a founder; the latter was responsible for mixing the ore and charcoal in the right proportions to produce iron with the desired properties.

Because iron production was a continuous-flow process, it demanded more discipline and regimentation than almost any other type of economic activity. Although the iron plantation had certain characteristics which made it a legitimate precursor of the nineteenth-century factory, this industry still retained a premodern profile, for it was tied to charcoal as a fuel, used water power to operate machinery, and was situated in a rural environment.

## SHIPBUILDING

Shipbuilding was likewise related to the forest since all vessels, large and small, were built with wood. The major northern ports—Philadelphia, New York, and Boston—had busy shipyards, and so did several outlying towns along the Atlantic coast. In-

FIGURE 2  Shipbuilding in Philadelphia (Source: New York Public Library Picture Collection)

dependent shipwrights organized construction under contracts from both domestic and English shippers. In addition to drawing up designs for vessels, shipwrights hired artisans to complete various stages of the work. Activity was seasonal and shipyards had few permanent employees.

The colonies possessed a comparative advantage in ship building over the mother country because wood was so much cheaper than in England. Even though wages and interest rates on construction loans were lower in England, lumber was so much cheaper that overall building costs were about one third lower in the colonies. By 1775, up to one half of all colonial contracts were from English merchants, and probably one third of the ocean-going vessels within the British Empire had been built in colonial shipyards.

## OCEAN RESOURCES

Despite the proximity of a large percentage of the population to the ocean, only the New Englanders were actively involved in gathering resources from the sea. The bountiful fishing grounds off the coast of Massachusetts had drawn Europeans to North America as early as the sixteenth century. These fishermen often went ashore to dry and cure their catch before returning home. In the seventeenth and eighteenth centuries, colonial fishing fleets sailed from New England ports and focused primarily on the huge schools of tasty cod. Fish were sold in local markets and exported to southern Europe and the Caribbean.

Another valued resource living in the ocean was not a fish but a mammal. Whaling became a large enterprise in the eighteenth century. By 1775 more than 300 whalers sailed out of Massachusetts ports, with Nantucket Island the main center of activity. Whales were hunted principally for their blubber, which was boiled down into an oil to burn in lamps and for use as a lubricant. Other products derived from whales included the head matter of sperm whales, used in making high quality spermaceti candles; ambergris, used as a base for perfume; and whalebones, used as stays in garments such as corsets and collars.

## WOMEN IN THE LABOR FORCE

Generally speaking, women performed the same type of work as men—farm chores of every variety. One of the major differences between this earlier era and modern economy is that home and workplace were not widely separated. Even if a man and his wife divided up economic tasks within the household, women were at least familiar with the skills necessary to run a farm. When a husband became disabled or died, his wife was often called upon to plow the fields, tend the crops, and reap the harvest. Economic considerations alone caused most widows to seek a new mate without a long delay. Colonial laws regarding the right of women to hold property were much more liberal than in most other societies. In Europe, women normally were not allowed to hold property in their own name. In the American colonies, however, they held about 10 percent of total wealth by the 1770s. Yet women did not enjoy the same degree of economic freedom and independence as men. Their civil rights were restricted as well, for they could not vote or serve on juries.

One type of economic activity was restricted largely to women and children, however. They produced crude textiles for home consumption. Relying on much the same technology in use since the Middle Ages, women spun thread and produced various pieces of clothing. Knit goods like mittens, stockings, sweaters, and caps were the major items made at home. Wool and flax, alone or in combination, were the two main fibers in homespun garments. The colonists made practical, everyday clothes at home and imported fancier cloth from England.

## ARTISAN WORKERS

Artisans, or craftsmen, were the second largest occupational grouping for males after farmers. Working with wood, leather, and occasionally metal, these skilled and semi-skilled workers provided specialized services and products for local customers and sometimes more distant markets. Artisans were found in largest numbers in towns and cities, but itinerant artisans and jacks-of-all-trades were fairly common in rural areas as well. On large southern plantations a few slaves invariably were trained as carpenters, blacksmiths, and in a whole range of crafts important to farming.

Free artisans were simultaneously laborers and small businessmen. Normally self-employed, artisans owned their own tools and frequently invested in the acquisition of raw materials. They worked at home or on the job, and were never grouped together in any factorylike arrangement. Artisans took great pride in their economic independence. The range of skills was wide and varied. A list of artisan occupations in the early 1770s from Germantown, Pennsylvania, a town of around 2,200 people five miles from Philadelphia included the following: weavers, tailors, hatters, dyers, shoemakers, tanners, saddlemakers, skinners, butchers, millers, bakers, blacksmiths, clockmakers, painters, printers, coopers, masons, carpenters, coachmakers, and wheelwrights. Technology changed very slowly in these crafts, and work methods remained very much the same during the entire colonial period.

Artisans occasionally took on apprentices. In return for an apprentice's labor services and the payment of a fee by his parents, the artisan agreed to teach the youth a marketable skill. The parties entered into a formal contract, much like those signed by indentured servants, which stipulated that the artisan would provide food and shelter, and perhaps even a small wage, during the life of the agreement. Some contracts were for a fixed number of years and others expired when the apprentice reached the age of twenty-one.

In England and most of Europe, artisans often banded together in associations called guilds, which restricted the entry of apprentices and outsiders into specific crafts through various licensing laws. The goal was to limit the supply of artisans and thereby raise wages. The modern counterpart is the "closed union shop," permitted in some states, which restricts employment in certain fields to union members only. In the colonial era, however, guilds were never firmly established, probably because wages were already higher than in Europe. The rapid growth of the economy kept artisanal skills in short supply without artificial manipulation of the labor market.

In the towns and port cities artisans held a middle rank in the economy between the wealthiest merchants and unskilled day laborers and seamen. They were respected members of their communities with the privileges of voting in elections, holding government offices, and serving on juries. In virtually every other society around the globe, craftsmen enjoyed none of the benefits of citizenship. Elsewhere skilled workers were totally excluded from the power structure of society. In the colonies, in contrast, independent workers with property were minor participants in the governmental process. What took earthshaking revolutions to accomplish in several European nations was already an established fact in North America long before the War of Independence.

## MERCHANTS

Following farmers and artisans, merchants were the third largest occupational group. They were intermediaries who coordinated the flow of goods between various producers of goods both at home and overseas with surpluses for sale in the marketplace. Individuals involved in some form of commerce were scattered across the landscape. Many were merely part-time storekeepers and farmers in remote areas, who stocked a small inventory of necessities for other frontier farmers. In the towns merchants conducted a larger volume of business, operating what we would today call general stores. In the major port cities the largest and most successful merchants were involved in domestic and foreign trade.

Irrespective of size or location, the tie of credit linked together much of the mercantile community. Because of the seasonal nature of this agricultural economy, merchants typically had to extend book credit to their retail customers between harvests. They, in turn, needed liberal credit terms from their suppliers—usually other mercantile firms in progressively larger towns and cities. Long chains of credit between merchants were common in this era, in large part because there were no banks to assist in financing inventories. (Banks were not organized until after 1775.) Much of the credit extended to the colonists could be traced across the ocean to English merchants. Capital was in greater supply there, which meant that borrowing was easier and interest rates were lower, too. The granting of credit to buyers at all levels from wholesalers to retail customers represented a technique designed for promoting sales volume. In our modern economy, the motive for the issuance of millions of credit cards to consumers is exactly the same—to induce customers to buy more goods by permitting a delay in payment.

All colonial business was small-scale and a very personal form of economic activity. Owners, workers, customers, and competitors all knew each other, at least as acquaintances. Mercantile firms were either proprietorships or partnerships among relatives and friends. The owners managed their enterprises and from a single office location; none had branches. Merchants rarely specialized in one or two types of goods, even in the largest cities, but carried a wide variety of merchandise. In rural areas barter trade was still a common form of exchange, and simply in the course of doing business merchants accumulated a wide range of goods. Most merchandise fell within the categories of foodstuffs, hardware, textiles, alcohol, and spices (especially salt for preserving meats). In the larger towns, merchants sold locally to retail customers and acted simultaneously as wholesalers for smaller merchants and storekeepers in outlying regions.

In the major ports, the most successful merchants were involved in overseas commerce. A wealthy merchant usually owned a few ships or took fractional shares —such as one-eighth, one-fourth, or one-half—in a group of ships. The use of fractional shares was an early substitute for insurance, since, if one ship went down at sea, the entire loss did not fall completely on a single merchant. Merchants rarely traveled overseas with their goods. When they believed someone in a foreign port could be trusted, that person was often named as an agent, with the authority to conduct business transactions for a commission ranging from three to ten percent. In other cases, the ship captain was designated to handle the business affairs or a third party, called a supercargo, was sent along on the voyage to sell the exported goods and, in turn, to buy a new cargo for the return trip. Most ships sailed directly to one port and then back home; a few vessels followed a triangular route between the colonies, the Caribbean, and England, but they were the exception, not the rule.

Long distance commerce was a very risky venture in this era. Both transportation and communication were slow. Information about market conditions overseas was almost always out-of-date. Goods arrived in haphazard order, which meant that prices tended to fluctuate much more than they do today, especially for perishable foodstuffs. Colonial merchants sending out cargoes in response to reports of foreign shortages often learned several months thereafter that others, through luck or better channels of communication, had already arrived to satisfy the demand. Large sums could be earned or lost on a single voyage.

Merchants were the primary financiers and managers of a series of small manufacturing ventures. These were ambitious merchants who saw profit opportunities in diversifying their investments. As a rule, the products manufactured were closely related to normal mercantile activities. For example, a merchant involved in the Caribbean trade might open a slaughterhouse to prepare meat for the outbound voyage and also a distillery to convert the sugar and molasses in the return cargo into rum. When the Brown family firm in Providence, Rhode Island—mentioned earlier as an investor in an iron plantation—created a small shop to produce spermaceti candles from the head matter of whales, it distributed them through other mercantile houses in New York and Philadelphia and overseas as well. No separate and distinct class of capitalist investors in manufacturing existed in the colonial era. Merchants sought the bulk of their profits from commerce, but they occasionally put money into small supplementary manufacturing ventures.

In the northern colonies, merchants were the wealthiest and most powerful men in society. In the absence of a class of aristocratic landowners (as in Europe) or wealthy planters (as in the southern colonies) to dominate government offices, merchants quickly assumed enormous political power. In Massachusetts, they held a majority in the upper chamber of the legislature during the eighteenth century. North America thus became the first region in the world where merchants and various business interests began to play a dominant role in governmental affairs. Merchants enjoyed not only economic strength but also very high social prestige and political influence.

## GREAT PLANTERS

In the southern colonies, a class of men existed who were both farmers and businessmen. They were called not merely planters, but "great" planters. To qualify for that designation, a person had to own thousands of acres of land and 50 to 100 slaves or more. Their economic strategy was to produce a large surplus of staple products for the international market. They made huge investments in indentured servants and slaves. Their estates were so large that most owners required the assistance of low-level salaried managers—overseers who helped to supervise the workforce. The great planters did not restrict their activities to agriculture but were also part-time lawyers, land speculators, and moneylenders; they even performed mercantile functions in transactions with smaller planters and family farmers in their locale. This group of very wealthy men comprised the dominant social and economic class in the southern colonies. Great planters held most of the elective offices in their region, including most of the seats in the colonial legislatures.

The great planters differed from the landholding aristocrats in England and Europe in several respects. In the mother country the owners of vast estates normally leased their farmland to a host of tenants. Then they lived in grand style off the rents. They not only failed to manage agricultural production, but they also shunned all varieties of business activity as socially degrading. Commerce was viewed as morally corrupting, or at least undignified for the high-born and the intellectually and socially refined. The only acceptable avocation for the English landholder was government service.

In the colonies the great planters were, in contrast, unrestrained in their entrepreneurial activities. No stigma was attached to the pursuit of business ventures. They organized the planting and harvesting of crops, kept their own account books, and invested in bonded labor. The owners of these estates were generally willing to pursue any line of economic activity that promised to return a substantial profit. Meanwhile, like their English counterparts, the great planters were active in political life. Out of this class emerged George Washington, Thomas Jefferson, and other great national figures. Great planters combined the traits of the educated and culturally conscious aristocrat with the business instincts of the calculating merchant. Large-scale agriculture as a business traces its roots to the colonial south.

*PEOPLE WHO MATTERED—William Byrd*

He finished building in 1691 his elegant residence, Westover, overlooking the James River in Virginia, and it remains one of the showpieces of southern colonial architecture. Born in 1652 in England, Byrd migrated to the newly established colony of Virginia as a youth under the protection of an uncle on his mother's side of the family. When his uncle died in 1671, Byrd inherited substantial land holdings on both sides of the James River. He expanded his estates and acquired English indentured servants and later African slaves to work in the tobacco fields and plantation shops. Active in the management of his vast holdings, Byrd was involved in other business endeavors including fur trading, dealing in slaves, importing English goods for sale to neighbors, and shipping. He became one of the richest men in the colonies.

He risked ruin in 1676, at the age of 24, by participating in Bacon's Rebellion, a major revolt against British officials in Williamsburg, the seat of government. The rebellion was eventually crushed and luckily Byrd escaped serious punishment. Elected to the lower branch of the legislature in 1677, he rose to the upper branch, the Council of State, in 1683, where he served for the next twenty years as one of the most powerful men in his society. Byrd's main area of expertise in government was Indian affairs, and he was active both in mounting military campaigns against tribes on the Virginia frontier and in negotiating peace treaties with Indian chiefs locally and as far away as the colony of New York.

In his role as plantation owner, entrepreneur, colonel in the militia, and powerful public official, Byrd typified the spirit of an emerging seventeenth-century Virginia aristocracy.

## BUSINESS VALUES

The elite classes in the northern and southern colonies—merchants and great planters—were very different from the dominant classes in other societies. The colonial elite had a very positive attitude toward entrepreneurship. They believed in the virtue of private property and encouraged individuals to take advantage of new opportunities for profit and advancement. A reverence for success in business actually became a part of the American culture. Although the majority in this society—small farmers and artisans—exercised less direct influence in the political sphere, they too tended to endorse these ideas about the value of pursuing economic success. Except for exploited slaves, most colonists were in basic agreement about a primary aim of society: the creation of an atmosphere conducive to the promotion of the economic goals of all individuals. These factors are important in explaining why foreigners have invariably viewed this country and its government as oriented toward the encouragement of business activities. In fact, no other nation has such a longstanding commitment to the values of private initiative and the legitimacy of business participation in the political and social system.

## SELECTED REFERENCES

BAILYN, BERNARD. *The New England Merchants in the Seventeenth Century.* Cambridge: Harvard University Press, 1955.

BRIDENBAUGH, CARL. *The Colonial Craftsman.* New York: New York University Press, 1950.

BRUCHEY, STUART. *The Colonial Merchant: Sources and Readings.* New York: Harcourt, Brace & World, 1966.

CARROLL, CHARLES. *The Timber Economy of Puritan New England.* Providence: Brown University Press, 1973.

GOLDENBERG, JOSEPH. *Shipbuilding in Colonial America.* Charlottesville, University Press of Virginia, 1976.

GREENBERG, MICHAEL. "William Byrd II and the World of the Market," *Southern Studies* (1977), 429–56.

HEDGES, JAMES. *The Browns of Providence Plantation: The Colonial Years.* Cambridge: Harvard University Press, 1952.

McMANIS, DOUGLAS. *Colonial New England: A Historical Geography.* New York: Oxford University Press, 1975.

MARAMBAUD, PIERRE. *William Byrd of Westover, 1674–1744.* Charlottesville: University Press of Virginia, 1971.

NORTON, THOMAS. *The Fur Trade in Colonial New York, 1686–1766.* Madison: University of Wisconsin Press, 1974.

PASKOFF, PAUL. *Industrial Evolution: Organization, Structure, and Growth of the Pennsylvania Iron Industry, 1750–1860.* Baltimore: Johns Hopkins University Press, 1983.

STACKPOLE, EDOWARD. *The Sea-Hunters: The New England Whalemen during Two Centuries, 1635–1835.* Philadelphia: Lippincott, 1953.

# CHAPTER FOUR
# THE IMPACT
# OF OVERSEAS TRADE

The colonies became involved in overseas trade soon after settlement. Commerce with foreign countries developed for two major reasons. First, trade was mutually advantageous since all participants, here and abroad, benefited. The exchange of goods permitted each country and its citizens to reap the rewards of regional specialization and comparative advantage. By foregoing self-sufficiency and concentrating on the production of a more limited range of goods, the colonies could exchange their surpluses and increase their aggregate incomes. The same principles are operable today.

## OCEAN TRADE

Ocean trade over great distances also occurred because of the relatively low cost of water transportation. Moving goods a long way across land in wagons was usually prohibitively expensive, unless items were light, small in volume, and very valuable —for example, spices and jewelry. Horses provided the power to move goods overland, and they had to be fed and generally maintained. Colonial roads were nonexistent or frequently in disrepair, since government did not raise revenues for road building or upkeep. By overland routes, little trade was conducted beyond distances of 50 miles or so.

Yet trade between ports separated by as much as 3,000 miles, or even more, was feasible. Why? Because water routes were already in place and required no construction or maintenance. Across the ocean there were no barriers to movement in any direction—except the delays of winter storms and summer hurricanes. Moreover, the power to move goods over water was free; the winds filled the sails of ships and carried them from one port to another. By modern standards, the holds of ships were very small, but they were still vastly larger than the carrying capacity of wagons pulled by horses. As a result, residents along the Atlantic coast were much more likely to become extensively involved in trade with people living in the Caribbean or Europe than with their neighbors just a modest distance through the forest. It was not until the nineteenth century that the building of canals and railroads broke the bottleneck in overland transportation and opened up the domestic American market.

## TRADING PATTERNS:
## NEW ENGLAND AND MIDDLE COLONIES

The trading patterns formed in the first half of the seventeenth century prevailed generally throughout the colonial period. The most complete information on colonial exports and imports comes from the late colonial period, and an analysis of that data reveals much about the direction and impact of foreign trade. The northern colonies shipped provisions to the Caribbean islands, where large plantations with huge slave populations grew sugar almost exclusively. Exports to the sugar islands included grain products (wheat, bread, and flour), fish, cured meats, horses, cattle, and candles. In return, the northern colonists received molasses, sugar, and rum. From 1768 to 1772 exports averaged £550,000 annually ($44 million in 1982 prices) versus imports of £595,000 ($48 million), leaving the northern colonies with a deficit of £45,000 ($4 million).

In the trade with southern Europe, the New England and middle colonies exported only two products—grain and fish. The value of these shipments was about one half of those sent to the Caribbean, but imports from southern Europe were quite small. Salt from the Spanish Mediterranean coast and wine from the Madeira Islands were the main products filling the holds of returning vessels. Overall, the northern colonies earned a surplus of £200,000 ($16 million) in the trade with southern Europe.

The trade balance with the mother country was, in contrast, highly out of kilter. Imports exceeded exports by a wide margin. With few exceptions the goods produced in the northern colonies were already available in England or, alternatively, the cost of shipment across the ocean was too great to form a basis for exchange. There was little demand in England for northern agricultural output. Lumber was in short supply there, but the price difference between the two regions was not large enough to justify the cost of overseas shipment. Ship masts over 100 feet long were exported, on the other hand, because trees with strong trunks of that height were rare in the English forest. The three most valuable products shipped to England in the late colonial era were potash, whale oil, and iron.

From England the northern colonies imported vast quantities of finished goods. Textiles, hardware, and luxury products of all varieties were the main items on the list of English imports. The value of these imports was seven times greater at £1.6 million ($128 million) than the value of exports to England, which was only £220,000 ($18 million). Since the northern colonies provided a substantial market for English manufactures, they were viewed as a vital part of the British Empire.

The overall trade balance of the northern colonies showed a large deficit. The small surplus in the commerce with southern Europe could not overcome the deficit with England and the Caribbean. The net deficit was over one million pounds annually between 1768 and 1772. That was the amount that the northern colonists owed foreigners for imported goods.

## SOUTHERN COMMERCE

In the southern colonies exports and imports were nearly equal in value. Direct trade with England was especially vigorous. Like their northern counterparts, the southern colonies provided a substantial market for English manufactured goods. At the same time, they sent large quantities of agricultural products to Great Britain. Tobacco, rice, and indigo accounted for 90 percent of exports. In the five-year period under scrutiny here, imports averaged £1.47 million ($118 million) and exports £1.4 million ($112 million), leaving a slight deficit of £70,000 ($6 million).

In commerce with the Caribbean and southern Europe, the main products included in outbound cargoes were wheat, rice, corn, and lumber. After the middle of the eighteenth century, the southern colonies had increasing amounts of wheat and corn available for overseas shipment. The ability to produce not only staple crops, like tobacco and indigo, but also surplus grains was one of the reasons that white incomes in the South were higher than in the North. On the return voyages, ships brought back rum, sugar, and molasses from the Caribbean and wine from European ports. Between 1768 and 1772 the southern colonies generated an annual trade surplus of £170,000 ($14 million) in commerce with these two regions. This amount was sufficient to overcome the deficit with England and give the southern colonies a favorable balance of trade overall.

## TRADE DEFICITS

The southern surplus was too small to make more than a dent in the huge deficit of the northern colonies, however. The thirteen colonies combined had a trade deficit of £1,120,000 ($90 million). In other words, the colonists bought almost a million pounds more from overseas merchants than they sold to them. But it did not end there, for the colonists incurred other foreign debts too. They paid £80,000 ($6 million) to buy the contracts of European indentured servants and another £200,000 ($16 million) to purchase slaves from the Caribbean and Africa. These sums increased American indebtedness to £1.4 million ($112 million) for the importation of goods and human beings.

How did the colonists finance these overseas debts? Over 60 percent of the deficit was made up by what economists call "invisible earnings." They were invisible in the sense that such earnings arose from the provision of services for the international trade sector rather than the sale of tangible goods. Many shipments were carried in the holds of American-owned vessels, and the northern colonies earned substantial amounts for providing these shipping services. In addition, colonial merchants earned income from insurance fees and sales commissions. These invisible earnings in the foreign trade sector totaled over £800,000 ($64 million), a sum larger than the proceeds from the sale of tobacco in the British market. Another source of foreign income was the sale of new ships to British buyers; very expensive items like ships are considered capital goods and do not usually get reported in lists of traded commodities. Ship sales brought in about £140,000 ($11 million). The application of earnings from shipping services and the sale of vessels brought down colonial indebtedness to around £400,000 ($32 million).

Sufficient revenues to cover most of the remaining deficit came from the expenditures of the British government on colonial defense and civil administration. Over 90 percent of these funds went to pay for the stationing of troops in North America and naval patrols to protect shipping in the North Atlantic. Parliament raised a small amount of tax money in the colonies to help offset the cost of these expenditures, but it authorized the spending of sums ten times greater from the pockets of British taxpayers. The British government was willing to spend this money in the colonies because of political and economic rivalries with other European powers, primarily the French and Spanish by the mid-eighteenth century. The expansion and maintenance of the British Empire had a very important priority in Parliament's budget. (At present the United States spends billions of dollars to station troops, ships, and atomic missiles around the world because of a political rivalry with the Soviet Union.) The colonists used these subsidies from British taxpayers to purchase an extra £400,000 ($32 million) worth of foreign goods annually.

This analysis reveals how the colonies balanced their accounts with foreigners in the years just prior to independence. Economists call such a statement of additions and subtractions a "balance of payments"; it goes beyond imports and exports to include all financial transactions involving foreigners. The debits and credits rarely came out even in any given year. There were years when the colonists increased their foreign indebtedness and other years when debts were reduced.

## COLONIAL DEBTS

At one time, historians generally put great credence in the following four propositions about colonial indebtedness to British merchants: that it was accelerating in the 1760s and 1770s; that such indebtedness signified the weakness of the colonial economy and its increasing dependency on England; that mounting debts were acquired involuntarily; and that a resolute desire to get out from under a huge debt burden contributed mightily to the independence movement. However, none of these propositions have held up over time. Historical interpretations of events frequently undergo change, or revision, as new evidence or the application of new research tools—especially mathematical and statistical techniques—reveal that old explanations of events are misleading or incomplete. Indeed, history is not a subject fixed forever in time and place, but a discipline constantly in flux. Historians build on the work of their predecessors, but they are constantly moving in new directions and questioning old assumptions. The controversy about the role of indebtedness in colonial history is a perfect example of how accepted explanations of events are modified by subsequent generations of historians.

Our review of the colonies' balance of payments indicates that long-term indebtedness was increasing only slightly, if at all, in the years just prior to independence. Substantial indebtedness had carried over from earlier decades but there is no reason to believe that it was advancing significantly. On the other hand, the amount of short-term credit, due in one year or less, that British merchants extended to colonial purchasers does appear to have risen rather sharply in the 1760s and early 1770s. The extension of these more lenient credit terms was not a sign of any weakness or dependency, but just the opposite. What it meant was that British merchants wished to boost their volume of colonial sales, and they used more favorable credit terms as an inducement to colonial buyers. They also were expressing greater confidence in the willingness and ability of the colonists to meet their financial obligations. At the same time, the colonists were also increasingly confident about the future of the economy and about their ability to service their debts. They bought more foreign goods on short-term credit voluntarily.

After the War of Independence ended, British merchants filed claims against American creditors for over £5 million ($640 million). This sum was allegedly the amount owed but not paid after the beginning of the war. It was a very large claim, for it represented almost two years worth of English imports at the prewar volume of trading activity. The very large size of these claims suggested to an earlier generation of historians that perhaps one of the prime motives for political independence and military confrontation had been the hope of escaping from this burden of debt.

Subsequent historical research has cast serious doubts on the validity of many of the claims. Historians now view them from a different perspective. In modern lawsuits, as we all know, creditors and other plaintiffs often make exaggerated claims for monetary compensation with the expectation that the sum finally awarded by the court, or in this case a government commission, will be deflated to a level more consistent with actual losses. It was no different in the eighteenth century. When the claims were filed in 1791, the alleged debts were over 15 years old, and the amount claimed probably included more accrued interest than original principal. The United States finally settled with the British for one eighth of the total requested. This amount was much closer to the real losses suffered by foreign merchants than the amount that they had initially claimed. In any event, these sums were not large enough to foment a revolution. The colonists had not been sinking under a burden of involuntary debts in the 1760s and 1770s. On the contrary, they were exceedingly prosperous and financially sound for a preindustrial economy— and they were becoming more so with every passing year.

## NAVIGATION ACTS

We must also revise our historical interpretation of the impact of the Navigation Acts, passed by Parliament beginning in the 1650s, on the economic life of the colonies. Again, historians previously believed that these laws had a very negative effect on the economy and that their continued existence was one of the major grievances of the colonists in the dispute with England. The modern judgment is that the net effect was only mildly negative and the overall impact almost negligible.

The motive for Parliament's passage of these laws was its desire to make certain that colonial trade coincided with the perceived interests of England. From the English and European view, this was the whole purpose in acquiring and maintaining an overseas empire—to enrich the mother country. According to mercantilist thinking, the prime value of colonies in the New World was to assist the mother country in securing specie (gold and silver) either directly or indirectly through the promotion of a favorable balance of trade.

During the first half of the seventeenth century, the colonists traded not only with English merchants and vessels but occasionally with the French, Dutch, Spanish, and Portuguese. In this early period, the number of settlers was so few and the volume of trade so small that the English were not very concerned about the direction of overseas commerce. During the 1650s and 1660s, however, the English began to have second thoughts about allowing their colonies so much economic freedom. The fear was that the colonies might be contributing to the welfare of European rivals and, thus, damaging the relative power of England. Although there was little hard evidence about the overall impact of unrestricted colonial trade on the English economy, Parliament finally decided to play it safe and enact a series of laws to guide colonial trade into more appropriate channels.

The Navigation Acts were designed to make certain that the flow of trade was in harmony with the goal of strengthening Britain and its empire. The main provisions of these acts were the following: 1) All colonial trade was to be conducted in ships built and owned by English or colonial merchants; vessels built and owned by foreigners were excluded from colonial ports. 2) The colonists were not permitted to import European goods directly from European ports but only after those goods had first passed through the hands of English merchants and paid English tariffs. 3) Certain commodities deemed especially valuable in promoting a favorable balance of trade for the mother country could be exported only to England or other points within the British Empire. These goods were said to be "enumerated," and included such items as tobacco, indigo, ship masts, furs, and rice bound for ports in northern, but not southern, Europe.

These laws had advantages and disadvantages for the colonies. The disadvantages were twofold. First, the colonists paid higher prices for imported manufactured goods because European merchants could not ship their inventories *directly* to colonial ports to compete with English goods. English merchants and manufacturers enjoyed what economists call a "protected" market—one protected from vigorous price competition by other potential producers. Second, the colonists did not receive the highest possible prices for some of their exports—the items on the enumerated list. They had to ship these items to British ports even if the prices offered in other countries were higher. The lost opportunities for greater profits were primarily in tobacco sales since the prices quoted on the European continent were consistently higher than the prices actually paid in England and Scotland.

The colonies benefited, on the other hand, from the rule restricting commerce within the British Empire to ships built and owned by residents of the empire. As a consequence, English merchants were not able to arrange transport for their goods on foreign vessels even if the rates were lower. In addition, they could not make contracts with shipbuilders in Scandinavia and other parts of Europe, where the cost of wood was lower. Much of this business came instead to colonial shippers and colonial shipyards. The navigation laws were thus instrumental in giving the colonists substantial earnings from the provision of shipping services. Meanwhile, the British navy assumed the cost of protecting the sea lanes and reducing thereby incidents of piracy.

On balance, the financial benefits and costs associated with the Navigation Acts were reasonably close. At the very worst, the total income of the colonies was penalized by no more than 1 percent annually. The greatest impact of the trade regulations was the internal shift in regional incomes. The southern colonies had the largest sales of items on the enumerated list, and its regional income was lowered by up to 2.5 percent. On the other hand, the northern region provided most of the shipping services and its income rose by up to 1.5 percent. Even so, white incomes in the southern colonies were still higher than in the North.

The Navigation Acts were not a major grievance in the relations between the colonies and England. The colonists themselves were influenced by mercantilist thinking and they understood its basic principles. Few colonial leaders disputed the right of Parliament to regulate the pattern and scope of foreign trade. That was widely recognized as a legitimate function of the government in England. What did raise the ire of the colonists in the 1760s was Parliament's interference in their monetary system and its effort to raise new taxes for the defense of the empire.

## IMPACT OF TRADE

From 8 to 10 percent of aggregate colonial output was sold in overseas markets. (The comparable figure in 1980 was around 8 percent of United States output.) Foreign trade boosted colonial incomes, but it was not essential for the health of the economy. The major strength of the economy was in its huge production of foodstuffs for domestic consumption and the productivity of skilled artisans. Even in the absence of a foreign trade sector, colonial living standards would have remained among the highest in the world. Over time, more of the country's productive capacity could (and almost certainly would) have been shifted into various forms of manufacturing to meet local demand.

Colonial participation in foreign commerce had a greater impact on the organization of society than on the level of income. The southern crops grown primarily for the export market were produced extensively by bonded labor. The existence of rising overseas demand for three crops ideally suited to plantation agriculture—tobacco, indigo, and rice—was the stimulus for the adoption and acceptance of the institutions of indentured servitude and slavery. Foreign trade was also responsible for the growth of the largest cities—the ports of Philadelphia, New York, and Boston in the North and Charleston in the South. These cities were centers of overseas shipping and shipbuilding.

Foreign commerce was likewise the key factor in bringing great wealth to the two most powerful economic and political classes in the colonies. Southern planters and northern merchants both looked to overseas markets for their prosperity. A huge proportion of the earnings from involvement in the foreign trade sector went into the hands of less than 5 percent of the total population. For example, North Carolina had a limited involvement in overseas commerce in the late colonial period, and its distribution of wealth and income was broader than in most other colonies. Meanwhile, in South Carolina, Virginia, and Maryland the great planters were oriented toward markets in the Caribbean and Europe. So were the rich merchants in Pennsylvania, New York, Connecticut, Rhode Island, and Massachusetts.

### SELECTED REFERENCES

DICKERSON, OLIVER. *The Navigation Acts and the American Revolution.* Philadelphia: University of Pennsylvania Press, 1951.

EVANS, EMORY. "Planter Indebtedness and the Coming of the Revolution in Virginia, 1776 to 1796," *William and Mary Quarterly* (1962), 511–33.

HARPER, LAWRENCE. "The Effects of the Navigation Acts on the Thirteen Colonies," in Richard Morris, ed., *The Era of the American Revolution.* New York: Columbia University Press, 1939.

PRICE, JACOB. "Economic Function and the Growth of American Port Towns in the Eighteenth Century," in D. Fleming and B. Bailyn, ed., *Perspectives in American History.* Vol. 8. Cambridge: Harvard University Press, 1974.

RANSOM, ROGER. "British Policy and Colonial Growth: Some Implications of the Burden from the Navigation Acts," *Journal of Economic History* (1968), 427–35.

SHEPHERD, JAMES, and GARY M. WALTON. *Shipping, Maritime Trade and the Economic Development of Colonial North America.* Cambridge: Cambridge University Press, 1972.

THOMAS, ROBERT PAUL. "British Imperial Policy and the Economic Interpretation of the American Revolution," *Journal of Economic History* (1968), 436–40.

# CHAPTER FIVE
# COLONIAL WEALTH
# AND INCOME

## INCOME GROWTH

From the dawn of civilization to the settlement of the New World, no society had ever experienced a sustained growth in personal incomes, or income per capita. There were earlier periods when unusually good harvests had raised living standards for perhaps a generation or two, but invariably one crisis or another drove living standards back down to near the previous level. The thirteen colonies were one of only three places in the world where that roller-coaster cycle was first broken in the seventeenth and eighteenth centuries. The other two were England and Holland. Within a decade or two of initial settlement, the free colonial population began to enjoy the benefits of continuous material advancement. And with only a few interruptions, the most notable the Great Depression in the 1930s, Americans have experienced rising living standards. This characteristic of perpetual income growth is a unique feature of American history, and it led the historian David Potter to describe Americans as a "people of plenty."

In the modern world most advanced nations aim for growth rates in living standards of 2 to 3 percent *annually* over the long run. In the colonial era, we are talking about fairly similar growth rates over an entire *decade*. In other words, progress was still very slow in this earlier period; the important point is that it was steady and uninterrupted. Different regions moved ahead at different speeds in certain periods. In New England, the most rapid era of growth was the seventeenth century, when the amount of good farm land per capita was highest. After 1700 population pressure placed more strain on natural resources. In the Chesapeake colonies, income growth was fast in the 1630s, steady between 1640 and 1670, nearly stagnant until 1750, and then quickened again in the third quarter of the century. For the entire thirteen colonies these rates of growth in personal incomes per decade seem reasonably accurate: 3 percent from 1650 to 1725; 4 percent up to 1750; and 5 percent up to 1775. The rate of increase was accelerating in the half century before independence. Between 1650 and 1775 living standards rose about 50 percent for the free population.

The evidence about rising income levels is varied, but one revealing source has become the value of probated estates at death. During the last two decades, historians have increasingly used old courthouse records in county seats to obtain a better understanding of economic status and progress. Where the volume of data is enormous, the use of statistical sampling techniques has helped to make research projects manageable. One careful study of probated estates in St. Mary's County, Maryland, in the seventeenth and eighteenth centuries has shown clear signs of rising living standards. In the initial years of settlement, the typical estate contained few personal amenities—usually a little furniture and a limited number of consumer goods. The only two items listed in at least half of all estates were earthenware and linen. By the eighteenth century the list of typical items had expanded to include knives, forks, and religious books. In the estates of very wealthy planters, clocks and watches, secular books, maps, and spices were found much more often in the eighteenth century. From 1700 to 1775 the value of probated estates doubled in St. Mary's County. More individual wealth was an indication of rising living standards.

## PRODUCTIVITY

Personal incomes rose because of increased productivity. Each individual was able to produce a little more each year. The changes were gradual because there were no major technological breakthroughs. Most progress was the result of trial and error experiments or what economists call "learning by doing." Farmers discovered better methods of growing crops and new ways to utilize their land. They matched more closely soils and seeds, applied labor more prudently between sowing and harvesting, and made hundreds of small improvements which raised the total output of their farmland. For example, the number of tobacco plants that one man could safely tend rose threefold between 1630 and 1700. The use of cradle scythes on wheat farms in the middle colonies after 1750 was an important innovation because it increased the amount of grain which could be cut at harvest. Another factor increasing total productivity was the farmer's greater utilization of formerly idle days to engage in nonagricultural production on a part-time basis.

We can also identify several factors causing increased productivity in the transportation sector. From 1675 to 1775 ocean freight rates fell by nearly one half. One reason for this drop in rates was that the number of seamen required to sail the typical vessel of 50 tons declined from 7 to only 5, a savings in wages of almost 30 percent. The increasing volume of trade and its better organization by local merchants lowered the number of idle days that ships spent in colonial ports and waters gathering full cargoes. Meanwhile, insurance rates fell because of improved safety on ocean voyages and the reduction of piracy in response to the effectiveness of British naval patrols. Tighter packing of tobacco in hogsheads raised the weight of cargoes and boosted the utilization of existing shipping capacity. These factors and others helped increase the income of the colonists.

## LIVING STANDARDS

By the 1770s the white population had the highest living standards in the world. Their gross incomes were not that much above those in England, but the English paid very high taxes for the defense of the empire (including, ironically, North America). The colonial tax burden was in contrast very low, probably lower than in any country in Europe, so that after-tax incomes available for expenditures on goods and services was up to one fifth greater than in the mother country.

The typical member of a white household had an income of about £13 a year, or roughly $1,040 in 1982 prices. One half of that income was realized through the direct production of foodstuffs, including up to 200 pounds of meat and dairy products. Since 1775, median living standards have risen about eight times, with white Americans now spending only about 15 percent of their incomes on foodstuffs. There were regional differences in colonial incomes. The living standard of the typical farmer in the southern and middle colonies was around one fifth higher than that in New England. The 30 percent of southern families who held slaves had the highest incomes in the colonies. Per capita income in the typical slaveholding family, with two bonded laborers, was probably around £14.5 ($1,160). White incomes rose as the number of slaves increased; the mean income for southerners was so high at £26 ($2,080) that many of the very wealthiest families must have enjoyed personal incomes of £100 ($8,000), or more, a figure on a par with the income of the typical American in the early 1980s.

There were differences in income according to legal status as well. Slaves normally did not earn money wages, but they did receive income in the form of food, clothing, shelter, wood for cooking and heating, and medical attention. A reasonable estimate of slave incomes suggests a figure about one half of that for free whites, or £7 ($560) per person. The largest source of income was the production and direct consumption of foodstuffs; diets contained little meat and not much variety, but the quantities of corn, rice, flour, peas, and other surplus crops were not deficient. Since 1775, the income of the typical black American has moved up nearly seven times. The incomes of indentured servants fell between free whites and slaves. Over and above the goods and services granted to slaves, servants received generous allocations of meat and alcohol, often a small wage, and freedom dues. They received incomes of about £9 ($720) annually.

Although colonial living standards were low compared to what we are accustomed to in the United States today, in comparison with other societies in the seventeenth and eighteenth century they were remarkably high. In most other parts of the globe, the population was concerned mainly about mere survival—escaping death from disease or inadequate nutrition. Even in the most prosperous European nations, the general population did not consume as much meat and dairy products, and it did not have as much excess production available for sale in the marketplace.

One of the most surprising facts about colonial white incomes is that they were around double the earnings of over one half of the world population *today*. The citizens of India, mainland China, most of the nations in Southeast Asia, and the bulk of the present African population all earned less than $600 annually in 1982. On a comparative scale, North Americans have always been an affluent and prosperous people.

## DISTRIBUTION OF WEALTH

A study of a large sample of probated estates left by deceased Americans in the early 1770s provides valuable insights into the distribution of wealth by region, class, and sex. The southern colonies held 55 percent of the total wealth, with slaves included in the calculations. With slaves excluded, the South was still the regional leader with 45 percent of all nonhuman wealth. The middle colonies followered with about one quarter of total wealth, while New England trailed with a one-fifth share.

The richest group were the great planters of South Carolina, where rice and indigo were the key crops. Some of them were already millionaires. One of the wealthiest Americans in 1770 was Peter Manigault, a South Carolina planter and lawyer, who died leaving an estate of £28,000, which translated into about $2 million in 1982. Some northern merchants, particularly in Philadelphia, also got into the millionaire class, but the large landowners and slaveholders in the South were the economic elite.

The most valuable single asset in colonial estates was, not surprisingly, land. It accounted for just over one half of all colonial wealth; in the northern colonies land was the source of 60 to 70 percent of wealth. For the thirteen colonies, slaves and servants were the next most important item with a 22 percent share of estates; in the south the figure was 34 percent. Livestock and personal possessions were the third and fourth most valuable items in colonial estates, with shares of 9 .and 7 percent respectively.

Although the colonies were a place where the typical farmer owned his own land, the distribution of wealth was nonetheless very uneven. The top 20 percent of all wealth-holders controlled 65 percent of all assets, while the bottom 20 percent accounted for less than one percent of the total wealth. Both the southern and New England colonies had very similar patterns of wealth distribution, which suggests that the existence of slavery was, in isolation, not a sufficient explanation for the concentration of wealth in the South. The middle colonies had the broadest pattern of wealth distribution, yet even there the top 10 percent of the population still claimed over one third of all assets. The colonies may have been a land of opportunity for enterprising whites, especially in comparison with Europe where social mobility was very low, but this new society was by no means classless. A minority of the free population held a disproportionate share of the total wealth, and this group maintained a tight rein on political power and framed the laws under which the economy functioned.

Free women were not permitted to participate in the political life of the colonies, and only a few held property in their own right. About 10 percent of all probated estates in the 1770s belonged to women. The average size of female estates was approximately one half of the amount for men. The discrepancy was caused primarily by the absence of land in most female estates. As a result, almost no women were enormously wealthy. One of the richest women to die in the 1770s was Abigail Townsend, a South Carolina resident, who left an estate of £2,600 ($208,000 in 1982 dollars).

One question that has interested historians in recent years is whether the concentration of wealth has increased over the course of the seventeenth and eighteenth centuries. It seems fairly clear that when villages grew into towns and later into cities, the pattern of wealth holding became more concentrated. The largest port cities—Philadelphia, New York, Boston, and Charleston—had the greatest degree of wealth inequality. A small percentage of the population gained ownership of large tracts of land within towns and cities, and a substantial portion of the urban population lived in rental housing. Nonetheless, for the thirteen colonies as a whole, there was no identifiable trend toward an increasing concentration of wealth in the eighteenth century. Why? Because patterns of wealth holding changed very little in settled rural areas and tended toward greater equality on the frontier. The rural and frontier population actually grew faster than the urban population after 1700. By 1775 over 90 percent of the colonists lived in a nonurban environment. Among the major changes in this country in later years was the movement of population from farm to city, and later the suburbs.


## CONCLUSION

American economic ascendency within a global context did not begin with the coming of giant industries in the nineteenth century; it was already an established fact long before independence from England and the subsequent application of new technology in manufacturing and agriculture. The new United States rose to pre-eminence in the world economic order rapidly in the nineteenth century because it started the climb from a very high base. The colonies possessed a skilled workforce, including white farmers and artisans and black slaves. No other contemporary society had so many enterprising, independent farmers, artisans, and merchants. No laws or traditions placed artificial boundaries on entrepreneurial activity. The free population was largely unrestrained in the pursuit of material advancement.

The colonies were operating at very near the optimum level of achievement for an agricultural-commercial economy. Personal incomes were already the highest in the world. Meanwhile, population growth was moving ahead at a very rapid pace; the number of Americans was doubling every twenty years or so. From the 1630s until the 1930s, a period of 300 years, this country had the world's most dynamic economy in terms of increases in aggregate output.

## SELECTED REFERENCES

ANDERSON, TERRY. *The Economic Growth of Seventeenth-Century New England: A Measurement of Regional Income.* New York: Arno Press, 1975.

BALL, DUANE, and GARY M. WALTON. "Agricultural Productivity Change in Eighteenth-Century Pennsylvania," *Journal of Economic History* (1976), 102–17.

CARR, LOIS GREEN, and LORENA S. WALSH. "Changing Life Styles in Colonial St. Mary's County," in G. Porter and W. Mulligan, eds., *Economic Change in Chesapeake Colonies* (Greenville, Delaware: Regional Economic History Research Center, 1978), 73–118.

DANIELS, BRUCE. "Long Range Trends of Wealth Distribution in Eighteenth-Century New England," *Explorations in Economic History* (1973/74), 123–35.

GALENSON, DAVID, and RUSSELL MENARD. "Economics and Early American History," *Newberry Papers,* No. 77-4E. Chicago, 1978.

JONES, ALICE HANSON. *American Colonial Wealth: Documents and Methods.* 3 Vols. New York: Arno Press, 1978.

_____. *Wealth of a Nation To Be: The American Colonies on the Eve of the Revolution.* New York: Columbia University Press, 1980.

KULIKOFF, ALLAN. "The Economic Growth of the Eighteenth-Century Chesapeake Colonies," *Journal of Economic History* (1979), 275–88.

SMITH, ADAM. *The Wealth of Nations.* London, 1776.

WILLIAMSON, JEFFREY, and PETER LINDERT. *American Inequality: A Macroeconomic History.* New York: Academic Press, 1980.

# CHAPTER SIX
# ECONOMIC ISSUES
# AND REVOLT

Historians have pondered for generations the underlying reasons for the political separation from England in the 1770s. A large number of explanations have been put forward, and several have focused on economic questions. Although the authors of this book share a predisposition toward identifying economic motives for much human behavior (probably more than is warranted), we do not believe, despite our general biases, that a fair evaluation of the evidence points toward granting a primary role to economic grievances or economic opportunism in fomenting the movement toward independence. In Chapter Four, we already examined the proposition that deep-seated resentment over the Navigation Acts and a desire to escape a heavy burden of debt to British merchants were factors in causing the break with England. In both cases, we dismissed them as insignificant factors in stirring up a revolutionary spirit.

At the same time, it can be said that conflicts with Parliament over matters with economic implications were crucial in precipitating colonial discussions about the merits of pursuing an independent course. These conficts were about the role of paper currency in the monetary system and the level and types of imperial taxes. Whatever the underlying reasons for separation from England, these were the two surface issues around which much of the debate centered in the 1760s and 1770s. The conflict over paper money was settled by 1773, and the dispute over taxation was mostly resolved as well. The tax issue continued unresolved in the minds of at least a small portion of the citizenry, however, because of the maintenance of the tea tax—a symbol of English authority and supremacy.

## PAPER MONEY

The contest with Parliament over paper money related to the terms of issuance. The colonies were among the first political units to use paper currency extensively in everyday business transactions as a supplement, but not a substitute, to specie. The Chinese had issued paper money at one time but gave up the practice in the fifteenth century. In England in the seventeenth and eighteenth centuries, gold and silver coins were the only medium of exchange. The financial sectors of the mother country and her colonies were still institutionally undeveloped. There were no banks where the average citizen could make deposits, obtain loans, and cash checks. Unlike today, most coins were high in value, which made small transactions difficult to negotiate.

Political leaders in England were skeptical about the use of paper money because they believed it would not be able to retain its value relative to specie. They feared that paper money would depreciate over time. Suppose, they hypothesized, England decided to issue paper notes with the value of one pound printed on their face. Although a one-pound note might be easily exchanged for a coin valued at one pound in the first year or so, it was generally accepted that the coin would retain its value, but not the paper substitute. Eventually, it would take notes with the face value of two pounds to obtain in exchange a one-pound coin; later the ratio, or exchange rate, would probably rise to 3:1, then 4:1, to 20:1, and even higher. Finally, the paper money would have no value at all relative to coins—and become "not worth the paper it was printed on," as the saying goes. The fear of depreciation prevented England and other European countries from adopting paper money as a feature of their monetary systems. But the colonists did not let the potential problem of depreciation deter them; they hoped to prevent it or live with it.

In the colonies, the legislatures were the issuers of paper money, not financial institutions, since none existed. There were two general types of paper money. In both cases, the assumption was that a given issue of paper money would not remain in circulation permanently, but would be withdrawn, or retired, within a period ranging from 2 to about 15 years. In the first category, the currency was issued to individual citizens in the form of a loan, with real estate as the collateral. To guarantee a broad access to these loans and a wide distribution of the paper money, limits were usually placed on how much one person could borrow. In New York, for example, citizens could borrow from £25 ($2,000) to £100 ($8,000) at 5 percent interest for up to 12 years. When the loans were repaid to the government, the paper money received in payment was retired from circulation. While the loans were outstanding, the interest provided a revenue for government, and thereby lowered taxes. Since the responsibility for repayment, and simultaneously retirement, rested with individuals, the paper money issued under these conditions generally retained most of its value.

The same cannot be said, however, about every issue of a second variety of paper money also authorized by the colonial legislatures. The paper money issued in this category was not loaned to individuals; it was paid out to cover government expenses or simply given to every eligible citizen according to a prearranged formula. In Maryland, for example, every taxable person was granted 30 shillings ($120), with the amounts allocated for servants and slaves turned over to their masters. This paper money was to be retired through taxation by a specified date, usually several years in the future.

The first issue of this variety of paper money came in Massachusetts in 1690. An underfinanced military expedition against the French proved a failure, and the returning soldiers demanded the payment of back wages. The colony's treasury was empty of specie, and with no banks to borrow from, the legislature fell upon the novel idea of issuing £7,000 ($560,000) in bills of credit—paper money. The terms of issuance made this money *legal tender* only in the payment of taxes, and not in private transactions between individuals. It meant that the government had to accept the paper money at face value but individuals had the option of refusing to recognize the paper completely and insisting instead on specie in the payment of debts. In other words, the notes had the legal status of money in government transactions, but not in the private sector. In this case the public demand for the paper money to use in the payment of taxes held up its value. As the paper money was received by the Massachusetts government, it was duly destroyed so that the size of the issue steadily diminished. Within a decade all of the original issue had been retired, and this temporary monetary experiment was widely heralded within the colony as a great success.

In fact, this financial experiment was so successful that over the decades notes were reissued again and again. Every colonial legislature eventually authorized the issuance of some form of paper money in this category. This medium of exchange proved so popular that many colonies never got around to collecting sufficient taxes to retire all the outstanding notes. The failure to assess ample taxation lowered the demand for paper money and usually led to its depreciation in value. The rate of depreciation varied by colony but reached very high levels in the New England colonies and South Carolina during the first half of the seventeenth century.

## PROBLEM OF DEPRECIATION

Concerned about the problem of an unstable paper currency, but lacking the will to impose the taxes required to sustain its value, colonial legislatures turned to other measures designed to slow down the rate of depreciation. They began to stipulate in the terms of reissuance that paper money would be legal tender in the payment of all debts, private as well as public. The rationale behind this proposal was that private demand would become a substitute for the absent public demand (taxes) and thus aid in propping up the value of the paper money. In colonies where the legislatures relied almost solely upon the legal tender in private debts feature to maintain the value of their paper money, the tactic failed to work. Instead the depreciation continued year after year. The net result was that the face value of the various notes was much greater than their real market value vis-a-vis specie.

This discrepancy between the face value of the currency and its market value was the issue which created tension between the colonial legislatures and Parliament. The problem arose because the colonists often attempted to pay longstanding debts to British merchants with depreciated paper rather than specie. The merchants usually expressed a willingness to accept the paper at its market value but not its face value. Their argument was that a debt should not be reduced in value through its payment in cheapened money. But the colonists pointed instead to the law, which stated that debtors had no choice but to accept the paper money at its face value.

Parliament struggled with this issue for over twenty years, and it attacked the problem in stages. First, in 1751, Parliament banned forever the issuance of any new paper money which would be legal tender in private transactions in all the New England colonies. Those were the colonies where depreciation had been the greatest and where British merchants felt most threatened. These colonies were permitted, however, to continue to issue paper money valid in public transactions. At this point, Parliament considered extending the ban to the middle and southern colonies. But in those locations (except South Carolina), the legislatures had been much more responsible about imposing taxes to retire their outstanding issues and the rates of depreciation were relatively low. British merchants were generally satisfied with how these colonies had managed their paper money. Thus, Parliament exempted the middle and southern colonies from the Currency Act of 1751, and they continued to authorize new issues of paper money which was designated as legal tender in both public and private transactions.

By the early 1760s, however, British merchants had become much more nervous about their position in these colonies. Virginia had issued paper money for the first time in 1755, with full legal tender provisions. Virginia planters bought huge amounts of English goods on credit, increasing the vulnerability of merchants to the risks of depreciating currency. Complaints arose about the alleged inequities of the colonial courts in cases involving the payment of overdue debts, especially in comparison to New England where all private obligations were strictly handled on a specie basis.

Meanwhile, with the ending of the French and Indian War, Parliament had become more interested in exerting greater control over the affairs of its colonies. This interest followed almost 150 years of salutary neglect. The government leadership considered for a short time a bill creating a comprehensive paper money system for all thirteen colonies, but the bias in Parliament against paper money finally prevailed. What emerged instead, almost inexplicably, was a law which banned the issuance of paper money with any legal tender provisions whatsoever, private and public, in the colonies not covered by the previous act. The Currency Act of 1764, for all practical purposes, took away from the legislatures in the southern and middle colonies the privilege of issuing paper money.

Colonial leaders in the affected colonies were outraged. In a combative mood, they set out to persuade Parliament to change its mind, and, in the meantime, to defy the law until it was repealed. Pennsylvania and New York had managed paper money emissions for almost half a century with modest depreciation, and they were completely perplexed and angered by the new currency act. Fundamentally, colonial leaders were not willing to let another legislative body over 3,000 miles away tell them to stop doing something that they had been doing successfully for decades. They viewed the composition of the monetary stock as an internal affair; it had nothing to do with international trading patterns and other mercantilist doctrines, which were considered the legitimate concern of Parliament.

Defiantly, the colonial legislatures continued to pass new laws creating more paper money, and with complete legal tender provisions. Then they intimidated the royal governors, the king's representatives in the colonies, and convinced them to approve tentatively the new emissions—despite the fact that these governors had explicit instructions from England to disallow all such bills. How were the colonial leaders able to exert so much influence over their governors? For one thing, they threatened to deny these governors their salaries, which, curiously, were paid by the colonial legislatures rather than by Parliament. Probably another reason the governors gave in to the demands of the colonists is that they had first-hand experience with the paper money system and realized that its benefits outweighed any disadvantages.

The colonial governors only had the authority to grant tentative approval to the new currency issues; final endorsement or disallowance rested with a powerful Parliamentary committee in London. British officials followed inconsistent policies, which further confused the issue. They summarily rejected two South Carolina acts and one New York law because of unacceptable legal tender clauses. Yet in 1770 the same officials let stand a Pennsylvania act which made newly issued money legally acceptable in the repayment of loans against real estate at government offices. New York, citing its long experience in managing paper currency, lobbied Parliament for an exemption from the act of 1764, and it was finally granted. Other colonies followed suit with similar pleas for an exemption from the stifling regulations. In 1773 Parliament amended the currency act to permit the issuance of paper money which was legal tender in all public transactions but not in the payment of private debts.

The settlement was a compromise of sorts. Parliament retained the ban on legal tender status in the private sector but permitted the colonial legislatures to make the paper money legal tender in the payment of domestic taxes and other government obligations. After decades of conflict, the issue was resolved generally to the satisfaction of British merchants, who remained protected from losses associated with the depreciation of colonial currency, and the colonial legislatures, who could now issue more paper money without harassment from British officials.

## IMPORTANCE OF PAPER MONEY

To understand the intensity of this conflict, we need to address the following questions. How important was paper money to the health of the colonial economy? How important were legal tender provisions in supporting the value of currency issues? Paper money proved convenient and useful in most colonies, but it was by no means critical for their economic development. The paper funds were only a supplement to the main component of the money supply throughout the period—specie coins. Virginia operated on a strictly specie basis up until 1755, without suffering any known disadvantages.

The major benefit of paper money in general was not that it boosted greatly the general level of economic activity, but rather that it made the negotiation of small, everyday transactions easier for the population. Paper money was issued in smaller denominations than specie coins. The lowest coin in circulation was valued at around 7.5 shillings ($30), or three days' wages for unskilled workers. In contrast, a large portion of the paper notes were under 5 shillings ($20) and some were as small as one shilling ($4). Even this lowest amount is very high by modern standards; you can image what it would be like today if a $4 bill or coin was the smallest denomination of change in your pocket. The net result was that the colonists had fewer problems negotiating small business transactions than the English, who remained on a strictly specie basis. A more convenient monetary system may have been one of the factors encouraging more exchanges of goods between individuals, or what economists would call market activity, but it is difficult to conceive of this system of paper finance making any more than the slightest impact on the total income of the colonists. Or, put another way, if Parliament had banned forever paper money in any shape or form, the incomes of the colonists would not have suffered very much—if at all.

Similarly, provisions in colonial currency acts making paper money legal tender in private transactions had little effect on the level of depreciation, irrespective of the claims of many colonial leaders. The designation of paper money as legal tender in public transactions was important in sustaining its value, however. The demand for these notes to use in the payment of taxes was the chief mechanism supporting their value. Where taxes were collected and the paper money retired in due course, depreciation was either avoided or was gradual and predictable. Paper money depreciated heavily in colonies where the legislatures failed to impose sufficient taxes to retire the outstanding issues on a regular basis. Yet even in these colonies, rapidly depreciating paper did not damage severely the economy or lower income levels.

The dispute with Parliament over the status of paper money was one of the two most hotly contested issues in the fifteen years before independence. After permitting the southern and middle colonies almost free rein for nearly half a century, British officials suddenly interjected themselves into what the colonists had long considered a domestic affair. Parliament's interference was resented and resisted. These colonies never stopped issuing paper money with legal tender provisions even after passage of the Currency Act of 1764, which forbade such issues. In the face of colonial defiance and constant badgering, Parliament finally backed off and agreed to allow the issuance of paper money which was legal tender in the payment of all public debts. After 1773, the regulations applicable to the colonies in the three major regions were the same for the first time since 1751.

The battle over paper money was primarily a contest of wills. In this instance a compromise was reached. The colonies retained paper money as a feature of their financial system, and British merchants were able to eliminate provisions making the currency legal tender in private debts. The confrontation over taxes was less easily resolved, and it eventually precipitated an outbreak of fighting between colonial and British troops.

## NEW TAXES

Throughout the colonial period Americans were probably the most lightly taxed people in the civilized world. Their status was ironic because free Americans also had one of the highest average income levels and thus possessed the financial ability to carry a healthy burden of taxes. In the middle of the eighteenth century the overall burden of taxes on the individual citizen was about five times greater in England than in the colonies. The colonists paid about 2 percent of their income for taxes compared to about 35 percent for Americans in 1982. This latter figure points up how much government in general has expanded in the last 200 years.

Why did the colonists pay so few taxes? The answer lies in the coming together of a unique set of circumstances. In this era central governments provided few social services for their citizens. The main expenses were defense-related, the maintenance of army and naval forces and the payment of interest and principal on huge debts incurred to fight past wars. All of the European powers had big national debts and continual defense costs. The colonies, in contrast, did not maintain standing armies and navies. Skirmishes with native American tribes were intermittent and not fought on a broad enough scale to saddle the colonists with a permanent debt structure.

The most important reason for such small outlays on defense, however, was that the British shouldered the bulk of the costs. The British navy patrolled the North Atlantic shipping lanes. Major military campaigns against the French, Spanish, and Indians in frontier areas were financed mainly by Parliament. In some cases the colonies advanced the money and Parliament reimbursed them at a later date for most of their expenses—or even more than they had spent since accounting systems were not very accurate in this period. The British assumed these costs because they were competing with other European rivals for empire and glory. Moreover, until the eighteenth century, the colonial population was too small to contribute very much to the overall costs of defending contiguous land and water. Thus by custom and tradition, the military costs in North America were assumed by taxpayers in Great Britain.

The colonists were the primary beneficiaries of this British policy. Over the years they became so accustomed to having their defense costs assumed by tax-payers 3,000 miles away that, by the middle of the eighteenth century, the colonists believed exemption from heavy taxation was virtually their birthright. Parliament had inadvertently encouraged this belief by subsidizing the colonies for generations.

It is only against this backdrop that we can understand the events of the 1760s and 1770s. After 150 years of granting their colonies almost a free ride, Parliament decided to shift a portion (not all) of military expenses in the North Atlantic and North America to the colonists. What precipitated this change in British policy was the astronomical cost of fighting the victorious French and Indian War (1755-60), which was also fought in Europe and other locations and was known across the Atlantic as the Seven Years War. Not only did the British run up a huge national debt in fighting this war, but they had increased expenses associated with protecting the vast new territories acquired in North America. To make matters worse, British leaders had agreed in advance to compensate the colonies for a substantial portion of the funds expended locally on the war effort. Making good on its pledge, Parliament sent £800,000 ($64 million) to the colonies after 1757. The colonies used these funds to retire their outstanding debts and lower tax rates, which were already minimal.

Meanwhile, the British national debt swelled. Interest payments on the debt soared to £5 million ($400 million) annually. Land taxes, already high, were doubled during the war years. British taxpayers sought relief. The cost of defending the colonies had risen to £400,000 ($32 million) annually and accounted for about 12 percent of the government's operating budget. Under extremely heavy pressure to lower taxes at home, British leaders finally decided in the early 1760s that the colonies would have to begin to absorb some of these mounting costs.

At first, Parliamentary leaders aimed at raising a tax revenue of £40,000 ($3.2 million) a year, or about 10 percent of the colonial defense budget. Later, they hoped to be able to shift, at a gradual pace, more of the financial burden to the colonists. But this strategy failed to work; the colonists resisted even Parliament's initial effort to force them to pay any taxes above a token amount. Pointing to over a century of de facto exemption from British taxation, the colonial legislatures viewed these new and unprecedented actions of Parliament as infringements on their rights and privileges.

The first effort to raise a small revenue in the colonies had a curious twist. In the 1730s Parliament had placed a tax of 6 pence ($2) per gallon on molasses imported from French and Spanish islands in the Carribean. The intent was not to collect taxes but rather to make the rate so high that very little molasses would be imported from French and Spanish possessions. The goal was to preserve the molasses trade for British sugar plantation owners in the Caribbean. In other words, the high tax on molasses was really a navigation act, in the sense that its prime aim was to control or influence the pattern of trade within the British Empire. A very high tax on imports is called a "protective tariff" because its goal is not to raise revenues but to inhibit or stifle trade.

The colonial response to this act of 1733 was smuggling. American merchants continued to import molasses from the French and Spanish islands but they avoided registering their cargoes with the customs collectors. Colonists caught engaging in smuggling usually had their cargoes confiscated and were fined as well. Beginning in 1764 Parliament changed its overall strategy. First, the tax on French and Spanish molasses was lowered to 3 pence ($1) per gallon and provisions were made to strengthen the enforcement of the law. The thinking was that colonial shippers would be willing to pay a reduced tax rather than run the risk of confiscation and fines. Then a few years later the tax was lowered again to one pence (33¢) per gallon and applied to British as well as foreign molasses. The generation of revenue now took precedence over protecting markets for British plantation owners in the Caribbean. The colonists realized the intent of the regulations had changed significantly and ominously, but they were hardly in a position to complain about a reduction in tax rates.

## STAMP TAX

Searching for other means of raising a small colonial revenue, Parliamentary leaders decided in 1765 to impose a stamp tax. Common in England, stamp taxes were applied to legal and government documents such as wills and deeds, plus a group of miscellaneous items—newspaper advertisements, playing cards, and dice. When news of the passage of the law reached the colonies, the reaction was harsh and violent. The colonists protested this unprecedented British effort to interfere in what they considered a strictly domestic matter. The tax itself was not burdensome, for it threatened to cost the typical American no more than 5 pence ($1.65) a year, or about 0.2 percent of per capita incomes. A major principle of self-government was at stake, however; the colonists raised the issue of "taxation without representation," irrespective of the amount of the levy.

Nine colonies sent representatives to a hastily called congress in New York. It issued a proclamation protesting the passage of the Stamp Act and challenging the right of Parliament to pass tax bills applicable to the colonies in general. The colonists threatened to cease purchasing English imports until the stamp taxes were removed. This threat of a sustained boycott frightened many English merchants who feared the loss of American sales. Meanwhile, Benjamin Franklin appeared before Parliament and told its members that the Americans were opposed to the stamp tax because it was an "internal" tax rather than an "external" tax such as the tariff on molasses. Franklin was dead wrong. He was either terribly misinformed or deliberately tried to mislead his audience.

But Parliament followed his lead. It repealed the stamp tax, and set to work looking for a substitute tax program less objectionable to colonial sensitivities. When the colonists learned that Parliament had rescinded the stamp act, they were overjoyed and heartened by their victory. This outcome strengthened their sense of power vis-a-vis Parliament and reinforced their belief in the righteousness of their arguments against British taxation. Few, if any, of them knew that Franklin had told Parliament they supposedly had no objections to higher tariffs or other so-called external taxes.

## TOWNSHEND DUTIES

In 1767, Charles Townshend, the new Chancellor of the Exchequer (comparable to our Secretary of the Treasury), pushed through Parliament a series of tariffs on such items as glass, paint leads, paper, and tea. The aim was to raise around £40,000 ($3.2 million) in taxes—the same amount as the doomed stamp levies. Since these were external taxes, Parliamentary leaders anticipated no serious objections in the colonies.

They were grossly mistaken. The protests were more vociferous than ever. Having successfully opposed British efforts to raise taxes in the previous two years, the colonists were in a mood to resist again. The arguments about representation in Parliament were repeated, and no distinction was made between internal and external taxes. The main weapon in the battle against the so-called Townshend duties was not rhetoric but an economic boycott of English manufactured goods. By the 1760s over 35 percent of English exports went to the North American colonies. The business lost by English merchants in 1768 and 1769 was enormous, over £1 million ($80 million) in sales foregone. That sum dwarfed the £2,700 ($216,000) collected in tariffs; the revenues were hardly large enough to pay the customs collectors' salaries. The colonists did without or found domestic substitutes for goods previously imported, and their resistance remained resolute. Finally, recognizing the futility of trying to raise a substantial tax revenue in the colonies, Parliament in 1770 backed down. It withdrew all the Townshend duties except one; the tea tax was retained as a symbol of British authority.

The Americans had shown the power of economic retaliation in a contest with a nation heavily dependent on overseas sales. The colonists had resisted taxation on two occasions and emerged almost completely victorious. After 1770 Parliament imposed no new taxes. It was reconciled to allowing British taxpayers to carry over 90 percent of the burden of defense costs in North America.

The colonists resented the continuance of the tea tax but they paid it. After dropping to only 108,000 pounds in 1770, tea imports climbed to 359,000 pounds in 1771. In the period from 1771 to 1773, the customs collectors received duties of about £34,000 annually on molasses, wine, sugar, and tea. This sum was large enough to pay for the cost of operating the customs houses and to provide a very small surplus for transfer to the English treasury.

## BOSTON TEA PARTY

Many people in both the colonies and England believed that the issue of colonial taxation had been settled. In the early 1770s neither side seemed anxious to renew the conflict. But then a series of unanticipated events, which initially appeared to have little connection with previous disputes, reopened old wounds and rekindled lingering resentments. The East India Company, a large English trading firm with friends and investors in Parliament, was on the verge of bankruptcy in 1773. Its warehouses were crammed with unsold tea. Seeking a plan to save the company, Parliament granted it a tea monopoly in the colonial market. At the same time, the government adjusted tariffs in England so that the price of tea for colonial consumers would be lower than previously, even after paying the American tax.

Instead of welcoming this opportunity to acquire tea at reduced prices, the colonists reacted very negatively to the new law. Historians and other scholars have never been able to agree about the exact reasons for this, even though these events occurred over 200 years ago and much research has gone into the subject. This is not unusual, for many historical events still seem to escape a full and convincing single explanation. History does not provide irrefutable answers to questions about the past, and events such as those occurring in the colonies in 1773 remain perplexing.

When the East India Company's ships reached colonial ports, the residents would not permit the tea to be unloaded. Here are some of the reasons cited by historians for their behavior. First, colonial shippers who had been involved in smuggling tea from Dutch suppliers into the country found that the new low prices for English tea threatened to undermine their illegal activities. Second, the English company planned to market the tea through its own wholesalers, thus diverting

*PEOPLE WHO MATTERED—John Hancock*

His most famous act was signing the Declaration of Independence in 1776 in huge script. Before his entry into politics, John Hancock was a successful Boston merchant. Born in 1736, he was adopted as a young boy, after the death of his minister father, by a childless uncle, Thomas Hancock, who ranked among the wealthiest men in Massachusetts. Following graduation from Harvard in 1754, Hancock entered his uncle's thriving mercantile firm, which was involved heavily in the trade with England. One of the partnership's major exports was whale oil, which was used in lamps as an illuminant until it was replaced by kerosene in the late nineteenth century. The American whaling industry was centered on Nantucket, an island off the southern coast of Massachusetts. By the late colonial period, whale oil accounted for about one half of the exports from New England to Britain. When his uncle died in 1764, Thomas Hancock inherited his fortune and continued the mercantile firm.

In 1768 one of Hancock's ships, *Liberty*, was seized by British authorities because of his alleged involvement in smuggling wine. Because feeling against England was so intense, the *Liberty* affair bolstered Hancock's reputation among local patriots. After election to the Massachusetts legislature in 1769, he was subsequently appointed a delegate to the Continental Congress and served as its president from 1775 to 1777. Returning to Massachusetts, Hancock held the governorship of the state for nine years and died in office in 1793 at the age of fifty-six.

business away from colonial merchants. Colonists in the port cities seemed to have been particularly inflamed by the monopoly issue. If Parliament could give the East India Company a monopoly on tea, what was to prevent other English firms from obtaining similar monopolies for the distribution of every item regularly imported into the colonies? Third, it has been hypothesized that many Americans were still angered by the continuance of the tea tax, and this new legislation associated with the importation of tea revived old animosities toward Parliament.

Whatever the reasons for their actions, a group of colonists in Boston raided a British vessel laden with tea and dumped it into the water in December 1773. The Boston Tea Party was a well-planned and well-executed three-hour operation involving 30 to 40 men. Tea valued at £9,000 ($720,000) went overboard. This destruction of English property was deliberately inflammatory; it represented another challenge to the authority of Parliament to control events in the colonies.

This time Parliament did not back down. It passed a series of punitive acts; it closed the port of Boston and stationed British troops in the city. In April 1775 shots were fired at Lexington and Concord, and the War for Independence was under way.

## ECONOMIC BURDEN?

These conflicts over paper money and taxes obviously revolved around economic issues, but it does not necessarily follow that the outcome of the debate had important economic consequences. The colonies could have functioned without paper money. Whether the existing paper money was legal tender in private transactions had little effect on its value. Likewise, the taxes proposed by Parliament in the 1760s were hardly burdensome. On the contrary, the rate of taxation would have had to increase tenfold before the amounts collected in the colonies equalled the sums Parliament was already spending for the defense of North America. Indeed, after independence, per capita taxes in the 1790s were approximately ten times greater than prior to the war, for Americans had lost the British subsidy.

The confrontations over money and taxes escalated into broader constitutional issues. What was the proper relationship among the colonies, Parliament, the crown, and even the colonies to each other? Subservience to a legislature meeting across an ocean where the colonies had no representatives offended American sensibilities and was ruled out as completely unacceptable. In every battle over money and taxes the colonists emerged almost completely victorious, yet they were still dissatisfied about their status in the British Empire. Parliament gave up its attempt to raise a substantial colonial revenue in 1770 after the Americans demonstrated the power of an effective boycott of British goods. The mother country was never able to mount a serious threat to the economic welfare of its colonies. Americans did not revolt because of economic hardships, but rather to achieve political independence.

## SELECTED REFERENCES

BARROW, THOMAS. *Trade and Empire: The British Customs Service in Colonial America, 1660-1775.* Cambridge: Harvard University Press, 1967.

BECKER, ROBERT A. *Revolution, Reform, and the Politics of Taxation in America: 1763-1783.* Baton Rouge: Louisiana State University Press, 1980.

BROCK, LESLIE. *The Currency System of the American Colonies, 1700-1764.* New York: Arno Press, 1975.

ERNST, JOSEPH. *Money and Politics in America, 1755-1775.* Chapel Hill: University of North Carolina Press, 1973.

_____, and MARC EGNAL. "An Economic Interpretation of the American Revolution," *William and Mary Quarterly* (1972), 3-32.

GREENE, JACK P., and RICHARD JELLISON. "The Currency Act of 1764 in Imperial-Colonial Relations, 1764-1776," *William and Mary Quarterly* (1968), 177-211.

HANSON, JOHN R. "Money in the Colonial American Economy: An Extension," *Economic Inquiry* (1979), 281-86.

LESTER, RICHARD. "Currency Issues to Overcome Depressions in Pennsylvania, 1723 and 1729," *Journal of Political Economy* (1963), 324-75.

MORGAN, EDMUND and HELEN. *The Stamp Act Crisis: Prologue to Revolution.* Chapel Hill: University of North Carolina Press, 1963.

NASH, GARY. *The Urban Crucible.* Cambridge: Harvard University Press, 1979.

PERKINS, EDWIN J. *The Economy of Colonial America.* New York: Columbia University Press, 1980.

WALTON, GARY M., and JAMES F. SHEPHERD. *The Economic Rise of Early America.* Cambridge: Cambridge University Press, 1979.

WEISS, ROGER. "The Issue of Paper Money in the American Colonies, 1720-1774," *Journal of Economic History* (1970), 770-785.

# CHAPTER SEVEN
# TRADE, BANKS, AND BUSINESS CYCLES IN THE NEW NATION

## WARTIME FINANCE

The War of Independence began in 1775 and six years later ended with the surrender of British forces at Yorktown. One of the major economic challenges facing American political leaders was financing the military effort. The new national government had no independent system of collecting taxes and was forced to appeal to the states for support. Little was forthcoming. With no banks and few domestic sources of loanable funds, congressional leaders turned to the expediency of issuing paper money to pay for military expenses.

About three quarters of the total cost of the war was financed by paper currency issued by Congress and various state legislatures. Because of the voluminous issuance of paper money and the absence of an effective tax system, this currency declined in value. Depreciation was moderate at first but accelerated rapidly after 1777. The national and state governments issued nearly $450 million in paper currency during the war years, and by the time the fighting ended in 1781, this money was virtually worthless. A popular saying for generations thereafter was "not worth a continental," meaning the paper issued by the Continental Congress.

The depreciation of the currency was simply an alternative method of taxation. Rather than collecting funds in advance through taxes to acquire goods and services, the government printed money to buy them. This means of obtaining goods and services was like a tax, however; in this case one imposed indirectly. The tax resulted from the decrease in value which individuals suffered between the date they voluntarily acquired and then voluntarily spent the paper currency. Each surge of inflation imposed a new tax on real spending.

Since most people knew the money was depreciating, they tended to hold it only for a short period of time. Thus, the tax extracted was usually fairly small on any given transaction. A good analogy would be the effect of the modern sales tax. In many ways the depreciation of currency was an equitable method of taxation, because the burden fell on a broad group of citizens. The wealthy paid the highest share since they were normally the most active in making business transactions involving cash, while small farmers on the frontier, who were not large participants in market activity, were generally exempt from this form of taxation.

One quarter of the funds required to fight the war was borrowed from lenders at home and abroad. In the 1780s some states made a serious effort to retire their debts, but the national government and other states permitted their debts to languish. The Articles of Confederation gave the national government no independent system of taxation, and the absence of taxing power was among the reasons cited for the drafting of a new Constitution in 1787. One of the first acts of the new government under President George Washington and his Secretary of the Treasury, Alexander Hamilton, was to guide through Congress a bill providing for the payment of interest and principal on the outstanding war debts. In the first major congressional compromise, it was agreed to locate the national government permanently in the District of Columbia, between Virginia and Maryland (two slave states), in return for the national government's assumption of the remaining state debts. The combined total was nearly $80 million, with the national government accounting for two thirds and the states one third. The revenues to pay the interest and principal on the national debt, plus all other government expenses, came from tariffs (taxes on imported goods) and the proceeds of land sales in the western territories. Until the ascendency of income taxes as an additional method of taxation after 1910, tariffs were the primary source of government revenues, which explains why their level was invariably one of the hot issues in political debates during the nineteenth century.

## DISRUPTION OF TRADE

The outbreak of hostilities with British troops in 1775 led to the disruption of overseas trade. In previous decades Great Britain and its Caribbean colonies had accounted for over 80 percent of foreign commerce, and that trade was abruptly cut off. The British navy also instituted a blockade of American ports which stifled early attempts to develop alternative trade routes. After 1778, however, the effectiveness of the blockade diminished, and direct trade with France, Holland, Spain, and their possessions began in earnest.

When the war ended, most of the new trading patterns established in the previous six years were retained. By 1790 one quarter of U.S. overseas commerce headed for non-British islands in the Caribbean, while nations on the European continent claimed another one third of United States exports. In the latter case most of the exports were tobacco, which could be shipped directly to continental ports following the ending of the old navigation acts. At the same time, much of the trade within the British Empire revived, in part because English merchants usually offered the greatest variety of quality goods at the lowest prices and because they granted favorable credit terms. By 1790 trade with Britain and its possessions accounted for 40 percent of American commerce.

Between 1770 and 1790 the monetary value of trade rose by one third but population grew much faster. Per capita exports declined by one quarter. The largest drop came in the lower South, primarily South Carolina, where per capita exports fell by one half. The value of rice and indigo exports both decreased in absolute terms, while naval stores showed almost no improvement. There were some bright spots in the United States trade figures, however, with the middle Atlantic states enjoying most of the benefits. Exports of corn more than doubled; wheat jumped two thirds; bread and flour climbed three quarters; and tobacco rose by one quarter.

In the last quarter of the eighteenth century, population continued to grow very rapidly, and growth was much faster in rural than in urban areas. The major seaports along the northern coast—Boston, New York, and Philadelphia—were nearly stagnant. Settlement was extensive on the western frontier, however, which was then just over the Appalachian Mountains. The transportation system in these newly settled areas was poor; few roads were regularly maintained and rivers were mostly unnavigable. The high cost of overland transportation discouraged farmers from making the maximum effort to increase output. Without easy access to distant markets in the east and overseas, the material living standards of those settlers who moved over 200 miles from the Atlantic coastline were low relative to seaboard residents, at least for a while. Indeed in the twenty years after the beginning of the War of Independence, per capita incomes may have fallen as much as 10 percent for the entire American population.

## PROSPERITY AND THE WAR OF 1812

During the first quarter century after the adoption of the Constitution in 1789, hostilities between England and France had a profound impact on U.S. trade. In 1793 these two European powers went to war, and many of their merchant vessels were converted into warships. The United States remained neutral in this conflict, and its ships took over a huge proportion of the carrying trade between the two belligerents and their respective colonies in the Caribbean. The suddenly increased volume of trade sparked a revival of population and income growth in the seaport cities and areas all along the Atlantic coast. Eventually, however, the American effort to maintain a neutral stance and thereby reap economic benefits clashed with the military aims of the British and French governments. Each side viewed the Americans as aiding the enemy, and both tried to clamp down on such activities through seizures of ships and cargoes and other tactics—such as the British impressment of U.S. seamen into its navy.

In an effort to secure greater respect for U.S. rights as a neutral, Presidents Thomas Jefferson and James Madison pushed through Congress a series of bills restricting trade with France and England. In 1807, for example, an embargo prevented all American vessels from sailing for foreign ports; it was subsequently lifted in March 1809. The strategy of using economic coercion to achieve political aims had worked successfully against Parliament in the decade before independence, but between 1807 and 1812 similar tactics failed to have the same effect. Indeed, their implementation eventually led the nation into an unnecessary, unwanted, and unwinnable military confrontation with Great Britain—the War of 1812.

Three factors accounted largely for the failure of economic coercion to achieve its aims in this era. First, foreign powers were more concerned about pursuing policies which damaged their immediate military rivals in Europe than in placating ruffled American feathers about abstract principles like neutral rights. Second, the restrictions were not painless for Americans since farmers lost markets and merchants surrendered potential profits, especially those in the port cities. Lastly, American leaders lacked resolve and were indecisive; they altered the scope of the trading regulations on three different occasions (1806, 1809, 1810) without giving any single strategy an opportunity to take full effect. The final irony was that, when a frustrated President Madison asked Congress for a declaration of war against Great Britain in the spring of 1812, Parliament had only a few days earlier agreed to accede to U.S. demands for the protection of its commerce. But communications moved slowly by sailing vessels in this era, and the news reached Washington after the first naval attacks on British warships had already occurred. The war neither side wanted went on inconclusively for a year and a half.

## EMERGENCE OF COMMERCIAL BANKS

One of the new institutions to appear on the American scene after the break with England was the commercial bank. In the colonial era, none had existed. Individuals needing money borrowed directly from other individuals who had surplus funds, while merchants extended book credit to their customers, both wholesale and retail. Beginning in the 1780s, however, banks were organized, which provided an alternative method of securing loans.

Banks served several functions. First, they were intermediaries between borrowers and savers. Banks offered a safe depository for those with surplus funds and often paid interest on such deposits. These funds were, in turn, loaned out to borrowers at slightly higher interest rates. The margin between the cost of funds on deposit and the interest received on loans was part of the revenue from which the bank paid its operating expenses and hopefully earned a profit.

But American banks did more than serve as mere middlemen between savers and borrowers; they also had the power to expand the volume of loanable funds beyond the existing monetary base. They could create new money! When banks took in specie from stockholders and depositors, they normally stored the gold and silver in their vaults and issued banknotes, which were a more convenient form of money for most borrowers. Banknotes were issued with the understanding that anyone could come into the bank at any time and exchange them for specie. This feature was called convertibility; it explains why so many people were willing to accept banknotes in payment for goods and services.

Banks did not, however, issue banknotes strictly on a one-to-one ratio to the amount of specie in their vaults. Instead, they issued banknotes in volumes three to five times greater, or sometimes even more, than their actual holdings of specie. Banks created this extra money because they wanted to make more loans and thereby earn more interest revenue. Meanwhile, they anticipated that the actual number of individuals demanding conversion of their outstanding banknotes into specie at any given period of time would be few enough to maintain their reserves. By using the specie in their vaults as *fractional* reserves, rather than one hundred percent reserves, commercial banks were able to make more loans and issue more banknotes than the stock of specie in the financial system had previously permitted.

The first American bank was established in Philadelphia in 1781. The chief organizer was Robert Morris, a member of the Continental Congress who had assumed the task of managing government finances during the last few years of the War of Independence. The Bank of North America made short-term loans to the national government, and it was instrumental in putting the military effort back on a solid financial basis. Two other commercial banks opened in the 1780s, and twenty-five more opened in the 1790s. By 1810, over 100 banks had been organized in the several states. They made short-term loans primarily to merchants in towns and cities and to farmers in rural areas.

In order to begin operations, banks needed to receive special charters of incorporation from the various state legislatures. Bank charters were issued on an ad hoc basis, and critics of the system frequently alleged that political concerns were instrumental in determining which group of citizens obtained the charter privilege. In subsequent decades, reform groups sponsored legislation designed to put more distance between politics and the power to authorize the opening of new banks. Bank charters usually placed some limitations on the liabilities of stockholders in the event of failure, and in the spirit of protecting the general public, they normally placed restrictions on the ratio of banknote circulation relative to specie reserves. The first quarter century after independence was a fairly safe period for American banking, since only a few institutions were unable to maintain convertibility between banknotes and specie.

## FIRST BANK OF THE UNITED STATES

Soon after the establishment of a stronger central government under the Constitution, Secretary of the Treasury Alexander Hamilton proposed the founding of a large national bank which would assist in funding the outstanding government debt and generally promote a sound United States financial system. A huge controversy immediately erupted about whether the Constitution contained provisions that would allow the federal government to create such a bank. The followers of Secretary Hamilton argued that since no articles explicitly denied this authority, the power to act was "implied." But supporters of Thomas Jefferson objected vigorously to this broad interpretation of constitutional authority. Since none of the articles called explicitly for the establishment of such an important national institution, they claimed its creation would be nothing less than unconstitutional. In this instance, President George Washington, after long deliberation, sided with Hamilton, and the bank bill received his endorsement and eventually was passed by Congress. However, politicians identifying with the Jeffersonian tradition remained skeptical about the constitutionality of the institution, and later on two occasions, in 1811 and 1832, they were in position to terminate the bank's national charter when it came up for renewal. Indeed, controversies about banking were among the two or three consistently debated political issues in the nation from independence up until the New Deal reforms of the 1930s.

The First Bank of the United States was capitalized at $10 million, with private investors purchasing 80 percent of the stock and the government assigned the remainder. At its inception in 1792, the national bank was as large as all the other existing fifteen states banks combined. Over the next twenty years, however, its share of total banking assets declined steadily, reaching a low of 15 percent in 1811. The bank had one charter privilege that distinguished it particularly from other institutions; it could open branch offices across the nation, and by 1805 seven were in operation in New York, Boston, Baltimore, Washington, Charleston, Savannah, and New Orleans. Its main office was in Philadelphia. In contrast, most state banks were restricted to only one location, and none had the authority to establish branch offices in another state.

The First Bank performed several different functions. It served as the fiscal agent for the federal government and held revenues collected from tariffs, land sales, and other taxes. The Secretary of the Treasury paid the government's bills by drawing checks against those deposits. Interest on the national debt accounted for one third to one half of the federal government's expenditures in the late eighteenth and early nineteenth centuries. The First Bank was also a general commercial bank, in the sense that it made most of its loans in the private sector. Urban merchants borrowed from the bank in order to finance their inventories and other short-term needs. The First Bank issued notes to borrowers that circulated at very near face value throughout the nation. It held a very large stock of specie so that conversions of banknotes were routinely made with little strain on reserves.

The First Bank also functioned as an unofficial and informal regulator of the operations of the numerous state banks. Because of its great size, its geographic distribution of branch offices, and its conservative lending policies, the First Bank accumulated in its normal business activities a substantial volume of notes issued by the state banks. By presenting these notes regularly for conversion into specie, the national bank kept sufficient pressure on the reserves of the state banks to prevent their managers from making an excessive number of loans and issuing, in conjunction with their lending activities, an imprudent volume of banknotes. At the same time there is evidence that the First Bank also aided state banks threatened with possible failure because of temporarily inadequate reserves. In these cases, the national bank refrained from presenting notes for conversion or actually made outright loans of specie to institutions desperately in need of reserves. When it made such interbank loans, the First Bank was acting as a "lender of last resort," a function normally associated with the services of a so-called central bank. Although it was never designated as a central bank or assigned the duties of a central bank, this institution did perform a number of central banking functions, and thus it can be considered a legitimate forerunner of the Federal Reserve System, which emerged in the twentieth century.

In 1811, when legislation to renew the national bank's initial twenty-year charter was put to a vote in Congress, it failed to pass. The First Bank's demise represents a perfect example of how the past rhetoric of prominent political leaders can come back to haunt them and prevent them from making adjustments to altered conditions. In the original debate about the creation of this financial institution in the 1790s, James Madison, then a congressman from Virginia, was among the bank's most fervent opponents. The proposed bank, he had claimed, was little more than a vehicle to advance the economic and political power of a monied urban, mainly northern, elite. But even more damning, the legislation to create the institution was allegedly an unconstitutional act. Madison and others in the Jeffersonian political tradition repeated this last argument over and over during the next two decades. Yet by 1808, when Madison was elected President, the bank could point to eighteen years of successful and responsible operations. None of the horrors predicted by its original opponents had come to pass.

Once in office, Madison began to modify his opinion of the bank, but he was still stuck with the old argument that, irrespective of its record of performance, the bank was unconstitutional. Finally he concluded that, as a practical matter, the First Bank genuinely deserved a renewal of its charter, and he gave it a lukewarm endorsement. But Madison's reversal of opinion came too late. The matter was left largely in the hands of congressional leaders, and after a series of very close votes in both houses, the bank bill died and the charter was allowed to expire in 1812.

## SECOND BANK OF THE UNITED STATES

Congress learned just a few years later that it had made a major blunder. The problems associated with financing the War of 1812 revealed how difficult it was for the federal government to borrow substantial funds in wartime without the assistance of a large national bank. As a result, with the almost unanimous support of all political factions, a new Second Bank of the United States received a charter in 1816. It had all the privileges of its predecessor plus a capital three and a half times larger at $35 million. The Second Bank also functioned unofficially as a quasi-central bank; it kept pressure on the state banks to restrict their lending activities to prudent levels by routinely presenting their notes for conversion into specie, and occasionally (but not always) it acted as a lender of last resort for smaller banks temporarily short of adequate reserves. Under the leadership of its third president, Nicholas Biddle, the national bank expanded its effort to smooth out the seasonal fluctuations in the domestic money market through its ability to transfer funds easily back and forth among various sections of the country. The Second Bank also became the largest foreign exchange dealer in the United States market, which meant that it bought foreign money (or claims on foreign money) from American exporters and then, in turn, sold foreign monies at slightly higher rates to importers with debts overseas.

Like its immediate predecessor, however, the Second Bank was unable to avoid political controversy. Only three years after its founding, the bank was accused of contributing significantly to the outbreak of the so-called Panic of 1819, which ushered in a long period of financial and economic dislocation. Although scholars have cast doubt on the actual role of the Second Bank in fomenting this period of economic unrest, a large number of people at the time—many of them looking for scapegoats—put much of the blame on bankers in general and the Second Bank, in particular, since it was the largest financial institution in the nation. Among the leading skeptics was General Andrew Jackson, who was later elected President in the election of 1828.

## BANK WAR: JACKSON VERSUS BIDDLE

In his inaugural address, President Jackson expressed doubts about whether the Second Bank should be permitted to continue operations when the existing twenty-year contract came up for renewal unless there was a complete overhaul of its charter. The matter came to a head in 1832. Representative Henry Clay of Kentucky, former Speaker of the House and a presidential aspirant in the Whig Party, along with other political opponents of Jackson convinced Nicholas Biddle, the bank's incredibly competent but occasionally haughty president, to apply to Congress for a renewal of the charter four years before the scheduled expiration date. A bill was introduced into Congress which called for the Second Bank to retain almost all of its existing privileges and powers.

The motive behind this premature application was political advantage. Supporters of the bank calculated that Jackson would not risk his political future by vetoing a bill to recharter the bank, which had the endorsement of the business community and most state bankers, in a presidential election year. In private, some of his political opponents actually hoped Jackson would act irresponsibly and reject the bank bill, because they believed it would certainly cost him the presidency.

The scheme to put the squeeze on Jackson backfired miserably, however. As anticipated, the bill to recharter the bank breezed through Congress, passing by wide margins (but not two thirds) in both the House and Senate. Jackson decided to meet the challenge head on; he rejected the bank bill and took the opportunity to deliver a ringing veto message, which subsequently became an important document in his successful reelection campaign. He sized up the situation succinctly in this memorable quote: "The Bank is trying to kill me, but I will kill it." Jackson listed a host of objections to the operations of the Second Bank and the terms of the charter, among them the old refrain about its unconstitutional status. He also asserted that the bank favored the rich over the poor and that it was a "monster" because of its alleged monopoly powers (a grossly overblown argument since there were hundreds of state banks providing competitive services).

After the veto message was delivered, the merits of the case and the future character of the American financial system were topics never seriously discussed by either side. A political power struggle was underway.

Supporters of the bank were in no mood for compromise. They made no effort to draft an alternative bill which might have satisfied the bulk of the objections cited in the veto message and still preserved the Second Bank in a slightly modified form. Instead, the bank faction held out for everything—and got nothing. When the vote to override the presidential veto was taken in the Senate, more Democrats deserted the bank bill and supported the President. The override vote failed, and Jackson went on to win the election handily. The Second Bank lost its national charter in 1836, and the United States had no commercial bank to provide central banking functions on a regular basis for over three quarters of a century.

The reasons for Jackson's animus toward the Second Bank have been the focus of a large number of scholarly studies. Historians are invariably interested in analyzing the underlying motives for important decisions and actions as well as describing the events themselves. Some researchers have turned to the new field of psychohistory in their efforts to find out why historical figures possessed certain attitudes and acted as they did. President Jackson has been the subject of one Freudian psychobiography in which the author, Michael Paul Rogin, traced Jackson's attitude toward the bank back to early childhood influences. According to this line of interpretation, Jackson, in battling the Second Bank, which exerted "control" over the economy and thereby undermined the independence of virtuous citizens, was actually reenacting his own struggle to escape the control of his powerful mother. Although many historians remain skeptical about the value, even the validity, of psychobiographies, they nonetheless represent another effort to apply the techniques of other disciplines to historical events.

A definitive conclusion about why Jackson was so determined to destroy the Second Bank, which most financial historians agree was performing a valuable service to the national economy, has remained elusive. In addition to psychological explanations, many other theories have been advanced over the decades. Some historians link Jackson's attitude to one crucial financial episode early in his career. In a transaction involving the sale of land in Tennessee, Jackson accepted in payment the personal note of a Philadelphia merchant for $6,000 (a large sum in those days). He then *endorsed* the merchant's note and used it to purchase inventory for his general store. When the Philadelphia merchant later went bankrupt and repudiated the note, Jackson as the endorser was called upon to make it good. This was a serious financial setback and it took him several years to pay off the debt. In the process he became subject to a series of allegedly excessive fees imposed by bankers and brokers, which angered him greatly. As a result of this unfortunate incident, Jackson purportedly came to despise banks in general and the Second Bank in particular, probably because it was the largest financial institution in the nation and therefore the biggest target for his animosity.

Other hypotheses appear equally plausible. Some historians have pointed to Jackson's increasingly antagonistic attitude toward Nicholas Biddle. The President apparently believed that Biddle was deliberately appointing large numbers of his political enemies to the boards of directors of the bank's branch offices. In truth, Biddle tried to conduct his duties in a nonpolitical manner but Jackson remained unconvinced. Other scholars have suggested that Jackson was simply jealous of the enormous economic power that Biddle, over whom the President had no direct control, could exercise over the economy. Although never a "monster monopoly" as depicted in the veto message, the Second Bank was by far the largest business enterprise in the nation in the 1820s and 1830s, and it did have at least the *capacity* for doing much harm if its administration fell into the hands of an incompetent or irresponsible president. According to this line of reasoning, the Second Bank was a threat to a democratic society simply because it possessed too much power, whether for good or evil.

Still other scholars believe that the key to understanding Jackson's general outlook lies in an appreciation of his attitude toward paper money. The President was what was called a "hard money" advocate; he favored a monetary system based largely on specie (gold or silver coins) rather than on substitutes such as banknotes and other forms of paper currency. Small notes under $20 were especially opposed by the advocates of a hard money system. The Second Bank was vulnerable to criticism on this score because, as the largest financial institution, it naturally issued the greatest quantity of paper currency. As President, there was little that Jackson could do to halt the issuance of paper money by hundreds of banks operating under liberal state charters, but within his own domain—the federal government—he could contribute to the cause and leave office knowing that he had done his utmost to curb the pernicious evil of paper money and small notes.

Finally, still surviving was the old argument that the bank was unconstitutional and therefore illegitimate. Jackson identified strongly with the fundamental tenets of the Jeffersonian political tradition, and he was suspicious of the commercial classes in the cities, where most (but not all) banks were located. By the 1830s the vast majority of the followers of Jeffersonian principles took a more practical view of the advantages of maintaining a large national bank, but some like Jackson were still under the spell of appeals to abstract ideals. He had adopted these principles early in his political career, and by the time he had risen to the highest elected office in the land, Jackson was rigid and uncompromising.

All of these hypotheses probably have some element of truth in them. Jackson's veto of the bank bill in 1832 was undoubtedly motivated by a combination of factors. Historians rarely put much faith in explanations of human behavior which place too much emphasis on a single factor. In analyzing the evolution of the U.S. commercial banking system, we must more often take into account the attitudes and prejudices of leading political figures, especially presidents, than in our discussions of the development of other sectors of the economy. This inclusion of the human element is vital because banks were always enterprises operating under some form of governmental supervision. Politics and banks were closely intertwined through the nineteenth and well into the twentieth century.

After Jackson won the election, largely on the basis of his veto of the bank bill, his vehement opposition to a nationally chartered financial institution providing numerous central banking functions was subsequently incorporated into the general ideology of the Democratic Party. That negative attitude toward a central bank was, for decades, a plank in the Democratic platform, and the major opposition parties—first Whigs and later Republicans—dared not advocate too loudly a third national bank for fear of losing at the polls. The Jacksonian legacy was thus a powerful force, which had a tremendous impact on the course of commercial banking.

## BUSINESS CYCLES

The development of an increasingly integrated economic system during the early nineteenth century laid the groundwork for advances in living standards, but its greater sophistication also brought some unpleasant side effects. These were periodic recessions, deep depressions, and financial panics. The economy began to go through a series of fluctuations in harmony with so-called business cycles. The upswings often led to booms, while the downturns, if especially sharp, frequently resulted in panics followed by depressed business activity. Cycles of steady advancement interrupted by recessions or depressions have characterized our economy for the last two centuries.

The first dramatic episode of heightened activity followed by a sudden nose dive came in the second decade of the nineteenth century. The War of 1812 curtailed the importation of British finished goods and set off an expansion in American manufacturing. As a result of a shortage of goods and an increased money supply, prices rose very fast, and they remained high for several years after the end of the war.

## PANIC OF 1819

In 1819, however, the economic boom suddenly ended. Prices fell dramatically to near their prewar level. Many firms went bankrupt and were unable to pay off existing loans. A panic atmosphere soon emerged. Citizens uncertain about the future of the economy and the strength of the financial system tried to convert a large percentage of the circulating banknotes into specie. Since all banks maintained only fractional specie reserves, a sustained effort on the part of the note holders of a single bank—usually called a "run"—invariably led to a suspension of payments. That is, the bank refused to redeem any more of its outstanding notes into gold or silver.

Commercial banks with depleted reserves and a host of bad loans on their books as a result of the recession were prime candidates for failure and liquidation. When a bank failed the losses fell not only on its stockholders, but also on its depositors and noteholders. When many institutions in one area failed within days or weeks of one another, the local population became panicky because everyone wanted to convert his or her paper currency into specie as quickly as possible. Only the lucky ones who got to the bank windows first were successful. Once the panic was underway, even soundly managed banks became vulnerable to runs and possible failure.

The Panic of 1819 was the first general economic crisis in United States history, but it was by no means the last. By the end of 1822, the economy had largely recovered. Except for mild downturns in 1825 and 1834, business conditions were generally favorable for the next fifteen years. In the early 1830s prices began to rise and the economy entered a boom period.

## PANIC OF 1837

Again, a correction was in the cards. The Panic of 1837 was one of the most serious financial breakdowns in our history; only the Great Depression a century later was a setback of greater magnitude. The panic was followed by a brief recovery in 1838 and then an aftershock in 1839, which ushered in three years of depressed business activity and declining prices.

An analysis of the factors leading up to the panic in 1837 represents another prime example of how historical interpretations of events long past remain subject to revision as a result of the uncovering of new evidence or the adoption of new methodologies. (No *definitive* history of any past event has ever been written nor ever will be written.) In the aftermath of the panic, contemporaries cited several factors they believed had made the economy ripe for a serious breakdown. For the most part, their on-the-spot critique was accepted by later historians, and it held up, with minor adjustments, for over one hundred years.

During the early 1830s prices did rise steadily, and contemporaries pointed to increases in the size of the money supply as the reason for the observed inflation. Banks were making more loans and thereby creating more banknotes to lend out to borrowers. Since banks were creating new money more rapidly than workers were producing additional goods and services, prices climbed. After the panic, critics of the banking system alleged that bankers had acted irresponsibly. According to this version of the origins of the crisis, banks had stretched their reserves beyond prudent limits. Thus, when the level of business activity dropped slightly, what should have been a mild recession became instead an uncontrollable panic. In their quest for more interest revenues and greater profits, bankers had placed the whole economy in jeopardy. They were therefore major culprits who bore much responsibility for the disaster which befell the country.

In addition to the banking community, President Jackson, who had just left office when the panic struck, also came in for a share of the blame for fomenting the crisis. Some charged that by destroying the Second Bank of the United States Jackson had foolishly removed the only means of restraint on the state banks. By eliminating the Second Bank, which kept constant pressure on the reserves of smaller state institutions, the President, one of the greatest opponents of paper currency and small notes, had unwittingly unleashed the flood gates of inflation. By this account, Jackson had simply reaped the bitter harvest of his own personal prejudices and bad judgment. In killing off the Second Bank, he had allegedly given birth to the inflationary boom, and thus he was ultimately responsible for the ensuing crises and depression.

President Jackson was also criticized for issuing the Specie Circular in 1836, which many contemporaries and later historians believed had triggered the panic. The circular was an executive order which stipulated that only gold or silver would be accepted by the federal government in payment for purchases of public lands in parcels over 320 acres in the western states (now the midwest). The intent was to slow down the sale of land, which had accelerated from $2 million in 1830 to $5 million in 1834 and then jumped to $25 million in 1836. The government had recently paid off the last installment of the outstanding national debt (a feat never accomplished before or since by any major power), and it had no compelling use for surplus revenue. Moreover, Jackson was convinced that much of the land was being purchased for speculative purposes, which he opposed, and that easy access to bank credit was fueling the speculative mania. Requiring payment in specie was designed to discourage buyers and also to help promote the use of hard money rather than banknotes. After the panic, which occurred soon after the issuance of his executive order, critics argued that the Specie Circular had drained gold and silver from the western to the eastern states, leaving western banks with lowered reserves and thus highly vulnerable to runs.

## ORIGINS OF THE PANIC: NEW INTERPRETATIONS

Within the last several decades, scholars have dismissed almost all of the previously accepted explanations of the origins of the panic and substituted new ones in their place. Jackson, for example, has received almost complete absolution—and so has the banking community. The reason banks extended their loans during the early 1830s was not because of their irresponsible attitude about the maintenance of reserves or because of the absence of the Second Bank as a restraining force. Rather banks stepped up their lending activity and created new money for the simple reason that their reserves of specie were actually increasing at a very fast pace. The inflation experienced during the early 1830s had its roots not in the domestic economy at all, but in the international flow of specie.

As incredible as it may sound, the changing business practices of Chinese merchants had more influence on the inflation rate in the United States than any action taken by President Jackson or anyone else in the United States. Prior to the late 1820s, the normal flow of silver was into this country from Mexico, after which substantial portions were shipped to China to pay for the importation of tea and other Far Eastern goods. By 1830, however, business practices in the leading Chinese ports had undergone a significant change. Foreign merchants no longer demanded silver in payment for their goods but expressed a preference for bills of exchange (something like a check) drawn on London. As a result, the Mexican silver which previously had gone to China now remained inside the vaults of American banks. Moreover, the American public had developed so much confidence in the American banking system that citizens came to prefer paper money over specie. They deposited more of their gold and silver coins in the banks, which boosted reserves even higher. With specie reserves building up rapidly, banks made more loans and issued more paper money. The net result was a high rate of inflation.

In addition, economic historians have largely absolved Jackson for precipitating the panic with the proclamation of the Specie Circular. A close review of the actual specie flows between western and eastern banks in the months immediately after the circular went into effect has revealed that no dramatic change took place. The reserves of state banks in the western states did not deteriorate.

Once more, we must look overseas to determine the most proximate causes for the actual panic. The focus this time is on Britain. In the middle of 1836, the directors of the Bank of England recognized that substantial amounts of specie were leaving the country. Normally, the response of central bankers in this situation would be to raise interest rates generally in an effort to attract more capital back into the national economy. On this occasion, however, the Bank of England made a judgment that the lost specie was going almost exclusively to the United States. We know now that the directors of the Bank of England were mistaken about the direction of the specie flow, but they based their decisions on what they believed was happening. Their solution was to discriminate in their lending policies against all the major English banking and mercantile firms known to be conducting a large volume of business in the United States. Restrictions on the credit of leading firms operating in the American trade left them extremely vulnerable to any pressure arising from an even modest decline in the prices of heavily traded goods, especially cotton.

In the winter of 1836–1837 British farmers suffered an unusually poor harvest. As a result incomes declined briskly. The local demand for textiles diminished and the price of cloth began to fall. By spring, the price of American cotton, the main raw material entering the English textile mills, had likewise dropped significantly. Several of the large Anglo-American firms heavily involved in the cotton trade discovered that the extent of their debts was greater than the value of the cotton inventory in their warehouses and in transit from the United States. Appeals to creditors and the Bank of England for relief fell mostly on deaf ears. Several of the largest cotton dealers could not meet their financial obligations, and their failures triggered a chain of bankruptcies in the United States. The Panic of 1837 was underway.

## THE INTERNATIONAL ECONOMY

The thrust of the new research on the financial disturbances of the 1830s has been to disregard domestic factors, which caught the attention of contemporaries and several generations of historians, and to emphasize instead developments overseas, which affected the United States less directly but much more decisively. The important lesson is that the United States was already a significant part of a rapidly emerging world economic system, and because it was tied to other national economies through the operation of gold and silver monetary standards, events far away could have a profound influence on American financial markets and ultimately the whole economy. Today it is commonplace to acknowledge that the size of harvests in India or the Soviet Union or the state of economies in Western Europe or Japan can have a major impact on farm prices and employment levels here in the United States. We are now beginning to realize the extent to which those overseas forces were influencing the course of the American economy in the second quarter of the nineteenth century as well.

## SELECTED REFERENCES

CATTERAL, RALPH. *The Second Bank of the United States.* Chicago: University of Chicago Press, 1902.

FENSTERMAKER, J. VAN. *The Development of American Commercial Banking, 1782–1837.* Kent, Ohio: Kent State University Press, 1965.

FERGUSON, E. JAMES. *The Power of the Purse: A History of American Public Finance, 1776–1790.* Chapel Hill: University of North Carolina Press, 1961.

HAMMOND, BRAY. *Banks and Politics in America from the Revolution to the Civil War.* Princeton: Princeton University Press, 1957.

MARTIN, DAVID A. "Metallism, Small Notes, and Jackson's War with the Bank of the United States," *Explorations in Economic History* (1974), 227–48.

NORTH, DOUGLASS. *The Economic Growth of the United States, 1790–1860.* New York: W. W. Norton, 1966.

REDLICH, FRITZ. *The Molding of American Banking: Men and Ideas.* 2 vols. New York: Hafner Publishing Co., 1951.

REMINI, ROBERT. *Andrew Jackson and the Bank War.* New York: W. W. Norton, 1967.

ROGIN, MICHAEL. *Fathers and Children: Andrew Jackson and the Subjugation of the American Indian.* New York: Knopf, 1975.

TEMIN, PETER. *The Jacksonian Economy.* New York: W. W. Norton, 1969.

# CHAPTER EIGHT
# EXPANSION
# OF THE MARKET
## *Transportation*
## *and Communications*

During the first half of the nineteenth century, the transportation system for carrying passengers and freight and the communications system for transmitting news and information underwent truly revolutionary changes. At the beginning of the century, transportation and communications moved in unison, and both traveled very slowly at speeds that had increased very little for thousands of years. In 1800 the fastest and least expensive means of moving people, goods, and information was by water—across oceans and lakes and down (but not up) rivers. The cost of transportation over land routes in wagons was so high that little exchange took place except at very short distances. News traveled no faster overland than a person on horseback could ride.

By the 1850s, however, dramatic changes had occurred. A completely new form of transportation, the railroad, carried goods and passengers up to 250 miles per day overland at reasonable prices. Meanwhile, the invention of the telegraph permitted communications to travel across the nation, and later around the world, at the speed of light in a system wholly independent of the transport sector.

Over this half century, the cost of transporting goods between the east coast and the newly settled middle western states dropped by 90 percent. Lower transportation costs opened up the entire U.S. market and encouraged huge increases in the volume of internal trade between urban areas and their hinterlands, within states, and between geographical sections. As costs decreased, the speed of transport increased. As late as 1825, it took one month for goods and news to travel from New York to New Orleans by ship. By 1840 the same trip by railroad took only nine days. A decade later faster locomotives delivered goods in five days, and information passed through telegraph wires in a matter of minutes. Improved transportation gave rise to greater specialization in the manufacturing, marketing, and agricultural sectors. When workers were able to concentrate on performing a limited range of functions, their skills improved and their productivity steadily rose.

Improvements in the transportation sector did more than speed the flow of goods and persons, they also gave birth to numerous institutional innovations. The railroads emerged as the nation's first big business. Prior to the building of the railroad network, the capital invested in even the largest manufacturing firms was counted in thousands of dollars, but the railroads required millions. Thus, the financial system was challenged to discover new ways of raising huge amounts of money. In addition, few early manufacturing firms had over one thousand employees and none possessed a hierarchy of administrators and staff personnel. Again, the railroads created new institutional patterns for the administration of business enterprises. The largest lines employed thousands of workers, and they required a new managerial class to oversee their operations.

## PRIVATE TURNPIKES

The first sign of improving transportation was a better system of roads. In the colonial era, neither government nor private individuals spent much money on the building and maintenance of roads. Goods and people moved overland on horseback or in small wagons. Forest trails were impassable in heavy weather. Because of poor transportation facilities, families living more than twenty-five miles or so from a navigable river or the Atlantic coast had limited opportunities to exchange their surplus agricultural production for other goods.

A breakthrough came in 1792 when a group of Pennsylvania promoters obtained a charter of incorporation from the state legislature to build and maintain a toll road from Philadelphia southwest to Lancaster, a distance of about 60 miles. Turnpike companies and commercial banks were among the first private organizations to receive incorporation privileges limiting the extent of their liabilities in the event of bankruptcy. The cost of construction was roughly $465,000—a sum raised primarily through the sale of stock to individual investors. The Lancaster Pike was completed in 1794, and it did sufficient business to inspire a host of imitators.

Between 1790 and 1830, turnpike companies built thousands of miles of improved roads, primarily in the northeast. Over 80 percent of all construction was in Pennsylvania, New York, and the six New England states. In this region over 750 chartered companies built around 10,500 miles of road costing over $23 million. Most of the funds came from local private investors who obtained corporate charters granting them the right of eminent domain in the selection of routes. They could seize private property and force owners to sell rights-of-way at the fair market value—a price established by mutual agreement or determined by an appropriate public body. Most farmers welcomed turnpike construction because it gave them easy access to markets and raised the value of their remaining property. Some states made direct investments of tax money in their turnpike companies. Pennsylvania was the most generous, with investments of over $2 million in public funds.

Although hundreds of turnpike companies were organized, few were profitable ventures. Teamsters discovered means of circumventing the toll gates, and gatekeepers often pocketed a healthy share of the funds collected. But the main difficulty was that too much of the volume came from passenger stagecoaches and not enough from freight-hauling wagons. Turnpikes made possible the physical movement of goods over intermediate distances throughout most of the year, but toll rates of 30¢ to 70¢ per ton/mile were just too high to attract and retain a steady traffic of freight. After 1820 much of the existing long distance traffic was lost to competitive forms of transportation which were cheaper and faster.

## NATIONAL ROADWAYS

For a brief period, it appeared that the federal government might devote a substantial share of its revenues to building and maintaining a network of interstate roadways. Congress passed a bill in 1802 which stipulated that 5 percent of the proceeds from the sale of federal lands in the Ohio Territory should be used for the building of local roads. Then in 1806 President Thomas Jefferson signed the National Road Bill, which called for the construction of a toll-free road starting at Cumberland, Maryland, and running westward 130 miles to Wheeling, Virginia, on the Ohio River. Work began in 1811 and was completed seven years later at a cost of $1.5 million, or $10,000 to $13,500 per mile. In the 1820s Congress authorized the extension of the road all the way to the Mississippi River, but construction was finally halted in the 1850s at Vandalia, Illinois, a mere 60 miles from the planned destination.

In 1808 Secretary of the Treasury Albert Gallatin drew up an extensive plan for a series of internal improvements designed to promote greater commerce between the states and overseas. Among the projects proposed for federal funding was a system of roads ranging from graded dirt surfaces to first-class hard surfaces designed for heavy traffic. But Gallatin's farsighted plans went largely unfulfilled—a victim of political and sectional rivalries. The western states were consistently in favor of the creation of a national system of roadways to connect them with the entire U.S. market. Other sections were opposed or wavered in their support. For example, New England had the best system of private turnpikes and did not want to permit public monies to be used to construct free roads elsewhere.

Politics also intervened. Some leaders attached to the Jeffersonian tradition of "little" government argued that internal improvement projects—like the national banks—were inherently unconstitutional, no matter what their merits. Presidents

James Madison, James Monroe, and Andrew Jackson vetoed various bills to provide federal funds for better roads wholly or partly on the basis of the constitutional issue. Meanwhile, one of the most prominent supporters of internal improvements, Henry Clay of Kentucky, whom we mentioned in the last chapter, never succeeded in his efforts to win election to the presidency. It was not until over a century later, under the administration of President Dwight Eisenhower in the 1950s, that the federal government finally funded a comprehensive plan for the development of a nationwide system of interstate highways.

## STEAMBOATS

Soon after the start of the turnpike era, the steam engine was successfully applied to water transportation. Steam engines were first used in factory production in England in the 1790s, but the substitution of wood and coal for wind and current in powering ships was not perfected until after the turn of the century. Several different men in Europe and the United States had experimented with the application of steam power to vessels, but Robert Fulton was the first to demonstrate the practical value of the steamboat in carrying passengers and cargo upstream over a long distance. In 1807 his steamboat *Clermont* paddled up the Hudson River from New York to Albany, a distance of 150 miles, in just over one day, traveling at an average speed of nearly five miles per hour.

The steamboat made the greatest impact on the Mississippi River and its tributaries, however. Regular upstream and downstream service began out of New Orleans in 1817, and by 1820 over 70 steamboats were in operation on western rivers. Initially, upstream rates were five times greater than downstream rates, but as more steamboats entered the market the gap began to narrow. By the 1830s freight rates were identical in either direction, and thereafter upstream rates actually were slightly lower.

What caused this turnabout in the rate structure? The answer lies, not surprisingly, in the operation of that economic perennial—demand and supply. Because of their much faster speed in getting to distant markets, steamboats were able to attract a large volume of downstream business in bulky products like foodstuffs in the north and cotton in the upper south. The upstream traffic was dominated by more valuable manufactured goods (by weight) which took up less cargo space. In building a sufficient number of steamboats to meet the high demand for downstream shipping, entrepreneurs eventually discovered that their vessels had too much unsold cargo space, or excess capacity, on upstream runs at existing prices. Thus, in an effort to compete with other steamboats and to generate new business, operators lowered their upstream rates. Between 1818 and 1840, the rate per hundred pounds of freight had fallen from $5.00 to merely 25¢. The downstream rate fell too, but not quite as sharply—from $1.00 to 32¢ per hundred pounds over the same period. The steamboat created a two-way, north-south market in the Mississippi River valley and stimulated settlement in the entire middle half of the continent.

FIGURE 3  New York City Docks and Wharves in the Early 1800s (Source: New York Public Library Picture Collection)

## CANALS

The construction of canals as a means of cheaply moving heavy freight over short to intermediate distances overland had been known by various civilizations around the world for centuries. England already had a fair number of canals between its major ports and manufacturing centers by the end of the eighteenth century. Prior to the War of Independence, the New England colonies were already the site of a few very short canal projects. Between 1785 and 1805 about 100 miles of human-made waterways were opened in the coastal areas of Massachusetts, Virginia, and the Carolinas. The crude techniques of canal construction were thus already a part of the storehouse of human knowledge. What was required in the new United States to create an extensive system of waterways was imagination, persistence, and very large financial resources.

It was clear to all that the greatest need was for canals to link the east coast port cities with the major rivers and lakes in the midwestern states. The distances between these points were measured in hundreds of miles, however, and in some locations the terrain was mountainous. No canal project on such a vast scale had ever been attempted in Europe. (The Chinese had constructed canals several hundred miles in length as early as 500 A.D. and possibly even before 200 B.C.) The federal government was probably the only entity with the financial resources to attempt such a bold project as an intersectional canal system in the first quarter century after independence, but because of constitutional reservations about the legitimacy of internal improvements and sectional rivalries, it failed to act. That left such projects up to the states since raising millions of dollars from private individuals was impossible in the absence of an organized capital market.

### Erie Canal

New York was the first state to meet the challenge. The dream of constructing a canal from Albany on the Hudson River westward to Lake Erie, a distance of over 350 miles, can be traced back to the middle of the eighteenth century. In 1808, Secretary of the Treasury, Albert Gallatin, recommended a canal across the state in his comprehensive report on the most advantageous internal improvement projects for public funding. The cost was estimated in millions of dollars, however, and many questioned whether the toll revenue would be sufficient to merit the investment. When Thomas Jefferson was asked to endorse the plan in 1809, he reportedly said: "It is a noble project, but you are a century too soon." Others shared his skepticism.

The main supporters of the canal idea were the merchants of New York City, which was already the largest city in the nation. The business community wanted to make their city the first eastern port to tap the rapidly expanding midwestern market. The single most important booster was Mayor DeWitt Clinton, who went on to become governor of the state in 1817. He made the canal project his first priority. The state legislature approved the plan for the Erie Canal in April 1817 and work began that summer. The "big ditch" was forty feet wide and four feet deep, with a tow path along one side for horses and mules to pull the canal boats. Sections were opened up as they were finished, and it quickly became evident that the canal would have considerable traffic.

Although the primary goal had been to facilitate trade with the western states, the most immediate impact of the canal was to open up the rich agricultural interior of New York itself. The entire 364-mile route of the canal, with 83 locks, was completed in 1825; the inaugural through trip, with Governor Clinton in the lead boat, took eight days, at an average speed of around two miles per hour. When the news reached Jefferson at his home in Virginia, he reportedly admitted to Clinton: "I now perceive that, in regard to your resources and energies, I committed an error of a century in my calculations."

The Erie Canal was a huge and instant success. Much of the east-west traffic which had previously moved down the Mississippi River to New Orleans and then around Florida to the Atlantic Coast went instead across New York state and down the Hudson River, saving thousands of miles and hours. Moreover, reductions in the cost of moving heavy and bulky farm products were so great—on the order of 90 percent—that new patterns of trade emerged which had never existed. More Americans were drawn into producing for distant markets, and in doing so they increased their total output and their incomes as well.

The Erie Canal cost over $7 million to build. It was financed from state taxes and the sale of bonds by the New York legislature. In 1826 the toll revenues were $700,000 and they rose to over a million dollars annually soon thereafter. Within ten years the construction costs were recouped, and plans were made to widen the canal to accommodate larger boats.

### Other Canal Systems

The success of the canal system in New York prompted other states to investigate similar opportunities within their borders. Pennsylvania and Ohio were the most active in this category. Indeed, over 70 percent of the total canal mileage was built in the three leading states. In Ohio, and Indiana to a lesser extent, canals were designed to feed traffic into Lake Erie and the Ohio River. Pennsylvania eventually constructed the largest canal system in the nation—nearly one thousand miles. The longest and most expensive project, at a cost of more than $10 million, was the 395-mile Main Line between Philadelphia and Pittsburgh. The terrain was so mountainous that at one point a 35-mile railway system, consisting of several inclined planes, was also needed to hoist the canal boats over the crest of the Appalachians.

Although the Pennsylvania Main Line and other large-scale projects were engineering marvels, few generated sufficient revenues to pay for themselves. In some cases, routine maintenance and flood repair ate up almost all of the tolls collected from users. If these projects generally fell far short of profit expectations, were the various state legislatures imprudent in the investment of public funds? Not necessarily. The building of canals stimulated a host of new economic activity and raised the value of farmland, factories, and other assets throughout the state.

Much of the money taxpayers lost on canal investments per se was recouped indirectly though lower transportation costs. The difference between what citizens had previously paid to move goods overland by wagon and what it cost to send them the same distance by canal were savings enjoyed by shippers in general. In the aggregate these sums were large and may have been high enough to justify public investment in many projects even if no tolls had ever been collected. The same principle applies today for the use of tax revenues to build and maintain toll-free roads and highways, and urban mass transit systems.

## RAILROADS

If canals made such significant reductions in the cost of moving goods overland between 1825 and 1840, why were so many unprofitable and why did they rapidly fall into disuse? The answer is that they were unable to meet the competition of a more effective mode of transportation—the railroad. The first spike in an American railroad tie was hammered down in 1828, only eleven years after construction had begun on the Erie Canal. Canals were just coming into their own when they were superseded by the railroad, which moved goods and passengers much faster and year-round as well since ice did not block their path during the winter months. The railroad was only a marginal improvement over canals, but in economic affairs, often only a slight difference is required to dictate the choice of one innovative idea over its nearest substitute. Several economic historians, among them Robert Fogel and Albert Fishlow, have argued, for example, that canals alone could have provided sufficient transportation to permit the United States to realize from 90 to 95 percent of the total economic growth actually experienced over most of the nineteenth century. In other words, railroads only needed to offer service just a little superior in order to attract the bulk of the traffic and eventually cause the abandonment of most of the canal mileage. Canals made a major breakthrough in opening up the American market for much greater internal trade, but they were surpassed almost overnight, figuratively speaking, by the railroads.

The first practical adaptation of the steam engine to haul freight and passengers over a fixed railway came in England in 1825. Three years later construction was begun in the United States on the Baltimore and Ohio Railroad, and by 1830 thirteen miles of its track were in operation. The three cities with the greatest initial interest in railroads—Baltimore, Boston, and Charleston—turned to the "iron horse" because they had no prospects of developing canal systems westward. By 1833 a railroad extended for 136 miles out of Charleston into the interior of South Carolina; it was at the time the longest road in the world under a single management.

During the 1830s more railroad than canal mileage was constructed. By 1840 both transportation systems had over 3,000 miles in operation. State and local governments assisted in financing many of the early railroads. Most rail lines were organized as private companies, but governments frequently made outright grants of cash or land, purchased a portion of the securities issued, or simply guaranteed the payment of interest and principal on the railroad's bonds. In the aftermath of the Panic of 1837, however, numerous railroad and canal projects suffered diminished revenues and were unable to meet their debt obligations. The losses fell in part on state and local taxpayers who were called upon by bondholders to come up with sufficient funds to make good on their earlier guarantees. Thereafter government assistance in financing internal improvements was substantially cut back. Between 1839 and 1843 few new projects were begun.

Railroad work bounced back with added vigor. From the mid-1840s to 1860 a new round of building, financed mainly by private funds, increased railroad mileage nearly tenfold. Meanwhile, canal digging virtually ceased. The expansion of the rail network occurred in three general stages. In phase one, construction was concentrated in the New England states. Then the focus shifted to the midwestern and middle Atlantic regions in the early 1850s. Later in that decade, railroad construction was active in the southern states. In the fifteen years before the outbreak of the Civil War, over 25,000 miles of new track were laid, and the entire area of the nation east of the Mississippi received its basic railroad network. Five states each held over 2,000 miles of track—Ohio, Illinois, New York, Pennsylvania, and Indiana. By 1860, the railroad had triumphed as the major form of intermediate and long-distance transportation for both passengers and freight.

Because of their giant size relative to other types of business enterprise, the railroads were stimulants for a host of new institutional patterns. Prior to 1860 the largest manufacturing plants rarely had more than $500,000 invested in capital and few employed as many as one thousand employees. In contrast, most railroad companies counted their capital in the millions of dollars; on the eve of the Civil War

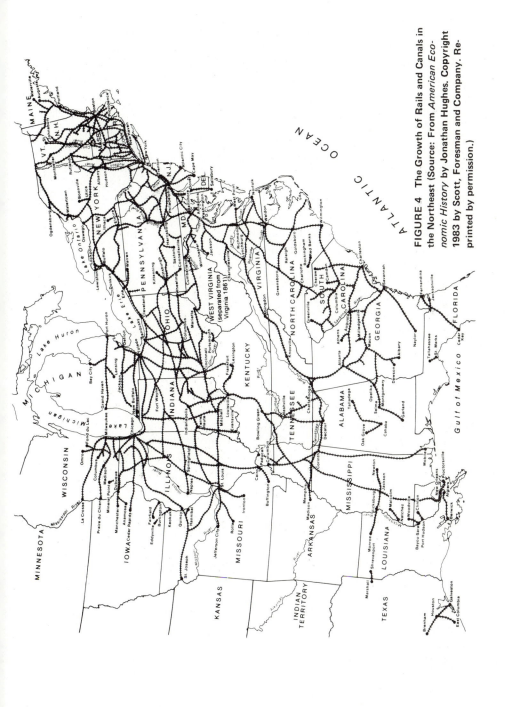

FIGURE 4 The Growth of Rails and Canals in the Northeast (Source: From *American Economic History* by Jonathan Hughes. Copyright 1983 by Scott, Foresman and Company. Reprinted by permission.)

five railroads each had over $20 million invested in their track and equipment and their employees numbered in the tens of thousands. People in the nineteenth century generally viewed the railroads as the most powerful business firms in the American economy.

### New Patterns of Finance

When government funds for financing railroad projects dried up significantly after the Panic of 1837, a capital market to tap the financial resources of the private sector suddenly emerged. A new type of banker—the investment banker—came forth to assist the railroads in raising millions of dollars for the construction of new track. Unlike commercial banks, the investment banker did not accept deposits or make short-term loans. Generally organized in small partnerships, these bankers performed the task of locating individual investors for the stocks and bonds issued by railroad companies. For their services they normally received a commission based on the total value of the securities sold, and, as a "sweetener," sometimes retained a portion of the stock. Investment bankers were financial specialists who concentrated on raising long-term capital for corporations, and they usually continued to provide some form of investment counseling for the investors who regularly purchased securities through them. Very successful investment bankers were able to identify and retain as customers a large number of loyal investors who could be counted upon to provide the funding for a whole series of new ventures.

As a rule, investment bankers sought out three general classes of investors. They solicited funds first from farmers and small businessmen along the proposed route of the railroad. These groups stood to gain most from the improvement in transportation facilities, and they tended to be avid purchasers of common stock, which carried with it an ownership position and opportunities for increased dividends in the event the railroad was profitable. A second group were wealthy families in the eastern urban areas who had made their fortunes in mercantile and real estate ventures.

Finally, American investment bankers were increasingly adept at attracting capital from overseas. European investors—primarily in England, Holland, and various German states—usually preferred bonds over stocks because of the safety factor; that is, railroads had to pay all the interest due on their debt obligations before any dividends could be declared on the outstanding stock, and bondholders also had the first claim on assets in the event of bankruptcy. The investment banking firms at the pinnacle were those with an extensive European clientele. Indeed the United States was a large importer of foreign capital throughout the nineteenth century. About one half of the bonds and up to one third of the stock issued to construct the United States railroad network were purchased by European investors. In the twentieth century, this position was reversed, and in conjunction with the rise of the American-based multinational industrial firm, the United States became a net exporter of capital.

In the 1840s, when railroad building was concentrated in New England, Boston was briefly a center for fledgling investment banking firms. When builders shifted their attention to the middle Atlantic and midwestern states, however, New York quickly became the prime location for investment bankers. By the 1850s many of the leading firms had established their offices on Wall Street in lower Manhattan, and a stock and bond exchange, where securities previously issued and still outstanding could be traded among individuals, was also located there. Eventually the term Wall Street became synonymous with the securities exchange and the entire investment banking field. For almost half a century, virtually all of the corporate securities listed on the stock and bond exchange were issued by the railroads. The coming of the railroads, in sum, stimulated the emergence of a very active United States capital market and secured for New York and Wall Street a permanent position as the financial center of the nation.

### New Patterns of Administration

The railroads were also a catalyst for changes in the administration of business enterprises. The railroad companies were so big that existing methods were inadequate. Prior to the development of huge rail systems, most business firms, including even the largest manufacturing plants, were still managed on a day-to-day basis by the owners themselves. In some cases owners hired a few persons to assist in supervisory tasks, but owners generally held a tight rein over business operations. The railroads had thousands of stockholders, however, which made such a system of owner control impractical. As a result a hierarchy of professional, salaried managers evolved to administer these huge new enterprises. Ownership and management were functions increasingly separated. The men who assumed managerial command were the forerunners of a new class in our society, the managerial elite, which has come to predominate in the modern business world. Now the participants are often women, but that was not true in the nineteenth century. In this earlier era, minorities, Catholics, and anyone who deviated from Protestant European stock was invariably excluded as well.

Faced with the unprecedented size of their enterprises, innovative railroad leaders developed a host of new management concepts and practices. The aim was to develop systems that would allow better coordination of the activities of thousands of employees who were running the trains, loading the freight, selling tickets, maintaining the track, and performing other vital tasks. Among the most original thinkers of the early railroad leaders was Daniel McCallum, president of the Erie Railroad, which ran along the southern border of New York state. In the 1850s, McCallum proposed a series of management principles applicable to every railroad and to other large business firms as well. He stated first that the authority of managers to make decisions should always match as nearly as possible their level of responsibility. In addition, McCallum called for internal reporting systems, which would identify trouble spots and lead to prompt solutions of pressing problems. He also advocated mechanisms which would routinely evaluate, for better or worse, the performance of employees and even managers themselves. These principles of management as proposed by McCallum have endured up to the present. In slightly modified form, his ideas are followed by virtually every large business organization in the modern world, and they are an integral part of the curriculum of every school of business administration.

Railroad leaders developed other ideas to cope with the strains of administering giant enterprises. They broke down operations into functional departments such as traffic, maintenance, finance, legal, and the like. They published manuals to keep all employees informed about the performance of regular business transactions. An organization chart (McCallum again) spelled out the chain of command within the company and revealed who reported to whom. The concept of creating staff positions to assist on-line managers in decision making also took shape on railroads. In meeting the challenge of administering their huge and geographically dispersed properties, innovative railroad leaders established institutional patterns which were later adopted by other large industrial firms.

## TELEGRAPH

The transfer of information speeded up at an even faster pace than the movement of passengers and goods. As late as 1840, improvements in communication paralleled those in transportation. Letters were delivered sooner using turnpikes, steamboats, canals, and railroads, but they still moved no faster than other tangible goods. In the 1830s, however, Samuel B. Morse experimented with the concept of sending messages over long distances through wires at the speed of light. He introduced a code of short and long taps (Morse code) to represent numbers and letters. The idea seemed promising, yet Morse could not raise funds in the private capital market to test out his invention on a commercial scale. Thus, he turned to the federal government, which agreed to provide the fairly modest sum of $30,000 for an experimental line of 40 miles from  Washington to Baltimore in 1844. The experiment was an immediate technical success, but interest in its commercial application still lagged. For the next two years, Morse's telegraphic department was located within the U.S. Post Office.

In 1846, however, the Post Office released its stagnant telegraph business to private developers who planned to invest substantial sums in an expanded system. Four years later the wires stretched over 12,000 miles and by 1852 exceeded 23,000 miles. Most of the wires were strung up along the rights of way of railroads, which explains why the system expanded so rapidly. Since the ability to communicate quickly over long distances was the most important feature of this new technology, a small number of regional companies dominated the industry from the very outset. By 1857 the six leading firms had divided the nation into designated territories, and they cooperated in clearing the path for messages sent to distant locations. Then in the 1860s the remaining firms merged into a single company—Western Union. In 1866 an undersea cable to Europe was successfully laid.

The capability of communicating within just a few seconds or minutes with distant points had a major impact on the economy. The railroads used the telegraph to coordinate the running of their trains and prevent accidents. Business firms in general used the system to keep abreast of prices in other parts of the nations and the world. For example, at the turn of the century general price changes in western cities like Cincinnati and St. Louis lagged behind those in New York and Philadelphia by almost a year. Yet by the 1850s the lag was only a week or so. Wholesalers and retailers discovered that they could maintain smaller inventories of goods because orders to replenish stocks could be transmitted to suppliers very quickly. The access to more accurate and up-to-date information about market conditions over a broad geographical expanse was one of the key factors laying the groundwork for a more efficient distribution of goods. As the cost of information gathering diminished, the economy advanced.

## SELECTED REFERENCES

CHANDLER, ALFRED D.  *The Railroads: The Nation's First Big Business.* New York: Harcourt, Brace, and World, 1965.

FISHLOW, ALBERT.  *American Railroads and the Transformation of the Antebellum Economy.* Cambridge: Harvard University Press, 1965.

FOGEL, ROBERT.  *Railroads and American Economic Growth: Essays in Econometric History.* Baltimore: Johns Hopkins University Press, 1964.

GOODRICH, CARTER.  *Canals and American Economic Development.* New York: Columbia University Press, 1961.

HAITES, ERIK F., JAMES MAK, and GARY M. WALTON.  *Western River Transportation: The Era of Early Internal Development, 1810-1860.* Baltimore: The Johns Hopkins University Press, 1975.

HUNTER, LOUIS.  *Steamboats on the Western Rivers.* Cambridge: Harvard University Press, 1949.

STOVER, JOHN F.  "Canals and Turnpikes: America's Early-Nineteenth-Century Transportation Network," in J. R. Frese and J. Judd, eds., *An Emerging Independent American Economy, 1815-1875.* Tarrytown, N.Y.: Sleepy Hollow Press, 1980.

TAYLOR, GEORGE ROGERS.  *The Transportation Revolution, 1815-1860.* New York: Holt, Rinehart and Winston, 1951.

THOMPSON, ROBERT.  *Wiring a Continent: The History of the Telegraph Industry in the United States, 1832-1866.* Princeton: Princeton University Press, 1947.

# CHAPTER NINE
# MANUFACTURING
# AND TARIFFS
# IN THE NEW NATION

Between the adoption of the Constitution and the outbreak of the Civil War, the United States was transformed from a country with only a few small factories to the nation with a manufacturing sector second only to Great Britain. By the end of the nineteenth century it had become the new leader. The total industrial output of the United States in 1900 was greater than the combined figures for the next three nations—Britain, Germany, and France.

Although agriculture remained the largest employer and accounted for the largest share of gross national product in 1860, about 18 percent of the total American work force was employed in manufacturing, which now accounted for over one third of GNP. Labor shifted steadily out of farming into factory work because annual earnings were up to 50 percent greater there for males; women and children also earned more in factories, but their pay was usually about one half of the amount for men. High labor costs in factories in turn encouraged owners to react quickly to new opportunities to invest in improved technology—usually labor-saving machines, which were increasingly made of metal rather than wood. This machinery was powered by new sources of energy: large waterwheels and hydraulic turbines erected on swiftly flowing rivers and steam engines which burned either wood or coal. During the first half of the nineteenth century, the United States took giant strides toward becoming an industrial nation. Some have called the net result of the multitude of changes an industrial revolution.

## HOUSEHOLD MANUFACTURE AND ARTISANS

When the nation entered the nineteenth century, much domestic manufacturing was still done in the home, as it was in the colonial period. Foods were processed on the farm. Meats were cured by drying, smoking, or salting. Everyday clothing was knitted from wool, while flax was woven into linen garments. Products which could not be made at home were normally bought from independent artisans, who worked in small shops aided by perhaps one or two apprentices. Artisans did not produce in bulk for district markets but accepted individual orders from local customers.

## PUTTING-OUT SYSTEM

An intermediary step between home production and the emergence of factories was the putting-out system. The aim was to boost the production of certain goods for distant markets without concentrating workers within a factory location. Enterprising merchants usually organized and financed the system. They generally concentrated on recruiting workers to weave cotton and woolen yarn into cloth or to cut and sew raw leather into boots and shoes. The merchant entrepreneurs purchased raw materials and delivered them to households of workers with instructions on how to produce the finished products. Periodically the entrepreneurs picked up the completed items, paid the workers on the basis of how much they produced (piece work), and left off more raw materials for further production. The participants in this system of work varied, but often included the whole family unit. Some highly skilled laborers worked year-round, whereas others participated on a part-time or seasonal basis—for example, during the cold winter months when little farm work could be done. This last factor may explain in large part why the putting-out system was organized almost exclusively in the northern states.

## FIRST FACTORIES: TEXTILE MILLS

For centuries in locations everywhere around the globe the production of cloth was done in the home. For hundreds of years the techniques of spinning yarn and then weaving on hand looms changed very little. Then in quick succession came a series of inventions in England during the eighteenth century, which made it possible to mechanize cotton textile production using water power and later steam engines as sources of vastly increased energy. By the 1790s the production of cotton textiles had begun to move out of the home and into British factories. A fair share of these British textiles were exported to the United States.

The adoption of new technology lowered the cost of making cloth and increased the supply very rapidly. As a result, prices fell. Price reductions in turn stimulated sales and led to even greater output, which was followed by another

**FIGURE 5**   Workers Weaving in a Textile Mill Around 1840 (Source: New York Public Library Picture Collection)

round of price reductions, more production, and so on. This outcome represents a classic example of how the forces of demand and supply interacted to propel forward a national economy.

Textile production underwent mechanization in the United States, but at a much slower pace. Samuel Slater brought knowledge of the new machinery across the Atlantic in 1789. In doing so, he committed a treasonous act, for the British considered this knowledge a national secret and tried to prevent its dissemination overseas. In cooperation with the Brown family firm in Providence, Rhode Island, Slater supervised the building of the first American spinning mill powered by water in 1791. The Brown family provided the capital and Slater contributed his knowledge of machine construction and operation. Over the next 15 years about 15 small spinning mills producing yarn were built in New England. When supplies of English textiles were disrupted during Jefferson's embargo of 1808, American entrepreneurs constructed at least 50 new spinning mills in an effort to meet the local demand for coarse goods. The technology of adapting water power to operate looms had not, as yet, arrived in the United States, which meant that most of this yarn was "put-out" to hundreds of independent weavers.

## BOSTON MANUFACTURING COMPANY

The War of 1812 again interrupted the supplies of British textiles and stimulated American entrepreneurs to make a renewed effort to carve out a larger share of the domestic market for themselves. Francis Cabot Lowell, a successful Boston merchant, envisioned one especially bold project. He was determined to accomplish something that had never been done before, not even in England. He made plans to construct a huge, integrated textile mill which, for the first time, would place both spinning machinery and power looms under the same roof. Raw cotton would enter the building and out would come finished cloth.

To raise what was then the astronomical sum of $600,000 for a single factory, Lowell solicited funds from other prominent Boston merchants. Organized as a large partnership, the Boston Manufacturing Company built a factory at Waltham, a few miles up the Charles River from Harvard University, in a then isolated, rural setting. The labor force consisted of hundreds of teenage women recruited from New England farms to tend the machinery. To house them, the mill owners built a town in the wilderness, complete with dormitories, cafeterias, medical offices, churches, and the like. The young women were supervised by upstanding housemothers who sent them to church regularly and forced them to save a substantial part of their wages, presumably for a dowry.

Most mill workers earned about $2.50 per week, and from that sum $1.25 was usually deducted for room and board. The other half of their pay could be spent on something other than food and shelter. Most workers saved some of their earnings. While these wages seem incredibly low today, they were reasonably high by the standards of the day! How do we know? Because it was high enough to attract thousands of young women away from their homes and farms to tend the textile machines in distant company towns.

Over the next several decades hundreds of integrated textile mills were constructed at sites with adequate water power across New England. American manufacturers concentrated on plain weaves for work and everyday wear. The output of cotton textiles expanded at a rate of 15 percent annually from 1815 to the mid-1830s, doubling every five years. Much of the increased demand sprang from the midwestern states which were undergoing rapid population growth following improvements in transportation. Indeed, what began to emerge was a new pattern of regional specialization. The northeastern states tended to become the location of factories and urban centers; the South specialized on the production of raw cotton both for export to Britain and shipment to the Northeast; and the Midwest became the supplier of food for many factory workers. By the 1840s male heads of households, many of them immigrants escaping the Irish potato famine, had replaced young women and children in the textile mills.

During the first half of the nineteenth century many other types of production moved out of artisans' shops and into factories. American entrepreneurs were especially interested in reducing labor costs by increasing the productivity of individual workers, and they led the world in the adoption of techniques based on the continuous flow of products through the factory using interchangeable parts. In Europe it soon became known as the "American system" of manufacturing.

The first products assembled from standardized parts were guns. Eli Whitney, who in 1793 also invented the cotton gin to remove seeds from fiber at a pace fifty times faster than by hand, and Simeon North both received contracts from the U.S. government to manufacture guns with interchangeable parts soon after the turn of the century. It was not until the 1830s, however, that the system was fairly well perfected. The use of standardized parts not only speeded up the assembly of new guns but also made it much easier for others with lesser skills to repair older guns. By the 1850s clocks and watches, sewing machines, and agricultural implements were among the products manufactured using interchangeable parts.

One of the factors critical to the development of factories based on standardized parts was the rise of the machine tool industry. Machine tools, rather than hand tools, could meet the requirement of stricter "tolerances," or mere fractions of an inch, and produce parts either of wood or metal that were generally interchangeable. Prior to 1820 almost all machines used in American manufacturing had been constructed of wood. The shift to metal meant not only that machines were more durable but also that they were able to produce products with much greater uniformity and precision. The United States was among the first nations to boast a large machine tool industry.

### PEOPLE WHO MATTERED – Cyrus McCormick

He was born in 1809 on a farm in Virginia's Shenandoah Valley, a wheat-growing region of the state. His father was always interested in experimenting with agricultural tools in order to reduce labor costs and increase total farm output. The elder McCormick developed a crude model of a reaper to cut wheat in 1831, and Cyrus, aged 23, made a number of major design improvements a year later. For centuries in the past, farmers everywhere had generally been able to plant and grow more wheat than they could harvest by hand since grain ripened quickly in the field. Pulled by horses, the mechanical reaper cut the grain at a much faster pace and thus permitted farmers to expand the scale of operations and produce larger surpluses for the outside market.

Cyrus McCormick constructed a few reapers for local markets in the decade following its invention. In 1843, for example, he sold just 29 machines. But McCormick thought he saw a huge market ahead, especially in the midwestern and plains states where the flat terrain seemed ideal for machine application. He decided to erect a factory in Chicago in 1847, even though the town was hardly beyond the frontier stage and had a population of less than 20,000. Ten years later sales surpassed 4,000 annually and continued to rise. McCormick sold through authorized dealers and emphasized service plus a credit plan to stimulate demand. Production rose dramatically during the Civil War; the industry total was over 80,000 annually in 1864 and 1865. By the later date over three quarters of United States wheat farms containing over 100 acres were at least partially mechanized. In the last quarter of the nineteenth century, commercial wheat farming spread as far west as California.

The McCormick harvesting machines were demonstrated and sold around the world after 1850. In 1879 the French Academy of Sciences added this American inventor and businessman to its membership because he had accomplished more for agriculture than any living man. McCormick died in 1884 at the age of seventy-three.

## NEW ENERGY RESOURCES

One of the main characteristics shared by all preindustrial societies, including colonial America, was the relatively low consumption of energy. Humans and animals such as horses and oxen converted foodstuffs into energy for application in agriculture and the production of goods. The wind caught the sails of ships, while small waterwheels operated by rural millers ground grains into meal and flour. Wood was burned to cook food and heat homes. In sum, energy technology had changed little before the end of the eighteenth century.

The first new source of increased and concentrated energy for manufacturing was the adaptation of an old technology, the waterwheel, to the factory. Using pulleys, chains, and belts, the first water-powered textile mill was operating in England by the 1770s, and two decades later it came to the United States. Complex hydraulic systems encompassing dams, channels, and sluices were built on many New England rivers to carry rushing water to textile mills with thousands of spindles and looms. Until the latter half of the nineteenth century, water provided well over half of the energy used in American manufacturing.

The second source of new energy to have an impact on early manufacturing was a fossil fuel—coal. The use of coal became practical after James Watt's invention of the steam engine in the eighteenth century. The first coal-powered factory in England was constructed in 1790, but over a quarter of a century passed before entrepreneurs began to exploit the huge U.S. coal fields. Why the lag? First, wood was much more plentiful and thus cheaper than in England. Locomotives on the early railroads normally burned wood to heat the boilers of their steam engines. Second, although coal was plentiful in eastern Pennsylvania, it was located in mountainous terrain. Until canals were built in the region after 1825, the cost of transporting coal to markets was prohibitive. Beginning in the 1830s, coal-powered factories increasingly became a feature of the American landscape.

The use of coal had a major impact on the location of manufacturing. Previously, most factories were situated in rural areas where water power was abundant. But with coal as a fuel, factories could be built anywhere with adequate transportation facilities, including many towns and cities. The shift to coal permitted owners to bring their manufacturing units to urban locations where the supply of labor was much greater. As a result, many urban areas became manufacturing as well as commercial centers.

## IRON PRODUCTION

The shift to coal affected iron production as well. From the colonial period up until the 1830s, the main fuel in the production of iron was the same as it had been for centuries—wood charcoal. Iron smelting was also a rural industry because it was only feasible at a limited number of sites where three natural resources all came together: iron ore, huge stands of timber, and water power. The American industry was unintegrated, for smelting ore into pig iron and its fabrication into finished products were done by separate firms. Indeed, all the firms associated with iron production tended to be small to medium sized establishments.

Although coal began to pour out of the eastern Pennsylvania mountains in the late 1820s, it was not until the 1840s that this fossil fuel was first used to produce iron in the region. The English had discovered that coal was a superior fuel in iron furnaces by the late eighteenth century, and English ironmasters had seized a huge share of the American market, including orders for most of the rails used to construct the U.S. railroad network. Some iron furnaces in the Pittsburgh area were using coal in the 1820s, but none in the East. Again, why the delay? The explanation can be traced back to differences in the types of coal and a technological bottleneck.

The fuel used in England and Pittsburgh was soft coal (bituminous) whereas the mines in the eastern United States held almost uniformly hard coal (anthracite). It was not until the 1830s that the invention of the "hot blast" technique made it possible to produce iron from hard coal deposits. The adoption of coal as a fuel coincided with the development of the integrated iron mill, where both smelting and fabrication took place, and a substantial increase in the size of such enterprises. Later in the nineteenth century, the iron foundries evolved into steel mills which consumed even more coal energy, both the hard and soft varieties.


## IMPACT OF TARIFFS

In 1828 Congress passed a tariff bill which placed on certain imports taxes so high that the act became known in some quarters as the Tariff of Abominations. Critics charged that the tariff schedule was sectionally biased because it penalized southern consumers and benefited northern manufacturing interests. What they meant was that southerners were unable to buy cheaply quality imported goods but were forced instead to pay inflated prices for similar, often inferior, goods produced by northern factories protected from foreign competition. Citing the alleged inequities of the tariff legislation, the state of South Carolina "nullified" temporarily the enforcement of the law within its borders in 1832 and ordered federal customs officials in Charleston to prepare to cease the collection of the tax on foreign goods. South Carolina invited other southern states to join in its defiance of Congress, but none complied. This first constitutional crisis involving the South was quickly resolved, however, when President Andrew Jackson threatened the use of military force to uphold federal law while he simultaneously maneuvered through Congress a revised compromise tariff with slightly lower duties. As a result, South Carolina backed off and accepted the tariff revisions.

As the so-called nullification crisis very clearly reveals, the level of tariff rates was one of the perennially controversial political issues in the nineteenth century. Tariffs were imposed on foreign goods for two different, and frequently opposing, reasons. First, taxes on imported goods were the primary source of revenue for the federal government in this era. Thus there was a general consensus that at least a modest level of taxes on imports, up to 20 percent of their wholesale value, for example, was necessary and appropriate just to generate sufficient funds to pay the government's normal operating expenses. There developed, however, a second rationale for the imposition of especially high tariffs, up to 50 percent or more of entering value, on certain specific goods. The justification was to protect newly emerging American industries from foreign competition until they were able to get their feet securely on the ground. Secretary of the Treasury Alexander Hamilton advanced this infant industry argument most succinctly in his *Report on Manufactures* submitted to Congress in 1791.

Because the United States had little manufacturing during the first quarter century after the adoption of the Constitution, the issue of protective tariffs for newly emerging industries lay dormant. It was revived, however, in the aftermath of the War of 1812. Cut off from regular supplies of foreign goods, Americans realized that Congress needed to stimulate the growth of domestic manufacturing. Moreover, during the war, several new textile mills, the most prominent being Lowell's Boston Manufacturing Co. in Waltham, Massachusetts, had already been constructed, so that now factories seemed worth protecting. Mill owners had a strong vested interest in securing protection. A bill placing high rates on relatively inexpensive cotton textiles and other specified goods was passed in 1816 with the almost unanimous support of all sections and political parties. The goal of the protective features was not to generate revenue but rather to keep out certain foreign goods altogether.

Problems began to arise in the 1820s, however, because northern manufacturing interests wanted to maintain indefinitely these high tariff rates. Southerners asserted that the "infancy" argument no longer held, for hundreds of textile mills were already firmly established in the northeastern states. Having become accustomed to the benefits of the absence of foreign competition, American textile manufacturers wanted to perpetuate their current status. Meanwhile, other special interests such as iron producers began to seek protective legislation as well. The net outcome was a continuing battle between the advocates of a high tariff structure to protect, either entirely or moderately, U.S. factories and the advocates of low tariffs which would benefit consumers by allowing them the option of purchasing goods produced overseas. The split was largely, but not completely, sectional with northern entrepreneurs opposed by southern planters. The fight over the Tariff of Abominations, followed by the nullification crisis and the compromise tariff of 1833, was a predictable outcome of the differing goals of competing groups.

Who was right in this dispute about the proper level of tariff rates? That is an extremely difficult question to answer, in part because the issue had political as well as economic implications. What can be stated, however, with a fair amount of accuracy is that both sides tended to overestimate the net effect of the tariff. Protective tariffs neither aided the northern manufacturers as much as most of them believed nor damaged the southern consumers as much as they protested. For example, cotton textile manufacturers did earn higher profits because of the protective tariff, but during the years of the industry's fastest growth American factories concentrated on the least expensive plain weaves, a market in which transportation factors gave domestic firms a decided advantage irrespective of the tariff level. In short, the tariff gave entrepreneurs some protection, but the American textile industry would have flourished in any event.

By the same token southerners paid prices only slightly higher for imported goods because of the protective tariffs. During the height of the controversy in South Carolina over the Tariff of Abominations, some prominent political leaders alleged that local income levels were up to one half lower because of the northern-sponsored protective tariff. Such charges were so patently absurd that they could have been considered laughable, had not so many local people believed these assertions; and they were even prepared to precipitate a constitutional confrontation with the federal government over the issue. A careful review of the politics of American tariffs in the nineteenth century reveals an important historical point: what citizens believe about the effects of certain laws and policies can be as important, or even more important, than the real underlying effects. Although, in retrospect, economic historians have concluded that the level of tariffs had little serious impact on the rate of growth of the American economy, it does nothing to diminish the heat of past battles over the justice and equity of tariff policy on the American political stage.

## IMPACT OF MANUFACTURING

During the half century from 1810 to 1860 the United States became a mighty manufacturing nation. Over this period the total value of manufactured goods increased tenfold. On the eve of the Civil War, output within five major categories accounted for over four fifths of the manufacturing total: textiles and apparel—25 percent; metals and machinery—24 percent; food processing—12 percent; lumber, wood, and furniture—12 percent; and leather and shoes—11 percent.

The rise of manufacturing also contributed significantly to a rearrangement of economic power between the northern and southern states. Factory workers earned more per year than farmers. Over 70 percent of manufacturing capacity was located in the Northeast compared to less than 10 percent in the South. The new Midwest made up the balance. On the eve of independence, when the nation was almost exclusively agricultural, the South had laid claim to almost three fifths of the total national income. But by 1860 its share had fallen to just over one quarter. Meanwhile, the Northeast claimed one half and the Midwest one fifth of national income. The northern states were already well on their way in the transition from an agricultural society to a new economic structure based heavily on manufacturing and complementary services.

## SELECTED REFERENCES

CHANDLER, ALFRED D. "Anthracite Coal and the Beginnings of the Industrial Revolution in the United States," *Business History Review* (1972), 141–81.

COCHRAN, THOMAS. *Frontiers of Change: Early Industrialism in America.* New York: Oxford University Press, 1981.

FREEHLING, WILLIAM. *Prelude to Civil War: The Nullification Controversy in South Carolina, 1816–1836.* New York: Harper & Row, 1965.

GALLMAN, ROBERT. "Commodity Output, 1839–1899," in *Trends in the American Economy in the Nineteenth Century.* National Bureau of Economic Research. Princeton: Princeton University Press, 1960.

GREGORY, FRANCES. *Nathan Appleton, Merchant and Entrepreneur, 1779–1861.* Charlottesville: University Press of Virginia, 1975.

LINDSTROM, DIANE. *Economic Development in the Philadelphia Region, 1810–1850.* New York: Columbia University Press, 1978.

LIVESAY, HAROLD. "Marketing Patterns in the Antebellum American Iron Industry," *Business History Review* (1971), 269–95.

POPE, CLAYNE. "The Impact of the Ante-Bellum Tariff on Income Distribution," *Explorations in Economic History* (1972), 375–422.

ZEVIN, ROBERT. *The Growth of Manufacturing in Early Nineteenth-Century New England.* New York: Arno Press, 1975.

# CHAPTER TEN
# LABOR IN TRANSITION

The use of new machines and energy sources in the production of goods had a profound effect on the ways in which many Americans earned a living. Gradually but steadily, workers moved out of agriculture and into various other types of jobs—manufacturing, commerce, transportation, and complementary services. Especially in the northeastern states, farmers abandoned their small tracts to enter the industrial sector of the economy. In doing so, they surrendered a certain amount of independence, but they often obtained year-round employment at relatively good wages. Women and children were increasingly drawn into unskilled factory work, thereby giving a boost to family income. A significant number of immigrants went into factory work in the urban port cities, rather than heading for the distant frontier. Meanwhile, artisans routinely left their homes and small shops to join together in bigger establishments to produce a much larger volume of goods for distant markets. Home and workplace were more frequently separate locations.

The increase in the size of business enterprises meant that relations between employers and employees became less personal. The coming of factories disrupted traditional patterns of work, and employees used various means to protest their increasing concern over their loss of independence and dignity. Nonetheless, to borrow a term from the vocabulary of Karl Marx, the father of communist ideology, American workers displayed little "class consciousness" in the first half of the nineteenth century. Few perceived that a permanent division between capital and labor was emerging. That split had occurred very quickly in industrializing Great Britain, but special conditions in the United States suggested to many Americans, if not most, that the gulf might be avoided, or at least forestalled, in their own land. Only a small percentage of the work force made any serious efforts to organize unions to bargain with employers over wages and hours, for example. Many of the unions formed were temporary bodies; once a disputed issue was settled, the union dissolved. Workers formed a few local political organizations in several northern cities, but they were never able to build a national following to compete with the major political parties.

Unlike industrial workers in many European countries, laborers in the United States rarely behaved in a revolutionary manner. American labor leaders who were active in political affairs focused instead on reform issues. Among the goals of these labor representatives in the antebellum period were better educational opportunities for their children, the end of imprisonment for debt, and shorter hours—usually for the same amount of pay.

Why were American workers so docile compared to their revolutionary European counterparts, who periodically challenged the whole structure of their societies? Probably the most important consideration was that in the United States white male workers already enjoyed almost full civil and political rights. By the 1820s they could uniformly vote in elections, hold office, serve on juries, and work and live largely independent of the power of government. In Europe, on the other hand, factory workers not only earned lower wages, but most were second class citizens as well, without the right to vote, and possessing limited civil rights. Thus, European laborers were frequently drawn to revolutionary ideologies that aimed not only at improved economic benefits but also more opportunities to participate in government and other civic affairs. In contrast, American workers were attached to the Constitution and the general principles of democratic government. Many skilled workers even succeeded in their efforts to be elected to local political offices. Here labor rarely threatened to topple the structure of society or the capitalist system.

## MILL WORK

The first large-scale exposure of Americans to factory work occurred in a very different environment and under very different circumstances than across the Atlantic. In Britain workers of both sexes and all ages went into the factories and often lived crowded together in dreary industrial towns where smoke from coal-powered machines billowed throughout the day and filtered out much of the sunlight. In the United States, in contrast, during the initial quarter century of development, the textile industry revealed another, almost utopian pattern. Americans initially tried to create a different type of industrial world, one less harsh and more democratic.

Following the model established by the Boston Manufacturing Co. at Waltham, textile mills in New England during the 1820s and early 1830s provided an almost idyllic setting for their female workers, at least by the standards of the day. The mills were built in rural areas where water power was readily available; thus no ugly smokestacks filled the air with soot and ashes. The owners built spartan but well-maintained dormitories for the young women recruited from farms all across the region. They constructed churches and libraries for the improvement of spirit and mind. Moreover, these mill towns were planned meticulously so that all the buildings, including even the factories, were surrounded by beautiful grounds in a parklike atmosphere. When European VIPs such as the novelist Charles Dickens visited the United States to see the sights, they often included on their itinerary, along with Washington and New York, mill towns like Lowell, Massachusetts, on the Merrimack River. They marvelled at how different the course of United States industrialization seemed in comparison to the degradation of industrial workers in their own countries.

During this early phase of industrialization, the American situation was truly unique. The initial collection of factory workers in the nation's largest industry was a very homogeneous and select group. They were hardly the roots of an industrial proletariat—to borrow another word from Marxian terminology. The mill girls were foremost temporary workers. None planned to remain in the mills indefinitely. By leaving their homes and going to the mill towns, they could temporarily avoid farm work and gain a measure of independence and some adventure. In place of parental supervision, however, the mill girls had to submit to the discipline of housemothers who got them up early, usually around 4:30 a.m., to begin work in the factories, and saw that they were in bed by 10 p.m. Eventually most expected to return with at least a modest dowry to their home counties, marry a local farmer, and begin raising children. If conditions became intolerable in the mills, they invariably had the option of returning prematurely to the family farm. They were not, in short, dependent entirely on the owners for their livelihood.

The mill girls worked long hours, usually 12 to 14 hours, 6 days a week. The repetitive tasks were tiresome and the setting was drab, but the slow speeds of early machines held down the work pace. Tending textile machinery was generally not overtaxing for women and older children. The letters of workers in the 1820s and 1830s suggest that most young women actually preferred the lifestyle of the mill towns to the boredom and isolation of the family farm.

The working conditions in the mills and life in the mill towns began to deteriorate in the 1840s, however. Competition between textile firms became more intense, and owners sought new ways to cut labor costs. Work loads increased. Improved machines operated at faster speeds, and workers were expected to tend more of them than previously. Meanwhile a new wave of European immigrants arrived in the northeastern states and swelled the supply of labor. Thousands of Irish came to the United States to escape the potato famine of 1845-1847, which deprived Ireland of approximately one half of its population, either from starvation or through emigration.

The Irish immigrants were normally uneducated and unskilled. Lacking the financial resources to set up farms, they rarely headed for the frontier but remained in the northeastern cities and towns. As the adoption of steam power brought more textile mills into urban areas, these recent immigrants increasingly sought work in the factories. Whole families went into the mills: husbands, wives, and their children. Generally willing to work at even lower wages than local farm girls, they steadily replaced native-born employees.

The character of mill work changed. Unskilled labor was no longer in such short supply. The new work force lived in crowded neighborhoods and received low pay for long hours. The paternalism of the owners faded. So did the utopian belief that industrialization in the United States would follow a different path than in Europe. Cotton textiles was the first industry to undergo extensive mechanization and the dominance of factory production, and it became also the first to witness the transformation of its labor force into an army of dependent and powerless workers.

## ARTISANS AND MECHANIZATION

In contrast to the impact of technology on workers in the cotton textile industry, its effect on workers in other types of manufacturing and on skilled workers, in particular, defies sweeping generalization—at least during the antebellum decades. The impact varied enormously between 1800 and 1860. Different groups of workers were affected in different ways, in different years, and with different results. Mechanization was an uneven process. In some cases machines displaced skilled workers; but more often the new technology aided the artisan in boosting output and raising incomes. The gap between the wages of unskilled and skilled laborers widened in this era.

In the colonial period, artisans had invariably performed all the tasks required to produce a single item using strictly hand tools. In constructing a chair, for example, a furniture maker did everything from simple jobs, such as cutting raw timber and sanding rough wood, to much more difficult tasks like tight fitting, fine polishing, and inlay work. The early machines were often welcomed because they generally did those routine but previously time-consuming jobs that required little special training. As a result, artisans in the furniture field had more time available to devote to tasks requiring the highest degree of skill. In this sense, machines complemented the work of the skilled laborer.

In response to new machinery and the increased size of markets following the transportation revolution, artisans began to move out of small shops and into larger establishments. In the first half of the nineteenth century, few of these work locations were big enough to classify as full-fledged factories. They were rather collections of journeymen brought together under one roof either by a merchant/entrepreneur or a master craftsman. Relations between employers and employees were not always cordial but no wide, impassable gulf divided labor and capital. The supervisors were master craftsmen who continued to work alongside journeymen in the shop.

As the volume of business increased, manufacturers initiated greater specialization within the workplace. An apprentice was no longer taught every task required to make a given product, but just a few, more limited skills. They usually received lower wages and had less job mobility than workers with a full complement of skills. To cite furniture makers again, machines performed the simple tasks while journeymen concentrated on a few parts of the chair—legs, seats, backs, inlay—which others then assembled into complete units. Workers contributed to the final product, but none carried the project from start to finish. As a result, the pride of workmanship diminished.

Another significant change accompanying the increased division of labor was the method of compensating labor. Previously, skilled workers had invariably received periodic payments for finishing a specific task, such as a completed chair. Under the new system of volume production, they were paid instead on the basis of time on the job—by the hour or day. As a result the discipline of the workplace became more rigorous. Reporting late to work or under the influence of alcohol were much more serious offenses because the offender often delayed or disrupted the work of others. The work pace became steadier too, since employers were loath to pay laborers for idle time.

In sum, employers were beginning to exert greater control over the workplace. Skilled workers who had always valued their independence from close supervision often found the adjustment to the tighter discipline of factory life difficult. They were rewarded with more regular, predictable, and, normally, higher wages, but many still resented the effect that machines and the impact distant markets had upon their status in the shop and community. Again, workers often protested such changes, but it was difficult for them to unite because change came at different times in different industries and in different locations. Workers in specific industries tended to view their problems within a narrow framework; few could perceive that these forces were affecting the working class as a whole. Major confrontations between workers and capitalists over the course of industrialization came much later in the nineteenth century, and we will discuss them in later chapters.

## UNION ACTIVITY

A few laborers did form unions in the early nineteenth century. The membership was composed of skilled workers in a single trade; members were white males. Craft unions were organized locally, usually in the largest cities, and they rarely survived more than a few years. The motives for their creation varied. They were partly fraternal. Meeting halls became locations for male socializing: drinking, gossip, and gaming. They were often mutual aid societies as well. Union dues went to establish modest funds to be drawn upon by members disabled or temporarily unemployed and to pay funeral expenses in case of death. In addition, unions were organized to bargain with employers over such issues as work rules, hours, and wages. No recognized mechanism for arbitrating dispute existed. Occasionally, journeymen called strikes in an effort to coerce employers into granting their demands. Some were successful; others failed.

Early craft unions increased in numbers and membership during prosperous times and then declined in recessions and depressions. When business was expanding and prices advancing, the leverage of skilled workers vis-a-vis employers was favorable. The demand for labor was high and employers either tolerated union activity or risked the loss of good workers and a disruption in production. Acting collectively, either through strikes or the threat of strikes, journeymen were frequently able to negotiate wage increases.

During the early 1830s union activity in the antebellum era peaked. The inflation rate was high and business was booming. Craft unions in several eastern cities were quickly organized, and many called successful strikes against employers in an effort to obtain real wage increases, namely those exceeding rises in the cost of living. (*Real* wages are wages adjusted for fluctuations in the value of money, whether from inflation or deflation.) A few of the most established craft unions made serious efforts to reach out beyond their local constituencies and create national organizations. The shoemakers and printers, plus three other craft unions, held national meetings in 1835 and 1836.

This progress toward a stronger union movement was severely interrupted by the depression following the Panic of 1837. With prices falling and business activity contracting, the initiative swung back to employers. The supply of labor was plentiful, and employers had no fear of unions or strikes. Workers who struck to protest cuts in wages could easily be replaced by others equally qualified. The failure of strikes led to the dissolution of many of the craft unions that had popped up in the early 1830s. From this experience, a trend emerged: unions had a difficult time surviving during business contractions in the nineteenth century.

When economic conditions improved in the mid-1840s and 1850s, craft unions made a comeback. Based on their experiences over the last quarter century, union leaders sought means of consolidating their strength. National unions were revived, and affiliated locals aided each other in acting as clearinghouses for information about job opportunities in their respective areas. Since there were no prolonged economic downturns between 1845 and the 1870s, several craft unions were able to fashion fairly strong organizations that were able to bargain effectively with employers. However, little effort was made to bring these independent craft unions together into a federation which might function as a central organization for all skilled workers. To reiterate, the absence of class consciousness prevented workers in different trades from appreciating the extent to which their problems were closely linked. That would come later.

## LABOR AND POLITICS

Disavowing revolutionary ideologies, most American workers identified with the programs of one of the two or three mainstream political parties in the antebellum era. For a brief moment, however, some labor leaders did try to form independent political parties. Separate Workingmen's Parties were organized in Philadelphia, New York, and a few other northern cities in the decade from 1825 to 1835. They concentrated on reform issues to attract voters. Their platforms called for expanding the system of free public education, since at the time only the wealthy could afford the cost of private tutors for their children. They also proposed ending the practice of imprisonment for debt and the enactment of "lien laws," which gave wages due to workers preference over other debt obligations in legal disputes in the construction industry and related fields.

One issue in which labor-oriented political parties and nonpolitical labor unions found a common cause was shortening the length of the standard work day. The goal in the first half of the nineteenth century was the 10-hour day. Many workers at that time were required to put in 12 to 14 hours on the job. Unions invariably bargained for shorter hours, and skilled workers in several trades were successful in achieving a 10-hour maximum by the 1840s. Unskilled workers and unorganized journeymen tended to seek a legislative solution. Their aim was to obtain the enactment of laws at the local or state level stipulating a 10-hour or shorter working day. Even when such laws were passed, however, enforcing them proved difficult.

Workingmen's Parties were reasonably successful in local elections in the largest cities for a few years in the 1830s. But like most third parties in American history, they were eventually coopted, or absorbed, by the traditional two party system. Their most appealing programs were adopted by the major parties, and their most popular candidates were persuaded to change affiliation once in office. The major parties offered opportunities to wield more influence in government and to control more patronage for supporters. Indeed, the success of the labor parties in getting their programs accepted by the majority parties was responsible in large part for their demise. Once the Democrats, Whigs, and Republicans had endorsed the demands of labor leaders for government action, the rationale for a permanent third party disappeared.

## SELECTED REFERENCES

DAWLEY, ALLAN. *Class and Community: The Industrial Revolution in Lynn.* Cambridge: Harvard University Press, 1976.

DUBLIN, THOMAS. *Women at Work: The Transformation of Work and Community in Lowell, Massachusetts, 1826–1860.* New York: Columbia University Press, 1979.

GUTMAN, HERBERT. *Work, Culture, and Society in Industrializing America.* New York: Knopf, 1977.

PESSEN, EDWARD. *Most Uncommon Jacksonians: The Radical Leaders of the Early Labor Movement.* Albany: State University of New York Press, 1967.

ROSS, STEVEN J. *Workers on the Edge: Work, Leisure, and Politics in Industrializing Cincinnati, 1788–1890.* New York: Columbia University Press, 1985.

SMITH, MERRITT ROE. *Harpers Ferry Armory and the New Technology: The Challenge of Change.* Ithaca: Cornell University Press, 1977.

# CHAPTER ELEVEN
# SLAVERY
## *Economics versus Morality*

When the Declaration of Independence, proclaiming that all men were created equal, was drafted in 1776, approximately one half million men, women, and children with black skins were still permanently enslaved. That dualism of freedom and slavery was one of the supreme ironies and certainly the single greatest tragedy in our nation's history. Congress ended the importation of new slaves in 1807, but slavery continued to expand because of the natural growth of the existing population. By 1860 their numbers had risen to nearly four million. The continued existence of slavery in a nation supposedly founded on the principles of democracy and equality represented an internal contradiction in which ideology and morality vied with economic advantage for supremacy. Because slavery eventually became entrenched only in the southern states, the stage was set for sectional conflict. The Civil War settled the question of secession and ended slavery—although not the economic and political consequences of racism.

### EMANCIPATION IN THE NORTH

In 1775 about 10 percent of the slave population lived in the northern states. Most acted as house servants in wealthy white households. By 1805 eight northeastern states had passed laws providing for emancipation of the slaves within their borders.

None, however, chose the course of immediate freedom. They opted instead for gradualism. Living slaves were not freed, but newborn children were slated for emancipation once they became adults. This plan imposed no cost on state tax-payers, and it did not cause slaveholders to suffer an immediate loss of property rights. Under these gradual emancipation programs the newborn were held in bond-age until owners had been largely compensated for their rearing costs. In their youth the value of a slave's annual output was less than the costs of food, clothing, shelter, and medical care. After the age of 10, however, the value of slave output exceeded annual maintenance costs, and by their mid-twenties slaves had usually fully compensated owners for the cost of rearing them. In the northern states the cost of emancipation fell largely on the slaves themselves. Thus, the ending of slav-ery did not come suddenly in the northern states as it finally did in the South; its demise was stretched out over a quarter century or more. Slavery did not finally ex-pire in New York, for example, until 1827, when all persons still held in bondage were declared free irrespective of age.

## RISE OF COTTON KINGDOM

While slavery was fading in the north, it was becoming more strongly entrenched in the southern states. During the colonial era, slave labor had been applied to three main plantation crops—tobacco, rice, and indigo. European markets for those three staple crops stagnated in the 1780s, however, and some liberal-thinking southerners

FIGURE 6   The First Cotton Gin in 1793 (Source: New York Public Library Picture Collection)

began to consider in a positive light the idea that declining economic opportunities might lead whites to give up voluntarily their attachment to the institution of slavery. That idea was quickly thwarted after Eli Whitney, a northerner visiting in the South, invented the cotton gin in 1793. Prior to this date the cost of slowly removing seeds from upland cotton was so high that farmers could not profitably grow it. The cotton gin, a relatively simply designed machine, removed seeds from cotton fiber *fifty* times faster than a person could pick them out by hand.

Immediately, cotton became a viable plantation crop since its cultivation was very compatible with the slave system. In the following decades cotton superseded tobacco as the great southern staple. This region became the chief supplier of raw material for textile mills in England and later in the northern states. Beginning in the western counties of South Carolina, the cotton kingdom moved steadily across Georgia, Alabama, Mississippi, Arkansas, Louisiana, and even into Texas by the late 1850s. Where the cotton fields spread, slavery followed. Indeed, it was primarily northern concerns about the continued expansion of slavery in western territories that stimulated the rise of the Republican party in the 1850s, the election of Abraham Lincoln in 1860, and the outbreak of the American Civil War.

## WAS SLAVERY PROFITABLE?

Since slavery survived for over 200 years on the North American continent and ended only because of the military victory of Union forces over the Confederacy in 1865, it may seem surprising to learn that during the first half of the twentieth century many historians questioned the profitability of the institution. This skepticism about the general level of profits and especially about the trend of profits in the 1850s can be traced back largely to the historian U. B. Phillips. He became the first professional historian to devote almost an entire career to the study of slavery and its consequences. When he published the results of his research and offered his interpretation of events in the antebellum South in books and articles during the first quarter of this century, his views had a powerful influence—almost unchallenged— on several generations of historians. Phillips argued that slavery was becoming increasingly unprofitable during the 1850s. He concluded that the institution was already dying a natural death and, therefore, fighting the Civil War to end it was unnecessary.

The primary basis for this interpretation was his observation that domestic prices for slaves were rising faster than the price of cotton on world markets. The price of a prime field hand rose, for example, from $600 to $1800 between 1845 and 1860. While slave prices tripled, the price of cotton only doubled in value. With little training in economic principles or theories, Phillips simply made a common-sense argument: if the net sales prices for cotton were climbing at a slower rate than production costs were rising (the cost of slaves) then it followed that profits had to be falling and, moreover, if that trend continued, slavery as an economic system would soon become obsolete.

But Phillips was dead wrong. Not only was slavery a strong and viable institution in the antebellum era, but its economic strength was actually increasing in the decade before the election of Lincoln. What Phillips failed to consider was that the underlying reason for the rising prices of slaves relative to cotton might be that enslaved workers were producing more per person—or increasing their productivity. That, in fact, was what was happening. How did we find this out? First, we now have better sources of knowledge about the slave south, including particularly access to raw data from the census in the nineteenth century. (The information we now give to census takers is held in strict confidence during our lifetime, but eventually, after the passage of a century, it too will be turned over to future historians for detailed analysis.)

The most important tool in changing our view of slavery in recent years has been the application of the computer and other quantitative techniques to historical research. The first field of history in which the computer had a great impact was the study of the economics of slavery. Beginning in the 1960s, economic historians applied sophisticated models to massive amounts of data using computers and other types of electronic hardware. The result was a radically different view of slavery—at least as an economic system. Owners generally profited handsomely from slave ownership. Slaveholders earned approximately the same amount from investments in human beings as northern manufacturers earned from investments in factories and machines.

The income levels of whites in the South were up to 50 percent higher than those of their counterparts in midwestern states in 1860. The strength of the slave system explains why white southerners were so willing to secede from the union and then fight a war in an effort to preserve their independence. Their behavior represents one of the worst examples of how individuals are sometimes capable of putting their own self-interest ahead of almost every other human emotion.

## EFFICIENCY OF SLAVERY

In addition to attacking slavery on moral and ideological grounds, abolitionists in the antebellum era condemned the institution because it was allegedly inefficient compared to the production realized by farms using strictly free labor. Frederick Olmsted, a northerner who traveled extensively in the South and who became a leading abolitionist, commented in 1861 that in comparison with slaves "white laborers of equal intelligence and under equal stimulus will cut twice as much wood, split twice as many rails, and hoe a third more corn." Olmsted's intentions were good; he tried to marshal every conceivable argument to convince his readers that slavery was an abomination. But on the efficiency issue Olmsted and the other abolitionists were mistaken. Again, the use of computer techniques has revealed a newer and more accurate interpretation.

From a strictly economic standpoint, slavery was an efficient system of production. First, if we compare free family farms in the South to other farms with from one to fifteen slaves, the output per worker was virtually the same for whites and blacks. That statistic alone is sufficient to refute the old argument about the poor quality of black labor. Second, plantations with over 50 slaves were actually up to 50 percent more efficient than smaller southern farms. How were these efficiencies achieved? The output of workers on large farms was raised by a combination of superior organization, the division of labor into many specialized tasks, and the implementation of a rigid discipline in the cotton fields. The operation of the southern cotton plantation was similar in many ways to the regimentation of the northern factory.

In theory, the same economies of scale could have been realized by hiring a sufficient number of free white laborers to work the plantations. But in fact, no big farms based on free labor evolved anywhere in the southern states. Presumably, free whites were unwilling to submit to the regimentation and discipline necessary to capture the efficiencies associated with large-scale production units. Whites uniformly preferred to labor on small farms where they could escape the direction of overseers and live independently. Indeed, it was only through the use of forced labor—slaves who involuntarily participated in the operation of the plantation unit—that production efficiency was optimized in cotton agriculture.

The superior economic performance of the large plantation was undoubtedly the primary reason why such units became so common in the antebellum South and why an increasing percentage of the slave population was concentrated on them. Cotton planters were thus acting rationally when they tried to expand the size of their farms and slave holdings. The southern plantation was a precursor of the modern commercial farm; in this earlier era the work was done by hundreds of slaves in which the owner had a fixed investment. Today that work is done mainly by machinery.

## EXPLOITATION AND SLAVE CONDITIONS

Slaves were exploited workers. Whatever slaves produced beyond the amount required to sustain their good health was kept by their owners. For the typical slave in his or her most productive years, usually between the ages of 18 and 55, the rate of exploitation was at least 50 percent. Over an entire lifetime that percentage was lower, however, because youths cost owners more to maintain than they initially produced and older slaves generated only small surpluses.

The treatment slaves received varied. Some owners were extremely harsh while others were paternalistic. Most slaveholders used some combination of fear and small rewards to control their bonded workers. Almost every slave was either whipped or witnessed a whipping. The ability to use physical violence against slaves was just one manifestation of the enormous, almost unrestricted power which owners exercised over their laborers. Troublesome slaves could be sold and permanently separated from family and friends; that means of vengeance loomed as perhaps the ultimate threat against uncooperative workers.

Although owners occasionally treated slaves cruelly, they rarely did anything to impair the health of their workers. A slave had value as a productive unit, and the maintenance of good health was in the financial interest of the owner—either for immediate work on the farm or as an asset for sale at slave markets. For that reason alone, owners provided reasonably adequate care for their work force on a regular basis. Meals were sometimes monotonous and contained modest amounts of meat, but the volume of food was plentiful. Some foodstuffs which whites normally disdained, such as sweet potatoes, are excellent sources of minerals and vitamins. Slave diets were not deficient and probably met modern nutritional standards. Workers were given plain but warm clothing. Housing was crude but not overcrowded or unsanitary; families usually lived in their own small units.

Slaves also received adequate medical care—or at least as good as was available in this era when most doctors still had rudimentary training. Sick slaves were not sent out to perform heavy labor in the cotton fields. Owners undoubtedly frequently suspected slaves of feigning illness—one method of resistance to oppression—but they were reluctant to take the chance that a genuinely sick laborer might die from overwork. Plantation owners were just as interested in keeping their workers in good health as northern manufacturers were in keeping their machinery in good repair.

The horror of slavery was not so much in the daily treatment of bonded workers, but rather on the limitations it placed on a whole population in terms of personal growth and development—the lack of education, the absence of political rights, and the inability to acquire property and enhance living standards. In the antebellum decades southerners became so paranoid about the possibility of slave rebellions led by individuals who had learned to read and write that they clamped down on opportunities for even the most elementary forms of education. In some states it was actually illegal to teach a slave to read. Of course, slaves had no political or civil rights. They could not vote, serve on juries, or even act as witnesses in court—certainly not to give testimony against a white person.

Southern apologists for the slave system often pointed out that living conditions on plantations were no worse and sometimes better than those endured by factory workers in the North. Moreover, planters generally cared for aged workers, whereas in the northern states those too old to work were simply fired and left to their own devices for survival. Yet these apologists missed the most crucial point: the northern factory worker had hope for a better life and the freedom to take advantage of opportunities when they came along—if not for themselves, then for their children. Slaves had no hope for themselves or their children; there was no possibility of upward social and economic mobility. The great tragedy of slavery was that future generations could never look forward to anything other than dependency, humiliation, and subjugation. The dream of economic success so vital to the welfare of white Americans was callously denied to the large proportion of the black population who remained enslaved. For those who were enslaved the institution was neither efficient nor profitable.

## SELECTED REFERENCES

CONRAD, ALFRED, and JOHN MEYER. "The Economics of Slavery in the Antebellum South," *Journal of Political Economy* (1958), 95–130.

DAVID, PAUL, HERBERT GUTMAN, RICHARD SUTCH, and GAVIN WRIGHT. *Reckoning with Slavery.* New York: Oxford University Press, 1976.

FOGEL, ROBERT, and STANLEY ENGERMAN. *Time on the Cross.* Boston: Little Brown, 1974.

GOLDIN, CLAUDIA. *Urban Slavery in the American South.* Chicago: University of Chicago Press, 1976.

OLMSTED, FREDERICK L. *The Cotton Kingdom: A Traveler's Observations on Cotton and Slavery in the American Slave States.* New York, 1861.

PHILLIPS, U. B. "The Economic Cost of Slaveholding in the Cotton Belt," *Political Science Quarterly* (1905), 257–75.

WRIGHT, GAVIN. *The Political Economy of the Cotton South.* New York: W. W. Norton, 1978.

# CHAPTER TWELVE
# THE CIVIL WAR
# AND ITS AFTERMATH

Most of us have probably heard or read in one context or another that, despite the ugliness and viciousness of previous wars, one positive effect has usually been the stimulation of the domestic economy. The best example is World War II, which—almost everyone concedes—pulled the United States out of the Depression years of the 1930s. For decades most historians had a similar belief about the effect of the Civil War on the United States economy, at least in every section outside of the South. First it was argued that the demands of the military stimulated northern industry. Second, several influential historians claimed that the emergence of the Republican party as the dominant force in American politics over the next 50 years coincided with the triumph of a capitalist ideology—which stressed societal change and economic development—over a planter ideology, which had emphasized agriculture and the maintenance of the status quo in politics, social relations, and economic life.

Over the last several decades, however, historians have altered their views about the impact of the Civil War on the American economy. The general consensus now is that the military conflict did more to retard than to stimulate economic activity. One of the main reasons for this change in historical interpretation is that we now know so much more about the status of the economy in the fifteen years prior to the war. The years from 1845 to 1860 witnessed a huge shift of workers out of agriculture and into manufacturing in the northern states. Industry was already expanding at a rapid pace without any stimulus from military spending. Indeed, the rate of increase of per capita output in manufacturing was lower in the 1860s at 2.3 percent annually than during the 1840s and 1850s when the percentage was over three times higher at 7.8 percent. In short, the United States needed no war or any change in its political alignment as prerequisites for reaping the benefits of accelerated economic progress. The rapid economic advancement after the war should be viewed more properly as a continuation of an earlier trend which had, in fact, been interrupted by the confrontation between the northern and southern states.

## THE SOUTH: THE WAR YEARS

The southern states were completely unprepared to fight a long, drawn-out war. The overwhelming majority of the region's productive capacity was in agriculture; it did not have a sufficient number of manufacturing plants to supply and arm adequately a huge military force for several years. In addition, the Confederacy had no navy of any consequence. Therefore, it was unable to break through the Northern naval blockade and export enough cotton to buy overseas the war material which might have permitted its generals to wage a more vigorous campaign. Even with limited supplies of men and guns, the brilliant military leadership of the South was almost able to avoid defeat. The best hope for the Confederacy was a short war, which of course everyone on both sides expected, but when it became a prolonged conflict the odds shifted heavily toward the Union forces. Once it had evolved into a war of attrition, the Southern states were seriously handicapped because of their unbalanced economic base, which had stressed cotton and food production over manufacturing.

The Southern states also faced severe difficulties in financing the military effort. Keeping armies in the field cost the region more than one half of its entire annual prewar income. An early effort to collect property taxes brought in very little revenue. The sale of Confederate bonds proved more successful in the first year of the war, but as the conflict dragged on bonds could only be sold at increasingly large discounts. Finally, with every other source of funds cut off, the Southern leadership turned exclusively to printing money to support the war effort. Inflation was rampant; prices climbed nearly 3000 percent between 1861 and 1865. The situation was fairly analogous to what had happened to the dollars issued by Continental Congress during the 1770s. The "real tax" fell on those who held the Confederate money while it was depreciating. The velocity at which Confederate dollars changed hands was very high because almost everyone wanted to exchange the paper for goods while the money still retained some purchasing power. By 1865 the money had virtually no value, and military officers were forced to requisition goods, primarily foodstuffs, from local citizens to maintain their starving troops.

## THE NORTH: THE WAR YEARS

In the short run the Union was not much better prepared to wage a major war than the Confederacy. Over the long haul, however, its much larger population and vastly larger manufacturing base gave the Union forces a decided military advantage. The population of the Northern states at 22 million was over three times greater than the free population of the South. Over 80 percent of the nation's manufacturing in 1860 was located in states that remained loyal to the Constitution. The Northern states also had a more developed transportation system—especially railroads—for the rapid movement of men and supplies. Despite all these economic advantages, the Union military effort floundered for several years because of indecisive, overly cautious military leadership. The war still had to be won on the battlefield, and victory came only after President Abraham Lincoln placed General Ulysses Grant in complete command of military strategy. Grant kept unrelenting pressure on the Confederate forces and thus relied on his inherent superiority in men and arms to defeat the enemy.

The Union faced an equally formidable task in raising the funds to wage war. Tariffs on imported goods and excise taxes were increased, and a new kind of levy, an income tax, was adopted. (The income tax expired soon after the war and was not revived again until the twentieth century.) As in most wars, however, taxes covered only a fraction of the cost of the fighting—in this case about 20 percent. Two thirds of the expenses of government between 1861 and 1865 came from the sale of bonds. In this situation, the earlier development of an investment banking sector to assist in raising vast sums of money for railroads during the 1850s proved beneficial to the Lincoln administration. The resources of investment bankers were mobilized, and one man, Jay Cooke, was extraordinarily successful in promoting the sale of war bonds not only to the wealthy classes but also to thousands of citizens of modest means.

During periods when the treasury was temporarily empty, the government also resorted to the printing presses to finance a portion of the war costs. Around $400 million in "greenbacks" were issued, and they covered nearly 15 percent of the total military expenses. Greenbacks were not exchangeable for gold and silver, and their issuance increased the money supply and drove prices in the North up to a level more than double what they had been in 1860. Because this form of money was not convertible into specie, the whole Northern financial and banking system soon abandoned the gold standard for domestic transactions. After the war some politicians favored the rapid retirement of these greenbacks but a myriad of groups opposed that policy because it would have caused a correspondingly rapid deflation in the prices of goods. After a period of indecision, the government decided to let most of the greenbacks remain in circulation and to wait until the general economy had grown into its enlarged money supply. Instead of falling quickly, prices fell gradually, and in 1879 specie convertibility was resumed for both banknotes and greenbacks.

The war had a surprisingly small effect on the Northern manufacturing sector. In general, the new markets created by the demands of the military were largely offset by the loss of previously existing Southern markets for a whole range of goods and services. The boot and shoe industry provides a case in point. The army placed orders for hundreds of thousands of shoes for its soldiers, but without any new orders coming in from the Southern states to provide footwear for its population of nearly four million slaves and six million whites, Northern firms cut net production and employment by one third. Iron for gun barrels and bullets naturally got a big boost, but the war disrupted previously planned railroad construction. As a result, iron production for rails and rolling stock declined. Without plentiful supplies of raw cotton from Southern plantations, textile mills were also underutilized. Manufacturing overall did continue to expand during the war, but its rate of growth in the 1860s was the lowest for any decade between 1840 and 1900.

To sum up, the Civil War had a negative effect on the American economy. It led to a huge decline in the output of goods and services in the Southern states, and it slowed down a vigorous growth in Northern agriculture and manufacturing. The war had no beneficial effect on free workers. The only clearly identifiable group to benefit were the freed slaves.

## THE POSTWAR SOUTHERN ECONOMY

The war had a devastating effect on the economy of the Southern states. At least 275,000 Confederate soldiers were killed and thousands more wounded. From one quarter to one third of the white males age 20 to 35 perished in the conflict. Before the war these men had been productive farmers; now their labor and entrepreneurship were lost forever. Southern livestock suffered similarly large losses—on the magnitude of one quarter to one half of all cattle, horses, and hogs in the region. Railroads were left in disrepair. Capital and credit were extremely scarce since few banks were in operation at the end of the war.

The emancipation of nearly 4 million slaves disrupted traditional institutional patterns in the Southern economy. Former slave owners were permitted to keep their land, but they had to absorb huge capital losses because of the freeing of their bonded workers. Some historians have put the property losses sustained by whites—including slaves, livestock, buildings, etc.—at a figure as high as 40 percent of their total wealth holdings in 1860. Of course, much of that loss represented simply a transfer of wealth within the section from slaveholders to the newly freed.

As a result of war damage and the sudden shift from a partially slave economy to a completely free economy, productivity in the region fell precipitously. Commodity output per worker dropped about 10 percent between 1860 and 1870. Income per capita for the total Southern population (free and slave) had been roughly 70 percent of the national average in 1860, but ten years later that figure had fallen to 50 percent. Although the region was able to recover sufficiently in the 1870s to match Northern growth rates, no substantial progress in closing the gap, which was opened even wider in the Civil War decade, occurred until almost a century later—during and after World War II.

Why did the Southern economy fail to rebound robustly in the postwar era? Economic historians have pointed to several factors related to both the demand and supply side of the economic equation. The demand for Southern cotton, which had been rising rapidly in the antebellum decades, began to slow down its rate of increase after 1860. English textile mills, which had taken up to 80 percent of the crop, now faced a leveling off in sales of cloth. In addition, other nations had expanded their cotton fields during the war years, in particular Brazil, Egypt, and India, and although the Southern states reclaimed part of their losses after 1865, they still were never able to recapture their former share of the world market.

The problem of a slower growth in demand for raw cotton could have been overcome if the region had been able to shift more of its productive resources into other pursuits—different crops or new industries. The region did begin to diversify its economy, but the change came slower than it should have. Several important reasons for this lag have been cited. The Southern states had placed less emphasis than the North on public education. The sums spent were modest for whites and nothing for slaves. As a result of the failure to provide more widespread educational opportunities, the population did not have sufficient entrepreneurial and labor skills to make an adjustment to changing demand.

Another reason often mentioned was institutional rigidities in the systems of sharecropping and of crop lien financing, both of which emerged in the postwar decades. Sharecropping was a method under which landowners and tenants shared in the risks of the market; it stressed safety, not daring and innovation. The crop lien system was (and still is) a system under which lenders provided funds to farmers throughout the year and took for security a lien against the upcoming harvest. In large part because cotton was nonperishable and a known quantity, lenders often insisted that prospective borrowers plant the same traditional crop year after year. Sharecropping and crop lien financing were not completely resistant to adaptation but they were not sufficiently flexible to permit the region to respond quickly to signals from the outside market.

The other major factor that accounted for the poor performance of the Southern economy was the reduction in the amount of labor supplied. Freed slaves did not participate in productive activities to the same extent as before. They now had a choice about how much of their time would be spent in economic pursuits or in leisure and recreation. Under slavery, black workers of all ages and sexes were forced to become active participants in the labor force. But granted freedom, women and children reduced substantially the amount of time allocated to field work. Despite the cutbacks in working hours, the typical black family still realized an income of up to 40 percent higher after emancipation. The fact that they could improve their living standards almost by one half with much less work reveals the extent of exploitation under slavery. The losses of slaveholders were counterbalanced by the gains of their formerly bonded workers, who now had the opportunity to keep the rewards of their efforts and to accumulate land and capital for future generations. Although the aggregate output for the Southern states declined, the income level of one specific group—former slaves—actually rose; for them, the postwar era did not appear to be an era of stagnation but rather one of opportunity.

Slavery ended, but not racism. After the end of Northern reconstruction in 1876, most Southern states passed laws which denied former slaves with artisan skills the right to ply their trade in local markets. The ordinances reserved for whites all jobs in such fields as carpentry, masonry, and a host of crafts. In addition blacks were systematically denied the right to vote, serve on juries, and hold political office.

Economic historians are divided at present about whether the effect of such extreme racism was great enough to cause black incomes to stagnate or even decline in the last quarter of the nineteenth century. Some scholars argue that prejudice was so pervasive that blacks simply could not take advantage of new opportunities for economic advancement. In addition to prohibitions on entering craft occupations, black farmers also found it difficult to borrow funds for seed and supplies except at very high interest rates. The net result was the evolution of a system of "debt peonage," under which farmers became the financial dependents of local lenders and lived in a status of quasi slavery. (It should be pointed out that many whites with small farms were equally caught up in this system of debt peonage.)

On the other hand, another group of scholars believes that, despite discrimination, markets functioned sufficiently well to permit blacks to enhance their economic status. Soon after the end of the war up to one third of black families acquired ownership of their own farms, purchasing land usually from their former owners, and the percentage of ownership climbed over the remainder of the century. Another complementary study has indicated that the aggregate value of black assets rose between 1870 and 1910 at about the same rate as white assets in the South over the same period. This latter data suggest that racism was primarily a negative force in the political arena but that its economic consequences were not substantial. In the future we should have a clearer picture about whether racism had a major or minor effect on the economic lives of black Americans in the Southern states during the postwar era. But until more research is completed, it would be unwise to try to make even a tentative judgment.

## SELECTED REFERENCES

COCHRAN, THOMAS C. "Did the Civil War Retard Industrialization?," *Mississippi Valley Historical Review* (1961), 197-210.
DeCANIO, STEPHEN. "Productivity and Income Distribution in the Post-Bellum South," *Journal of Economic History* (1974), 422-46.
ENGERMAN, STANLEY. "The Economic Impact of the Civil War," *Explorations in Economic History* (1966), 176-99.

GOLDIN, CLAUDIA, and FRANK LEWIS. "The Economic Impact of the American Civil War: Estimates and Implications," *Journal of Economic History* (1975), 299–326.

HAMMOND, BRAY. *Sovereignty and an Empty Purse: Banks and Politics in the Civil War.* Princeton: Princeton University Press, 1970.

HIGGS, ROBERT. *Competition and Coercion: Blacks in the American Economy, 1865–1914.* New York: Cambridge University Press, 1977.

RANSOM, ROGER, and RICHARD SUTCH. *One Kind of Freedom: The Economic Consequences of Emancipation.* New York: Cambridge University Press, 1977.

TEMIN, PETER. "The Postbellum Recovery of the South and the Cost of the Civil War," *Journal of Economic History* (1976), 898–907.

WALTON, GARY M., and JAMES SHEPHERD. *Market Institutions and Economic Progress in the New South, 1865–1900.* New York: Academic Press, 1981.

# CHAPTER THIRTEEN
# AGRICULTURE
# IN A CHANGING ECONOMY

From the Civil War to the 1980s, United States agriculture followed a variable and paradoxical course. This sector of the economy enjoyed huge successes and faced some major difficulties. In terms of increasing productivity, agriculture has been enormously successful, especially since the 1940s. For example, the labor required to produce 100 bushels of wheat fell from 152 hours in 1880 to under 10 hours in 1980. Aided by new machines, genetically superior plants and animals, plus refrigeration and canning, the farm community has provided American consumers with a diverse diet at very reasonable prices. The share of the total work force engaged in farming dropped from slightly over 50 percent in 1880 to under 4 percent, and it continues to decline. Americans now pay out a lower percentage of earnings for food, from 15 to 17 percent, than any society in the capitalist world.

Ironically, this record of productivity eventually brought much hardship to individual farmers. They suffered first because of the volatility of commodity prices and, after 1920, because of chronic surpluses of farm products which led to the difficult transition of workers out of agriculture and into other sectors of the economy. In response to mounting difficulties, farmers organized political parties and numerous pressure groups to agitate for reform of the economic system and subsequently for direct government financial assistance. Eventually farmers were able to use their voting power to convince Congress to enact a whole series of programs designed to curb farm output and support crop prices. In the post-World War

II era the public came to accept the proposition that farmers had a legitimate claim on government to protect them from uncontrollable market forces and to guarantee a substantial rate of profit. No other special interest group, not even defense contractors, has been so successful in persuading government to serve its purposes. Moreover, the farm bloc has been able to achieve its goals while continuing to espouse the tenets of individual initiative and free enterprise. Farmers came to view government support not as a form of public welfare but rather as an expression of economic justice within the context of an advanced technological society.

## EXPANSION AND PROTEST: 1870-1895

During the last quarter of the nineteenth century, farmers and ranchers continued to press westward across the Mississippi River into the plains, southwestern, and Pacific coast states. The amount of land under cultivation in the country more than doubled from 408 to 840 million acres between 1870 and 1900. Using the expanded railroad system to ship their products to market, wheat farmers from Oklahoma to North Dakota, cattle ranchers from Texas to Montana, and fresh vegetable and fruit growers in Florida and California all entered the national market in full force. The rapid urbanization of eastern and midwestern cities provided increased demand for agricultural products, while European markets were expanding too.

Not only did the number of farms increase but the output of individual farm workers rose as well. For centuries, humanity had realized very slight increases in its capacity to produce more food per person. The main bottleneck was the harvest. Beginning in the 1840s, and accelerating after 1870, American farmers were able to purchase various types of horse-drawn equipment to boost productivity. For example, the reaper was very adaptable to the flat plains, and it increased the ability of the family farmer, with a limited supply of labor at harvest season, to cut more grain before it rotted in the fields. Wheat production per farm increased swiftly since more acres could be planted for harvesting.

Despite the progress in raising output, farmers were not completely satisfied with their economic status during most of the last quarter of the nineteenth century. Many farmers had borrowed money to purchase land, and they protested the deflationary trend of prices after the end of the Civil War. Deflation meant that money increased in value relative to goods; therefore loans had to be paid off in the future with money which was more valuable than when originally borrowed. Farmers believed this outcome was inequitable, and they were attracted to political movements which espoused inflationary policies such as the issuance of more greenback dollars or the inclusion of more silver coins—free silver—in the monetary system.

In addition, farmers frequently called for governmental oversight of the railroads or even their outright ownership by government. The main complaints were first that rail rates did not fall in unison with declines in farm prices and second that freight rates for short distances were invariably proportionally higher than for longer routes. This so-called "long haul–short haul" differential upset farmers enormously because they failed to understand why the rates per mile were not essentially the same for all railroads irrespective of location. The agricultural sector was absolutely convinced that it had become the victim of a monopolistic transportation system which always charged "all the traffic will bear"; farmers interpreted that rate to be the highest possible, and thus one which was unfair and exploitative.

## ANALYSIS OF FARM COMPLAINTS

Were farmers justified in their complaints? The modern judgment is no. Although farm prices did fall in the post-Civil War decades so too did the prices of manufactured goods, and by about the same amount over the long run. True, farmers and other debtors generally repaid loans with money more valuable than when it had been borrowed, but since the pace of deflation was gradual and *predictable,* the anticipated change in its value was reflected in reduced interest rates, which were lower than they otherwise would have been.

The case against the railroads was likewise overstated. There were legitimate reasons for the differential in rates for short and long hauls. Short hauls were usually made over railroads serving remote areas where the volume of traffic was extremely seasonal—usually large only in the harvest months. Therefore rates had to be relatively high since revenues over only a limited period of heavy traffic had to cover the fixed costs for a whole year of operation. Meanwhile, railroads making long hauls from Chicago and other points in the Midwest directly to New York and other large eastern ports could offer lower rates per mile because they had a substantial amount of business all year long.

In addition, the general level of railroad rates went down about as much as farm prices fell in this era. But whereas railroad rates decreased gradually from one decade to the next, farm prices fluctuated wildly from year to year. In years when the prices for crops dropped precipitously, transportation costs suddenly became a much higher percentage of a farmer's total operating costs, and it was during these years that agricultural protest was loudest in the midwestern and plains states.

Although farmers often blamed the wide swings in crop prices on such bogeymen as railroad leaders, monopolists, and Wall Street bankers, the underlying cause stemmed from their increased participation in world markets. Exports of foodstuffs to Europe rose dramatically after 1880. As the transportation and communication systems improved, the price for wheat, for example, was determined not merely by demand and supply forces in the domestic market but in the global market as well. As a result, prices could be affected, and often were, by weather conditions in locations as distant as western Europe and Russia. Short crops overseas drove up wheat prices very quickly; but later when good weather permitted the production of bountiful harvests in large wheat-producing areas such as the Russian Ukraine, the price could just as suddenly plummet. Thus one of the goals of agricultural interests in the United States became governmental protection from the negative influences of foreign market conditions—but not, of course, from anything positive that might occur in international food markets.

## REVIVAL AND PROSPERITY: 1896–1920

After decades of complaints about the alleged failure of agriculture to share properly in the material progress of American society—which was becoming increasingly industrialized—farmers unexpectedly enjoyed a quarter century of genuine prosperity beginning in the mid-1890s. The first decade of the twentieth century witnessed the arrival of the largest number of immigrants in the nation's history, mostly from eastern and southern Europe. They swelled the cities and created a huge demand for food. Farm prices rose relative to those for other goods and services, and they remained high with only modest fluctuations through 1920. Indeed, the ratio of farm to industrial prices was more favorable for the agricultural sector in the years from 1910 to 1914 than during any other comparable peacetime period in American history. Many historians subsequently labeled it the "golden age" of United States agriculture. The total number of Americans actually living on farms peaked at over 32 million in 1910. In later decades, when crop prices headed down again, farmers tried to induce the government to reestablish the "parity" which had existed between agricultural and industrial prices in these most favorable years.

## COLLAPSE AND STABILIZATION: 1920–1950

The post-World War I recession signaled the end of a quarter century of agricultural prosperity. Between 1920 and 1921 both crop prices and net farm income dropped by over 40 percent. Wheat fell from $2.58 a bushel to 93¢ and corn was down from $1.86 to 41¢ per bushel. The prices of nonagricultural goods also fell in the early twenties but not quite so steeply. During these difficult years farm debt rose by one-fourth. Adding to the farmer's plight, property taxes on farm acreage went up slightly. With interest costs and taxes climbing while gross farm receipts were falling, millions of farmers faced a financial crisis.

In the mid-twenties, however, crop prices stabilized and started to move upward again. From 1925 to 1929 net farm income recovered somewhat, increasing to over 80 percent of the income prevailing at the beginning of the decade. But the optimism about the future of farming had dimmed. The value of farmland declined by almost one-third. For the first time in the nation's history, the total number of people actually living on farms declined significantly, falling from 32 to 30.5 million. The rate of foreclosures jumped from 3.8 per one thousand mortgages in 1920 to between 14 and 17 per thousand in 1929.

The productivity of individual farmers expanded by about 10 percent during the twenties. The gasoline-powered tractor began replacing horses and mules in the field and around the farm. Thousands of acres previously planted in hay and other feed grains for draft animals were freed for the production of foods for human consumption. Meanwhile, trucks could be used to carry crops more swiftly to waiting markets.

Then came the Great Depression. The overall index of farm prices between January 1930 and February 1933 was off over 60 percent; net farm income dropped similarly. Recovery was slow, and the prospects were bleak for farmers with little capital. Thousands of small farmers were threatened with the loss of their property because they could not generate sufficient cash income to make their mortgage payments. On the other hand, most farm residents at least had enough food to maintain a proper diet, which could not be said of many of their fellow citizens in the cities who were unemployed and hungry.

During the 1930s the federal government assumed a much more active role in trying to prop up farm prices and incomes. Previously, government aid had been focused on assisting farmers in raising production. In the late nineteenth century, the national government had provided financing for agricultural research stations and the establishment of land grant universities, which stressed agricultural education. Later, in 1916, the federal government established a system of banks to serve specifically the needs of the farm community. But the activities of the new Roosevelt administration, elected in 1933, went much further to rescue farmers from bankruptcy and despair.

New Deal farm programs aimed both at reducing the production of food and the surpluses already in storage. To lower stocks in silos and warehouses, the government promoted nutritional programs and export subsidies. In the nutritional category were such programs as free or inexpensive school lunches for children, low-cost milk distribution, and food stamps for destitute families. In addition, the government gave farmers subsidies to boost agricultural sales overseas; the subsidy was the difference between prevailing food prices in the domestic market and the even lower prices on world markets. (In a curious twist, an issue of sharp contention between the United States and the Common Market countries in the early 1980s was the American objection to the payment of export subsidies by some of our European allies to their farmers—because, of course, such subsidies hurt United States agricultural sales overseas.)

The programs which made the greatest impact on the farm economy, however, were plans to reduce the acreage under cultivation. In 1933, the Agricultural Adjustment Act (AAA) created an acreage allotment system, which aimed at limiting the amount of land planted in major crops. With food supplies reduced, it was hoped that prices would recover. Individual farmers who voluntarily participated received "benefit payments," one of the numerous euphemisms invented to avoid the use of the correct word—subsidy.

In 1938, Congress passed a new AAA bill which directly supported crop prices. The government agreed to loan farmers a certain fixed amount per bushel against crops placed in storage. Subsequently, if market prices rose above the amount borrowed, farmers could sell their crops, pay off their debts, and keep the profits. On the other hand, if prices remained below support levels, farmers could simply default on their loans and allow the government to assume ownership of their crops. In effect, the loan levels became minimum prices, or a floor below which government and taxpayers rather than farmers suffered any additional losses.

The various New Deal programs designed to raise farm prices and incomes were effective. Between 1933 and 1937 crop prices more than doubled. The ratio of farm prices to industrial prices prevailing in the favorable 1910-1913 period—commonly called simply "parity"—was restored. Net farm income climbed from a low of $2 billion in 1932 to $4.5 billion in 1940. Grateful farmers returned the favor and voted heavily for Roosevelt in the 1936 and 1940 presidential elections. Indeed, from this point onward, agricultural production was, except for very short periods, never guided completely by free market forces again.

During World War II, the demand for agricultural output rose substantially, and suddenly the goal of government shifted from the limitation of production to expansion. As an incentive to farmers, the Roosevelt administration sponsored legislation which authorized most price supports at 85 to 90 percent of parity. During the war years, farm output increased at about 5 percent annually, despite the loss of over 6 million men and women (or 20 percent of rural population) who either went into the military or moved to the cities to take advantage of high paying jobs in defense industries. Net farm income climbed to over $12 billion in 1945 and then peaked at nearly $18 billion in 1948.

## THE MODERN ERA: 1950-1980s

Since mid-century, American agriculture has undergone a new series of dramatic alterations. Perhaps the one change which has made the greatest overall impact was the application of the biological sciences to crop and livestock production. Agricultural scientists and technicians made huge strides in improving the genetic makeup of plants and animals. As a result, yields of food per acre and per animal began to rise substantially. For example, the average yield per acre of wheat only went up from 15 to 17 bushels between 1800 and 1950, but over the next twenty-five years, average yields climbed to over 30 bushels, an improvement of more than 80 percent. Similarly, the development of hybrid corn, the nation's largest food crop, helped increase yields from under 40 bushels per acre in 1950 to over 80 bushels in 1975. Biologists also discovered methods of boosting milk and meat production per animal and at lower costs per pound. Increases in yields of this magnitude have come only very recently in the United States and around the world.

The combination of higher yields and more efficient machinery meant that fewer workers were needed in the farm sector. Farm employment fell from 10 million workers in 1950 to just under 4 million in 1980. The number of farms decreased by one half after 1950, while the average farm size doubled to around 400 acres. The total amount of land under cultivation remained roughly the same, however, ranging from 1.1 to 1.2 billion acres. Farm population declined from 15 to 3.5 percent of total United States population between 1950 and 1980.

During most of the post-World War II era, agriculture was plagued by the same fundamental problem which had emerged in the 1930s: the threat of chronic surpluses. Individual farmers often suffered, especially in marginal areas, because of the success of farmers as a group in improving their productivity. Net farm income fell by one third over the next two decades after reaching its post-World War II high in 1948. Again, the federal government assisted the farm community through nutritional programs, price supports, and legislation designed to take cropland out of production.

Under the administration of President Dwight Eisenhower in the 1950s, the so-called Soil Bank program was introduced; it paid money to farmers for not planting crops on up to 20 percent of their productive land. The misleading name was deliberately chosen because government officials wanted to disguise what was primarily a subsidy to farmers as a conservation measure adopted in the public interest. Such deceptive nomenclature was necessary partly because conservative Republicans opposed providing welfare payments, another form of public subsidy, to poor people living in urban areas. Politics was at the root of this double standard, for farmers generally voted heavily in national elections and controlled several key states important in congressional and presidential elections.

During the administrations of Presidents John Kennedy and Lyndon Johnson, a food stamp program was initiated and later expanded. Under the law poor families received stamps which could be used like currency to purchase foodstuffs at grocery stores. This legislation proved very popular with congresspersons from both rural and urban areas, since it met the needs of several different constituencies. Urban representatives favored the food stamp program because of its humanitarian aspects, while rural representatives voted for the legislation because it increased the demand for food and thereby reduced surplus stocks. During the administration of President Ronald Reagan, funding for food stamps exceeded $10 billion annually.

Historians have expressed differing views about the wisdom of extensive government intervention in the agricultural sector. Critics of subsidies and production control programs have objected that such intervention disrupts the normal functioning of the pricing and profit systems, which guide the operation of other sectors of our economy. While such critics have expressed approval of temporary emergency programs to alleviate genuine suffering, they do not believe that agriculture should have been singled for special treatment year after year. Without subsidy programs, it was argued, food prices for consumers would have continued to decline.

Another objection focuses on the inappropriateness of the formulas devised for distributing subsidy funds. Government aid was invariably justified by arguments stressing the plight of small farmers with inadequate financing who were unable to compete with their neighbors who had larger holdings and more capital. But, in actuality, for decades—until the law was changed in the 1970s to place limits on sums given to individual farmers—most of the subsidy payments went to large farmers who were already prospering. Many critics thus found the inequities of the program and the hypocrisy of its advocates unpalatable.

Yet the farm programs had staunch defenders too. They pointed to the fact that food prices for American consumers remained fairly steady in the 1950s and 1960s and were generally much lower than prices prevailing in other advanced nations. Net farm income likewise was probably more stable than in any other period over the last century, ranging from a low of $10.5 billion to a high a $14.6 billion between 1953 and 1971. Moreover, the subsidy payments were not sufficiently high to distort labor markets and halt the continuous shift of workers out of agriculture and into other sectors of the economy. By 1980 less than 4 percent of the United States population lived on farms. Two hundred years ago it had taken four to five farm workers employed full-time to feed themselves and just one additional urban resident; but in the present economy a single farmer produces enough food to feed 25 fellow citizens plus several more people overseas.

Indeed, there were those who argued that, to the extent that subsidy payments to American farmers slowed that transition of workers out of agriculture, the United States government was performing a humanitarian service for millions of people in other countries who were periodically threatened with starvation. Surplus crops were stored in government silos and warehouses where they then became available on short notice for shipment overseas to people in Asia, Africa, and Latin America who, because of unexpectedly poor harvests or war dislocations, needed food from outside sources for survival. In the absence of farm subsidies, United States surpluses and reserves would have very likely disappeared and millions of men, women, and children around the world would have faced death from starvation.

## RECENT DEVELOPMENTS

In the 1970s and early 1980s, however, fluctuations in the demand for agricultural goods on world markets had major repercussions in the United States. The Russians suffered a series of poor harvests during the early 1970s, and, rather than abandoning plans to continue a scheduled build-up of livestock herds, Soviet leaders decided to purchase substantial amounts of grain in the American market. Several other countries also experienced setbacks in agricultural production and increased imports. Between 1970 and 1975 United States crop prices more than doubled; net farm income jumped from $14 billion in 1970 to $33 billion in 1974. Farm prices climbed far above parity levels, making government price supports unnecessary and inoperable. Land lying fallow under the Soil Bank program was quickly brought back into production. Even the exodus of workers out of agriculture was temporarily reversed. Opinionmakers around the globe began to talk about potential crises that lay ahead for humanity because of the depletion of reserve stocks of food.

This upward shift in the fortune of the United States farm sector was short-lived, however. The crisis atmosphere stemming from the fear of shortages passed almost as suddenly as it had emerged. Supplies rose rapidly after nearly 20 percent of American farmland was brought back into production. Meanwhile, the rest of the world experienced improved harvests. With foreign demand falling and supplies soaring, prices and income began to fall. Prices fell back to support levels again, and government storehouses were bursting at the seams by 1982. The cost of storing excess food reached into the billions of dollars annually.

In 1983 acreage control programs were reintroduced with added vigor; under the "payment-in-kind" (PIK) program, farmers who voluntarily agreed not to plant anything on much of their existing cropland were permitted to take, at no cost, sufficient amounts of grain from government surplus stocks to compensate for their "lost" production. They could then sell the freely acquired grain on the open market and keep the proceeds. The aim was to eliminate the surplus food stocks "hanging over" the market and to bring demand and supply back into equilibrium at currently prevailing prices. The plan proved enormously popular with farmers who signed up for participation in the voluntary program in record numbers.

By the 1980s, therefore, the American farm sector looked for its prosperity on two fronts. It hoped for a new surge of foreign demand, but it sought relief through government programs to restrict domestic production. Meanwhile, the movement of workers out of agriculture into other occupations had resumed. Given the increases in farm productivity, some economists were predicting that as small a fraction as 2 percent of the total work force might soon be all that was required to keep Americans well-fed at reasonable prices and still maintain a high level of agricultural exports.

## EMPLOYMENT PATTERNS IN THE FARM SECTOR

Among the most interesting developments in the rural economy in recent decades has been the rise in nonfarm income. Like their urban counterparts, farm families have also sought to augment their income with multiple employment. Farmers have taken on other part-time or seasonal jobs, while their spouses have driven to nearby cities and towns to seek out full-time positions in manufacturing plants or in merchandising and other service industries. Except in a few remote regions, the isolated farm family is a relic of the past. In the early 1980s the federal government reported that almost two-thirds of net farm family income, in fact, came from nonfarm sources. During the 1970s over 50 percent of American farms, largely the smaller units, reported net losses from farm operations; yet the net family income for those same farms averaged over $13,000. The discrepancy was explained by the huge impact of income generated from nonagricultural pursuits.

Multiple employment has permitted farm families to maintain many of the virtues of a rural lifestyle without sacrificing opportunities for higher income. For centuries after the settlement of the United States, urban incomes were invariably higher than rural incomes. By the 1980s, however, there was little difference in income between farmers and other groups in our society; moreover, most farm families claimed higher net wealth.

## SELECTED REFERENCES

BOGUE, ALLAN. *Money at Interest.* Ithaca: Cornell University Press, 1955.

COCHRANE, WILLARD, and MARY RYAN. *American Farm Policy.* Minneapolis: University of Minnesota Press, 1976.

HIGGS, ROBERT. *The Transformation of the American Economy, 1865–1914.* New York: John Wiley, 1971.

JOHNSON, H. THOMAS. "Postwar Optimism and the Rural Financial Crisis of the 1920s," *Explorations in Economic History* (1973/74), 173–92.

MAYHEW, ANNE. "A Reappraisal of the Causes of Farm Protest in the United States, 1870–1900," *Journal of Economic History* (1972), 464–75.

SCHLEBECKER, JOHN T. *Whereby We Thrive: A History of American Farming.* Ames, Iowa: Iowa State University Press, 1975.

SHANNON, FRED A. *The Farmer's Last Frontier.* New York: Holt, Rinehart and Winston, 1963.

# CHAPTER FOURTEEN
# THE EMERGENCE
# OF BIG BUSINESS

The era from 1870 to 1910 is best known in historical annals for the emergence of the large industrial firm, or "big business." The big firms which prospered were more efficient than smaller competitors, and they sold better quality products at lower prices. Some of the most prominent names in the history of American business enterprise reached the apex of their careers during this era—John D. Rockefeller, J. P. Morgan, Gustavus Swift, and Andrew Carnegie, to name a few. At the turn of the century Morgan and Carnegie negotiated a business deal that created the first corporation in the world with over one billion dollars in capital; its name was United States Steel.

Several big business leaders built huge industrial empires and earned enormous amounts of money. Damned by some because of the allegedly ruthless tactics used to defeat competitors, these late nineteenth-century entrepreneurs were subsequently called "robber barons" by their critics. But others viewed them primarily as "captains of industry" and role models for enterprising people who dreamed of making a fortune through their own initiative.

Horatio Alger was the most prominent of a group of American writers who found a wide audience for fiction glorifying the rags-to-riches rise of determined and imaginative youths. Such stories in fact rarely happened in real life, but were a one-in-a-million long shot. In most other societies around the world, however, class divisions were so rigid that absolutely no one born into poverty had any chance of becoming wealthy, drive and ambition notwithstanding. Thus, the United States still was a land of opportunity for prospective immigrants, because it was a country where upward social and economic mobility and the acquisition of vast riches was at least a possibility, even if the odds were very long for any given individual.

## PRECONDITIONS FOR BIGNESS: BEFORE 1870

Prior to 1870, every manufacturing firm in the United States was either small or moderate in size. A single firm shared any given market with many competitors of comparable size. Their production costs were usually not vastly different. Meanwhile, the cost of transportation to distant markets within the continental United States was normally great enough to prevent firms outside of one state or region from trying to compete with local manufacturers who produced goods at sites closer to consumers. Since no firm was large, none had any significant influence over the prices of raw materials they purchased or the end products they sold.

Because the capital required to enter any field of endeavor remained reasonably low, new entrepreneurs were not discouraged from starting up additional manufacturing firms whenever they perceived fresh opportunities for profitable operations. Indeed, the existence of a number of prospective manufacturers on the sidelines ready to jump quickly into any given market whenever conditions appeared favorable was the main factor which kept profit rates at about the same general level, irrespective of the type of enterprise. Smallness, freedom of entry, and the unrestricted functioning of the price system—these were three of the main ingredients reflected in the economic principles espoused by Adam Smith, the famous, influential Scotsman who is recognized as the father of so-called classical economics. These principles guided the course of the American economy through the 1860s, with the exception of the railroads, some of which were already large firms before mid-century.

The railroads were a very important exception, however, because their prior existence provided the setting for the emergence of big industrial firms. With reliable year-round and relatively cheap transportation available, it became possible for a factory in one region or city to ship its goods long distances and still compete with local manufacturers elsewhere—many of which had previously enjoyed a local monopoly. The railroads created a national market—or at least the potential for one—and it remained for business leaders with foresight to take advantage of the new opportunities for growth. An improved transportation system was a prerequisite for bigness elsewhere.

## BIG BUSINESS

Beginning in the 1870s, a new type of industrial firm emerged which ultimately altered the competitive structure of certain sectors of the economy. No longer small, these new enterprises were financed with millions of dollars in capital and employed thousands of workers. Not every big firm proved profitable, however; in some industries bigness rarely paid handsome dividends for investors. But in others the big enterprises were usually able to drive small firms out of the market and retain almost all the business for themselves. In these cases, the market became concentrated into the hands of just a few firms, usually three to ten. We call such a competitive structure an oligopoly—a position between pure competition, where numerous firms all have a very small share of a market, and monopoly, where only one enterprise handles all the business.

Why did some industries become oligopolistic and others remain competitive? Contemporaries, and even historians for many years, generally pointed to the unparalleled entrepreneurial skills of certain greedy business leaders, who seemed to hold the fate of some industries in their hands. Carnegie in steel and Rockefeller in oil are prime examples. The modern interpretation is somewhat different. While conceding that certain entrepreneurs were particularly talented, business historians today stress the fact that oligopoly came only in specific industries with common underlying characteristics. Bigness paid off only in industries subject to "economies of scale." This means that, as the size of a business got larger, the cost of producing and distributing individual units—a ton of steel or a barrel of refined petroleum —fell per unit. With lower costs, the big firms were able to undersell their small competitors and reap most of the profits. They used their enhanced earnings to build even larger factories and thus lower their costs even further. Soon smaller competitors without the capital to expand were threatened with bankruptcy. After an initial shakeout period, industries in which economies of scale were technologically achievable normally settled down into an oligopolistic structure.

On the other hand, in situations where technology did not permit economies of scale, industries never lost, except very briefly, their competitive structure. Textiles probably provides the best example in this category. The oldest and one of the largest United States industries prior to 1870, textiles would appear on the surface to have been a prime candidate for concentration. But oligopoly never emerged. The reason is that, although improvements were made in machinery over the years, no vast changes occurred which permitted larger mills to obtain lower production costs per yard of cloth than hundreds of medium-size factories. As a result, the larger firms could not consistently undersell their competitors. Without the characteristics of economies of scale in production, the textile industry remained competitive, with many different firms supplying the needs of American consumers.

## STRATEGIES FOR FIRM GROWTH

The firms which became very large usually pursued two different general strategies toward bigness. There are two somewhat technical terms used to describe these processes—horizontal combination and vertical integration—but both can be explained in plainer language. Horizontal combination means the joining together of two or more business enterprises performing very similar operations—for example, two shoe factories or two oil refineries. Firms that expanded through horizontal combination usually closed their smaller plants and enlarged their more efficient, large factories.

Vertical integration means that a single firm begins to perform different, but related business functions. Prior to 1870, businesses usually performed a single function. They gathered raw materials or manufactured goods or were involved in sales, but none did all three or even two of these things. In the era of the rise of big business, however, enterprises broadened the scope of their operations. Instead of hiring an independent selling agency to distribute its goods, a factory employed its own salespeople; rather than buying raw materials from independent suppliers, a factory acquired raw materials from its own properties. In doing so, a firm integrated its operations. Many big businesses increased their size through both vertical integration and horizontal combination, sometimes simultaneously, but more often at different stages in their development.

## VERTICAL INTEGRATION: SWIFT & CO.

One of the very best examples of a firm that grew through vertical integration is Swift & Co., the Chicago meatpacker. Although techniques for preserving pork had been known for centuries, beef was a meat that usually spoiled fairly quickly. To meet the increasing demand for fresh beef during the 1860s and 1870s, thousands of head of cattle were shipped in boxcars from the western states to stockyards in eastern cities. There local butchers purchased the live animals and walked them back to their shops for immediate slaughter and sale to the public. The beginning of the perfection of refrigeration equipment in the 1870s, however, provided the opportunity for a complete restructuring of the entire industry.

Gustavus Swift was the first person with the imagination and determination to alter the fresh beef business. He perceived that, if cattle could be slaughtered at a central point in the Midwest so that only the carcasses were shipped eastward in refrigerated railroad cars, then vast cost savings were possible. The meat would be cut into uniform sections by specialized laborers working at the same routine tasks throughout the day. With the use of refrigerated cars, it would no longer be necessary to ship hundreds of miles across the country that one-half of the animal which was inedible, and thus unsaleable, upon arrival. Moreover, chilled carcasses, usually called "dressed beef" within the trade, could be packed much more tightly in a railroad car than live animals. The potential savings in transportation costs alone were enormous.

Swift's most monumental problem was that the existing distribution network for goods of all varieties could not accommodate highly perishable items such as fresh beef for shipment over long distances or subsequent storage. No wholesalers in the eastern cities owned, or were willing to construct, refrigerated warehouses to store the meat on arrival. No railroad was willing to invest in building expensive refrigerated cars for an untried venture which might prove a complete flop. If

Swift was really serious about entering this new business, he would have to set up his own slaughterhouse in the Midwest and then build a distribution network from the ground up—including his own refrigerated railroad cars and his own warehouses. He took a chance and made the investment. Swift faced some resistance from individuals with a stake in the continuation of the status quo, primarily eastern stockyard owners and butchers who were by-passed by the new system of distribution, but good fresh beef at much lower prices found favor with consumers and soon won out. Other meatpacking firms rose up and followed Swift's initiative. By the end of the century, the vast majority of the dressed beef business was in the hands of just four or five firms, all of which developed vertically integrated structures.

## HORIZONTAL COMBINATION: STANDARD OIL

One excellent example of an enterprise that grew through horizontal combination was John D. Rockefeller's Standard Oil Co. Until the middle of the nineteenth century, petroleum was normally considered little more than a potential pollutant of water wells in many areas of the world. In what seems like a comical and irresponsible usage today, patent medicine peddlers in the 1830s bottled the crude oil and sold it as a remedy for almost every illness under the sun; a typical dosage recommendation was three teaspoons, three times daily.

In the 1840s, however, a method for refining crude petroleum into kerosene was developed by an American, George Bissell. Kerosene was a superior product for illumination, substituting for candles and replacing whale and coal oil in lamps. (Until the 1910s, the main use of petroleum products was as illuminants, not energy for powering machines or heating homes.) Once petroleum was proven to be a valuable product, the problem became obtaining large quantities for refining. Edwin Drake decided to try drilling a well, and he selected northwestern Pennsylvania as the most likely location because crude oil was oozing out of the ground in many spots. In a drilling operation at Titusville, about 100 miles north of Pittsburgh, Drake struck oil in 1859.

Among the investors in refineries in the early 1860s was John D. Rockefeller. As a teenager, Rockefeller started out his business career employed by a wholesale grocery firm in Cleveland. Often cited by historians as a prime example of the financial rewards which occasionally accrued to persons who were frugal, diligent, disciplined, and religiously devout, he became a partner in this enterprise during his early twenties. Cleveland was a minor refining center, and Rockefeller decided to invest some of his capital in this new venture in 1863.

During the first ten years, the kerosene refining business was exceedingly risky because prices fluctuated wildly. At first consumers at home and abroad rushed out to buy this new illuminant, driving up prices and encouraging many budding entrepreneurs to construct additional refineries. Then, however, new discoveries of crude oil swelled supplies and prices fell dramatically. Many refineries were threatened with bankruptcy. Lower prices attracted new customers, and soon demand climbed to a higher plateau, forcing up prices again. More drilling brought in new wells, and predictably prices plummeted one more time, bringing the fear of multiple bankruptcies. This cycle of sharp rises and sharp declines was characteristic of the kerosene industry in the 1860s.

Rockefeller sought ways to lessen competition and to bring greater stability to the industry. He noticed that refining seemed subject to economies of scale: the larger refineries had lower costs per barrel. With that factor in mind, Rockefeller initiated a plan to expand his existing firm through the strategy of horizontal combination. Sometimes he bought out local competitors with cash, but more often he persuaded other refiners to join him as minority stockholders in an enlarged enterprise. He promised not only the prospect of lower refining costs, but also the enhanced ability to bargain with railroads for reduced rates on a higher volume of kerosene shipments. Lower transportation costs were normally achieved by rebates, which railroads granted to large shippers. By 1870, Rockefeller had consolidated almost all of the refineries in the Cleveland area into one firm. Yet, prices and production remained unstable across the nation, because Cleveland handled only 10 percent of the total kerosene business in the United States.

Rockefeller next attempted to arrange a cartel agreement with refiners in other states to regulate prices and production. Created in 1872, its name—the National Refiners Association—sounded innocent enough (like OPEC), yet its goal was to control the industry, thereby substituting cooperation for competition and assuring every firm in the cartel an agreed-upon share of the market. Rockefeller soon found that his creation had serious flaws; the agreements with competitors were little more than "ropes of sand." Some refiners produced kerosene beyond their quota in an effort to enhance their profits at the expense of other firms, and there was nothing that Rockefeller could do about it. The United States courts refused to recognize the validity of the cartel agreement, calling it illegal according to the common law concept forbidding monopolistic anticompetitive behavior. (In most European countries, incidentally, such cartel agreements usually were legal and enforceable through the courts.)

After finding the cartel arrangement unworkable, Rockefeller decided to pursue the strategy of horizontal combination on a national scale. The major impediments were laws in numerous states which did not permit those corporations chartered in other states from owning the stock of a company located within their borders. For example, it was impossible under existing law for Rockefeller's Standard Oil Co., chartered in Ohio, to acquire the stock of refiners in Pennsylvania and other important refining states. The main purpose of such laws was to keep out so-called foreign competition (emanating from other states, not nations) and to preserve local markets for local manufacturers. Eventually, the Supreme Court ruled that such laws violated the Constitution because they acted as barriers to trade across state lines. But in the 1870s and 1880s these laws still prevailed and Rockefeller needed a method to circumvent them.

Rockefeller pursued the course of horizontal combination through the creation of a new type of business organization called a trust. During the late nineteenth century, the term *trust* became a synonym for big business, and its creation incited the wrath of a substantial part of the American public. Since Rockefeller could not at the time acquire the shares of other refining companies outside of Ohio through an outright purchase or exchange of shares, he and his lawyers devised a mechanism which achieved virtually the same effect. Again citing the advantage of economies of scale in the production of kerosene and transportation savings, Rockefeller convinced a majority of his competitors to join him in a single enterprise. They did not sell out their enterprises but rather transferred their stocks to Rockefeller "in trust," and he, in turn, issued to them trust certificates which paid healthy dividends. At first such transactions were carried out in secrecy, but in 1882 Standard Oil's trust arrangement was formalized and became a matter of public knowledge.

For a decade or more in the 1880s and early 1890s, the Standard Oil Co. controlled around 90 percent of the petroleum refineries in the United States. The firm was more than just a legal consolidation; the inefficient refineries were closed and the more efficient ones expanded. At one point in time, a single East Coast refinery was actually producing up to one third of all the kerosene for the entire world market. Rockefeller was reasonably successful in stabilizing the kerosene industry, and he did so without gouging the public, irrespective of his new monopoly position. Throughout this period, the price of kerosene to consumers continued to fall since production costs were declining and the firm was trying to attract new customers who had traditionally relied upon candles and coal oil lamps. In addition, the firm wanted to ward off the inroads of another new invention of the 1880s—the electric light.

FIGURE 7   John D. Rockefeller (Source: New York Public Library Picture Collection)

## "UNFAIR COMPETITION"

Rockefeller eventually aroused an enormous amount of public hostility primarily because of the tactics he used after deciding to engage in vertical integration as well as horizontal combination. Standard Oil caused only a minor stir when it moved backward into drilling and oil production, but not so when it moved forward into marketing and distribution. Initially, independent wholesalers had exercised unlimited freedom in choosing the sources of their kerosene supplies. Prior to 1880, most wholesalers carried kerosene produced by several different refiners; they selected suppliers on the basis of price, credit terms, availability of the product, and other factors normally considered in routine business transactions. After Standard Oil began refining an overwhelming majority of the kerosene in the country, it became the major supplier to wholesalers everywhere. Yet there were always a few independent refiners outside of the Rockefeller trust which still held a small share of the market and needed a distribution outlet.

In an effort to promote more effectively sales of kerosene and to deny remaining competitors market outlets, Standard Oil took a more active role in the distribution end of the business. It attempted to persuade wholesalers to carry only Standard Oil products. When that tactic failed, it shifted to threats and coercion. Company salesmen demanded that wholesalers sign contracts which waived the right to carry any other refiner's kerosene no matter how attractive the price and terms. If a wholesale firm refused to sign an "exclusive agreement," the oil company threatened to cut off its supplies of Standard kerosene and take other disruptive action.

Recalcitrant wholesalers were often the object of escalated competitive practices. When they tried to obtain kerosene from other refiners, Standard Oil intervened with the railroads to divert, delay, and occasionally even destroy such shipments. If all else failed, Standard Oil was alleged to have engaged in "selective price wars." According to these reports, if a dealer in one locality defiantly resisted signing an exclusive contract, Standard Oil would lower drastically the price of the kerosene supplied to other dealers in the area so that they could consistently undersell the lone holdout. The oil company was so big that it could afford to lose money in one small market almost indefinitely, but the wholesaler under attack was not in such a position. Eventually independent wholesalers usually came around and signed exclusive agreements, at which point Standard supposedly raised the price for its kerosene back up to the previous level.

Recently, scholars have questioned whether the firm actually initiated selective price wars. Nonetheless, contemporaries, and subsequently many historians, were convinced that this tactic was one weapon in Standard Oil's arsenal. This case may represent another example of how important what the public *believes* about the activities of a certain firm can be in the determination of government policies, irrespective of the absence of solid evidence. Standard Oil was widely accused of engaging in selective price wars, and Congress eventually enacted legislation designed to halt such practices in the future.

Meanwhile, wholesalers who were coerced into signing exclusive agreements deeply resented the intrusion of Standard Oil into what had been heretofore their realm of independent decision making. Now a big firm was telling them how to run their businesses, or at least a part of it. Many began to describe the power to demand exclusive agreements as an example of "unfair competition." These tactics were viewed as unfair because they did not emerge in the course of competition among firms of fairly equal size and strength—as had traditionally happened in the American economy. These new competitive practices could only be employed by giant enterprises which seemed to hold the power, if not of life and death, then of profit or bankruptcy over a legion of small businesses in the distribution and marketing chain.

## CARNEGIE STEEL

Another firm to expand its operations both through horizontal combination and vertical integration was Carnegie Steel, the forerunner of United States Steel. The founder, Andrew Carnegie, was one of the very few highly successful American entrepreneurs who actually came to this country as an immigrant. His father was a wool weaver in Scotland who became a victim of technological advancement; he lost his job to a power loom and fled to the United States for a new start in the 1840s. As a youth, Carnegie started work as a lowly bobbin boy in an American textile factory. During his teenage years, he learned the skills of a telegraph operator and landed a job with the Pennsylvania Railroad. Soon he became personal secretary to the railroad's president, and while still in his twenties Carnegie was promoted and given complete command over an entire 100-mile section of track. The railroads had the most advanced managerial structures of any American business enterprises in the 1850s and 1860s, therefore Carnegie was in the perfect spot to become knowledgeable about administering a large organization, adapting to technological change (in sharp contrast to his father), and, perhaps most important of all, the value of taking advantage of the new managerial tool called cost accounting. Carnegie took what he had learned on the railroad and transferred that knowledge to the iron and steel industry.

In the first half of the nineteenth century, the American iron industry had fallen far behind the British in terms of technology and output. Most of the iron rails used to build the extensive United States railroad network prior to 1870 were British imports. Steel rails were potentially much superior to iron rails since they lasted for twenty to thirty years rather than merely three to five. But steel was extremely expensive to produce and thus too costly to use in most industrial applications. In the late 1850s, however, the technology for producing steel at a much lowered cost was discovered nearly simultaneously by William Kelly in the United States and Henry Bessemer in England, with the latter receiving most of the credit and having the process named after him.

When Carnegie entered the iron business in the late 1860s, it was being

FIGURE 8    The Bessemer Steel
Workers in Pittsburgh, **1881**
(Source: Culver Pictures)

FIGURE 9    Andrew Carnegie
(Source: New York Public Library
Picture Collection)

rapidly transformed by the Bessemer furnace into a steel industry. Carnegie was at the very forefront of that movement. Steel mills were subject to vast economies of scale. Carnegie was extremely cost conscious and stayed on top of the most current technology. He aimed at gathering the lion's share of the huge American market for steel rails. In addition to expanding the size of existing mills, Carnegie pursued the strategy of horizontal combination, acquiring other firms to expand his capacity.

Carnegie Steel also integrated its operations forward and backward. Iron ore was the primary raw material and some of the richest fields were in northern Minnesota. Carnegie not only acquired the ore fields but also built a fleet of boats to bring the ore over the Great Lakes and constructed rail lines to make deliveries to the gates of his mills. Coking coal was the main source of energy in steel making, so the firm got control of its own mines in western Pennsylvania. Later, in the 1890s, when structural steel for buildings emerged as a substantial market, Carnegie by-passed the traditional iron wholesalers in the big cities and employed his own sales personnel. Over a period of several decades, Carnegie had built a huge busi-

*PEOPLE WHO MATTERED—Jay Gould*

He was a nineteenth-century railroad entrepreneur whose competitive tactics led to his inclusion in a small group of ambitious and wealthy business leaders labeled "robber barons" by a later generation of historians. Gould profited mainly because of the absence of any effective laws related to the manipulation of security values on the stock exchanges. Gould had a general plan of operation. First, he bought controlling interest in a railroad suffering from a low volume of traffic and low profits, or losses. After he had assumed managerial control, Gould immediately started a rate war with rival railroads in order to build traffic and boost profits—at least temporarily.

When the financial condition of his railroad had improved, its stocks and bonds rose in price. Eventually, however, the rival railroads retaliated with competitive rates, and Gould's railroad retreated back toward its originally weak financial condition. Even though Gould knew the position of his railroad was deteriorating, he continued to release glowing reports to the public based on falsified information. Secretly, he also began to unload his personal holdings of securities to unsuspecting buyers. By the time the news got out that a Gould railroad was again heading toward bankruptcy, the master manipulator had already sold out and taken his profits on the fluctuations in security values.

Today there are stringent laws to prevent potential manipulators from operating in such a cavalier fashion. Corporate officials who give misleading information to the public are liable for criminal prosecution. Moreover, they must report regularly to a government agency the extent of their so-called insider transactions—their purchases and sales of stocks issued by the companies in which they hold top management positions.

ness enterprise, which helped propel the United States to a position of leadership in world steel production; indeed, by the turn of the century, his firm alone had greater output than all of the steel mills in Britain combined.

In 1901, the Wall Street investment banker J. P. Morgan convinced Carnegie to merge his firm with several other medium-sized steel mills to create the first billion dollar business enterprise—United States Steel. Carnegie retired with nearly one half a billion dollars in bonds. He was probably the richest man in the world, and he spent most of his remaining years in philanthropic activities. He established the Carnegie Foundation to fund educational projects and in addition distributed millions of dollars in individual gifts to schools, churches, and libraries primarily in the United States and Europe. Other wealthy American families—the Rockefellers, Fords, and others—subsequently imitated this model and created privately funded foundations to support various projects for the public welfare.

## STRUCTURE OF INDUSTRY

What developed in the United States between 1870 and 1910 was a two-tiered business system. Many industries, probably the majority in terms of sheer numbers, continued to be highly competitive. They generally were guided by the principles of classical economics. Yet, there also developed sectors of the economy dominated by oligopolistic firms: steel, oil refining, meat packing, and others. In these industries the application of the principles of classical economics was modified. The entry of a new firm into an oligopolistic market was rare. The capital required to start up a new business to compete effectively with giant enterprises was enormous and difficult to raise. Moreover, the prospects for earning an adequate profit were not very attractive. People with money to invest in new ventures looked elsewhere to markets which were more open and competitive. The closing off of certain fields of business endeavor because of the huge, almost impossible, demands placed on any conceivable new entrant seemed to many Americans unjust and not in the democratic spirit of equal opportunity.

## ANTITRUST MOVEMENT

In response to this altered business climate, a movement emerged to roll back the clock to the era before 1870 when, except for the railroads, almost every field of economic endeavor was relatively easy for budding entrepreneurs to enter with a moderate amount of capital. Organizations like Rockefeller's trust company and its imitators, which sprang up so suddenly in the 1880s, were highly visible symbols of this new trend toward concentrated market structures. Thus this movement became known as "antitrust," but it was really aimed at breaking up all big business firms contributing to the shift away from free competition toward monopoly. The word *monopoly* had a particularly odious ring to American ears; it was a legacy that went back at least as far as President Andrew Jackson's attacks on the Second Bank of the United States in the 1830s for allegedly behaving in a monopolistic fashion.

Bowing to public pressure, Congress passed the Sherman Antitrust Act in 1890. The legislation was vaguely worded, stating merely that actions of firms which fostered monopoly were illegal. But the act never defined monopoly nor stated precisely what types of business activity were illegal. It did not legislate the break-up of any existing big businesses into smaller firms, as some of the original supporters had hoped might happen. Instead, Congress just endorsed the principle of antitrust and left to the courts the interpretation of the law.

Ironically, for the first decade after the passage of the Sherman Antitrust Act, the Supreme Court interpreted the law in such a manner that bigness was actually encouraged. The majority on the court in the 1890s were conservative in their outlook, and these justices had no intention of taking a stand on vaguely worded legislation that might disrupt the organization of much of the United States economy. In fact, they initially ruled that while it was illegal for two separate firms to conspire to restrain trade through the division of markets and price fixing, if those two firms decided to merge together into one enlarged business enterprise, then the antitrust law would no longer apply to them. The handing down of this decision actually encouraged mergers among competitors—the very opposite effect intended by the critics of bigness and oligopoly.

Finally, in a ruling in 1904, the Supreme Court altered its interpretation of the Sherman Act to correspond more closely with the goals of the antitrust movement. In the Northern Securities case, a proposed merger of the two leading railroads in the northwestern states, the court ruled that a merger between large companies in a market that was already very oligopolistic was per se illegal. This decision was a landmark because it has halted the mergers of large firms competing within the same markets up until the present. The courts have not, however, prevented mergers among large companies competing in *different* markets. For example, two large steel firms could no longer merge, but a steel company might be allowed to acquire a shoe manufacturer, or a computer firm, or any other business unrelated to metals. We call these large, diverse businesses "conglomerates," signifying the variety of their product lines. Many conglomerates were formed beginning in the 1950s.

Since the ruling in 1904, the courts have also broken up a few companies considered to be too large and thus approaching monopoly status. Among those successfully prosecuted were Standard Oil, American Tobacco, and Dupont. One of the main reasons these firms were singled out was that they were found to have engaged in competitive practices believed to be "unfair," such as the creation of cartels, dictating coercive agreements, and the like. U. S. Steel, in contrast, escaped intact in large part because it had not engaged intensively in any of these allegedly unsavory tactics. In announcing the so-called "rule of reason," the Supreme Court stated that huge size or a dominant position in a given market was not necessarily illegal. The path to bigness was considered pertinent evidence, and in cases such as U. S. Steel, where few "predatory" practices were uncovered, a firm might be allowed to continue operations even it if accounted for over half of the sales in a given market.

## PERMANENCE OF OLIGOPOLY

In those cases in which big businesses were broken up (less than ten during the entire century), the guilty firm was never divided into hundreds of small businesses. The successful prosecution of a monopolist did not restore markets to their pre-1870, competitive status. Instead, the very biggest business enterprise in an industry was divided into three to ten smaller but still relatively large companies. Rockefeller's original trust was broken up into separate Standard Oil Companies based in New Jersey, New York, Ohio, California, Indiana, and other states. Industries that had been very oligopolistic became less oligopolistic, but their fundamental structure was not radically altered.

The Supreme Court ratified what technology had first dictated, namely that business activities subject to vast economies of scale were best suited to an oligopolistic structure. Although some small business entrepreneurs were hurt in the process and certain areas of the economy were virtually closed to new entrants, the American consumer benefited from lower production costs which translated into lower prices for quality goods. Moreover, the public accepted the big firm in certain sectors of the economy after 1910 more readily than in the late nineteenth century. Americans began to realize that big businesses were not destined to gobble up every market since many huge enterprises hastily thrown together in industries unaffected by economies of scale had proven miserable failures. Small entrepreneurs found they could adjust their strategies to complement the big firms as suppliers or by discovering a new niche in an expanded market. Indeed, opportunities in the aggregate do not appear to have diminished for the typical citizen because, for every market big business closed off, it opened up several new ones for others to enter.

## DUAL ECONOMY

By the 1920s the American public had come to accept, for the most part, the new dimensions of the economy. In a certain number of markets, mostly at the core of the industrial sector, in fields such as steel, oil, and later automobiles, oligopoly was the rule. But monopoly was thwarted, except for public utilities, which were regulated by government. Oligopolistic firms competed with one another primarily on the basis of product quality, fashion, or novelty, rather than price. Their profits were substantial, but not exorbitant. Meanwhile, thousands of small manufacturers, service firms, and retail stores continued to conduct business in competitive markets just as in the past. The United States had developed a dual economy: oligopoly alongside the traditional competitive sector.

## SELECTED REFERENCES

AVERITT, ROBERT. *The Dual Economy: The Dynamics of American Industry Structure.* New York: W. W. Norton, 1968.

GALAMBOS, LOUIS. *The Public Image of Big Business in America, 1880-1940.* Baltimore: Johns Hopkins University Press, 1975.

KIRKLAND, EDWARD. *Industry Comes of Age: Business, Labor, and Public Policy, 1860-1897.* New York: Holt, Rinehart and Winston, 1961.

LIVESAY, HAROLD. *Andrew Carnegie and the Rise of Big Business.* Boston: Little, Brown & Co., 1975.

McGEE, JOHN. "Predatory Price Cutting: The Standard Oil (N.J.) Case," *Journal of Law and Economics* (1958), 137-69.

PORTER, GLENN. *The Rise of Big Business, 1860-1910.* New York: Thomas Crowell, 1973.

SEARS, MARION, and THOMAS NAVIN. "The Rise of a Market for Industrial Securities, 1887-1902," *Business History Review* (1955), 112-16.

TARBELL, IDA. *The History of the Standard Oil Company.* New York: McClure, Phillips & Co., 1904.

WILLIAMSON, HAROLD, et al. *The American Petroleum Industry.* 2 Vols. Evanston: Northwestern University Press, 1959.

# CHAPTER FIFTEEN
# LABOR
## *Successes and Failures*

As the United States continued to build its manufacturing sector in the post-Civil War period, the number of laborers engaged in factory work accelerated. The status of workers in a more industrialized society underwent significant change. The self-employed artisan of the previous era became the skilled laborer working under the direct supervision of foremen and low-level managers. Meanwhile, factories provided employment opportunities for millions of semi-skilled and unskilled men, women, and children. Some of these new laborers left their farms and came to the cities; others were recent immigrants who headed for the factories and never left. Between 1860 and 1920, the total number of factory workers climbed from 2 to 11 million, and their share of the total American work force rose from 18 to 26 percent.

The rise of large, national business organizations sparked a greater interest among workers in uniting to pursue common goals. Certain parts of the labor force began to realize that their status as independent workers had probably been irreversibly altered, and they exhibited increased class consciousness. Most workers had previously seen themselves as collaborating with owners in joint business ventures, but by the late nineteenth century the atmosphere had changed in many industries to one of confrontation and antagonism. Dissatisfied workers protested in different ways. In big cities they frequently called mass rallies and sponsored parades through downtown to demand a shorter workweek. They also formed diverse types of unions, with different goals and tactics, which promised to meet the needs of workers—or as they often preferred to call themselves in this era, the producing classes.

## WAGES AND HOURS

Between 1860 and 1920, the *real* wages of workers generally doubled, rising about 1.3 percent annually. (Real wages are adjusted for inflation and deflation.) The standard workweek of most laborers was shortened as well. In 1860 the average time worked per day in nonagricultural employment was nearly eleven hours, six days a week. By 1890 the typical workweek in manufacturing had declined to 60 hours. In 1920 most workers put in 50 hours on the job; a typical pattern was five days of 9 hours plus Saturday mornings. Yet there were exceptions. In the skilled trades, 44 hours weekly was already typical. At the other end of the spectrum, unskilled labor in an industry like steel punched in for 12 hours daily, with only every other Sunday off, when the day shift and night shift exchanged places.

Despite the steady increases in living standards, many workers remained unhappy about their economic position compared to the owners of capital. The productivity of labor in many industries, especially those subject to economies of scale, moved ahead even faster than wage rates. The extra revenues accrued to the benefit of owners, many of whom became enormously wealthy and lived in grandiose and ostentatious splendor. Workers laboring for long hours and often in danger of serious accidents believed that the division of the productivity gains associated with new technologies was inherently unjust. One of the main pleas of nineteenth-century workers caught up in technological change was for greater "justice," meaning a more equitable division of the revenues of large firms between wages and profits.

Were the workers' complaints about their alleged failure to share properly in the fruits of material progress valid? This is a very tricky question to answer because it extends beyond the mere issue of dollars and cents; it touches as well on the public's image of how our society should be organized. It depends, in large part, on an individual's vision of the main attributes of a good society. For those workers who believed there was a link between the American democratic system of government and the narrower economic gap that existed between the extremes of wealth and poverty in the United States and in Europe, the trend of events in the late nineteenth century seemed unjustified and very threatening. These critics were not out to overthrow capitalism or deny factory owners a reasonable return on investments, but they did believe that too many business leaders had exceeded traditional bounds of fairness and equity. Indeed, they claimed that the creation of a class of extraordinarily wealthy capitalists contradicted the spirit of the American principles of democracy and equality.

But there was also another point of view. Defenders of the factory owners argued that no feature of the American system of government was ever designed to place restraints on the accumulation of wealth by individuals. They viewed as perhaps the most pronounced virtue of the American political system the unlimited opportunities provided for economic advancement. From a more practical standpoint, the defenders of wealth espoused the argument that factory owners reinvested most of their profits in expanded operations and more productive plant and equipment. As a result, they continually created new jobs and upgraded the wages, steadily if not spectacularly, of existing jobs. Without the entrepreneurial contributions of wealthy factory owners, their defenders argued, the living standards of workers would have been lower than actually realized. Moreover, it was pointed out that despite the existence of very high profits, the wages paid by big business were usually equal to or higher than wage rates in other business firms.

In a recent study, economic historians estimated that if all the allegedly excess wealth of big business leaders in the nineteenth century had been completely taxed away and redistributed to the general population, the typical working family would have realized a one-time increase of less than 2 percent in its annual income. In subsequent years, the resulting shift of expenditures away from new capital investments toward personal consumption would have almost certainly contributed to declining employment opportunities and eventually lower wages. Although a definitive answer to a hypothetical situation is always elusive, it seems safe to state that most economic historians would endorse the proposition that the denial of large profits to big business leaders would not *in the long run* have improved the wages of the working class.

## IMMIGRATION OF WORKERS

Between 1865 and 1920 over 25 million new immigrants arrived in the United States. Over this period, the foreign-born remained a fairly constant 14 percent of the total population. These arrivals came from a different part of the world than previous immigrants. Until the middle of the nineteenth century, the British, northern Europeans, and west Africans composed the bulk of the population stock. After 1880, however, immigration was heavily from Eastern Europe: Russians, Poles, Greeks, Italians, Swedes, and others.

The shift of location within Europe occurred for two main reasons. First, economic opportunities in northern Europe were improving and fewer people there were attracted by a risky overseas venture. In eastern Europe, in contrast, economic life remained generally stagnant. Reduced transportation costs across the Atlantic lured many peasants to take a chance on a trip to a new country where wages, even for unskilled labor, were much higher than at home. Steamboat and railroad companies also directed much advertising and promotion material toward these areas in order to generate more business.

Previously most immigrants (except for the Irish) had gone into farming, but the new immigrants from eastern Europe were drawn primarily to the cities. Many became unskilled factory workers. In fact, as late as 1920, one third of all employees in manufacturing and one half of all miners had been born overseas. More men than women and children crossed the Atlantic; many males came with the intention of saving a substantial share of their American earnings and then returning to their native countries. Over one quarter of all new arrivals in this era actually returned home, frequently departing during recession years. There was a tendency for all members of an immigrant family to enter the work force, including wives and children. In 1880, prior to heavy immigration, about a third of the total population was in the labor force, but by 1920 that figure had risen to 40 percent. The majority of the new arrivals crowded into unsanitary tenement housing in slum areas.

Were the new immigrants, unaccustomed to the new environment, discriminated against by employers seeking a supply of cheap and vulnerable workers? The current judgment of historians is no. Immigrants generally congregated in lower paying jobs because they lacked the skills and education of other workers, not merely because they were foreign born. We know this is true because native-born workers with similar skill levels earned about the same income. Moreover, as immigrants improved their language and job skills, their earnings definitely rose. Of course, there were some employers who refused to hire immigrants or pay them a fair wage simply because of their nationality or religion, but there were not enough prejudiced employers to make a significant impact on the status or advancement of the majority of these new Americans and their children. It was not easy to get ahead and it certainly did not come all at once, but the second and third generation of these European immigrants eventually became prosperous citizens in their new land.

## LABOR DISCIPLINE: SCIENTIFIC MANAGEMENT

In addition to complaints about the general level of wages and the length of the workweek, labor was also disturbed by the trend toward greater discipline and regimentation in the workplace. The more relaxed on-the-job atmosphere of an earlier era gave way increasingly to a faster and steadier work pace under the supervision of management representatives. Two developments illustrate the changes occurring during this period. First was the introduction of "scientific management" and how it was used to exert greater control over workers, and second was the perfection of the moving assembly line, especially in the new automobile industry.

The father of the discipline of scientific management was Frederick W. Taylor. Born into a socially prominent Philadelphia family, Taylor had little interest in the traditional Ivy League education planned by his parents. Instead, he disavowed college and enrolled in an apprenticeship program in a machine shop. In this factory environment he advanced rapidly, and within a few years rose to the position of chief engineer (largely self-trained) of Midvale Steel Co., a medium-sized, well-managed fabricator of raw steel into finished products.

In addition to his managerial duties, Taylor was an inventor of various types of machine tools, especially high-speed cutting tools for strong metals. He was an athlete of some ability as well, and his penchant for invention and improvement spilled over into that realm too; Taylor introduced the spoon-shaped tennis racquet, and he and his partner won the United States men's doubles championship in 1881. His two-handed putter was subsequently banned by golfing associations, however.

As these anecdotes suggest, Taylor was dedicated to improving the ability of people to perform almost any task, whether for work or leisure. His main goal was to increase efficiency. When he examined the shop floor of the steel manufacturing firm, Taylor was appalled by the gross inefficiency which seemed to prevail. His management peers blamed most of the low productivity on the poor quality of the work force. But Taylor thought otherwise. The problem, as he viewed it, was the absence of system—both in the design of the workplace and in the carrying out of specific work tasks. What was lacking was a genuinely scientific approach to factory production. Through scientific management, Taylor hoped to improve efficiency, with the prospect that improvements would lead both to higher wages for workers and higher profits for owners.

One of the main reasons for frequent worker idleness during the day was that raw materials and semi-finished products usually flowed through the factory in a haphazard manner. Taylor wanted to rearrange factories so that productive activities could be conducted at a steady, uninterrupted pace. He instituted formal job descriptions so that workers would know exactly the nature of their responsibilities. Using close observation and a stopwatch, Taylor studied each task within the factory. The aim of these "time-and-motion studies" was to determine, first, if a new way to perform a task more efficiently could be discovered, and, second, to estimate exactly how much work could reasonably be expected each day from the typical worker. Once he was able to conclude what represented "a fair day's pay for a fair day's work," he made that a standard. Workers who met standards received regular wages; those above standard were supposed to receive bonuses; those slightly below standard had their pay docked; and those far below standard were fired. In actuality, few employers adopted the Taylor system of labor management in its entirety, but they did borrow from it piecemeal.

Workers invariably objected to the introduction of these new techniques of control. The Taylor system and its imitators aimed at harmonizing the interaction of workers and machines. In so doing, people were treated as though they were themselves a part of the factory machinery—living machines. Time-and-motion studies and the regimentation of the work process was condemned as dehumanizing. On another level, workers complained about the tendency of management to raise performance standards periodically. A standard that perhaps began as a reasonable measure for the average worker was often pushed up to match the output of only the very best workers.

## MOVING ASSEMBLY LINE

Another development that led to greater control of management over the work process was refinement of the moving assembly line, primarily in the automotive industry. Assembling products using interchangeable parts can be traced back to the first half of the nineteenth century, when it was applied to guns, clocks, and other products. The idea of moving a product slowly along a fixed track to stationary workers who performed one or two simple operations was first introduced in the meat-packing industry. Hogs were pulled forward by overhead hooks to laborers who debristled and skinned the carcass and then chopped up the pork to pack in barrels for shipment to distant points. These two concepts—interchangeable parts and moving products to stationary workers—reached the culmination of their development with the opening of Henry Ford's Highland Park plant in 1913, where the Model T was produced.

Ford was a contemporary of Taylor and they shared a number of characteristics. Ford was the son of a farmer, not a Philadelphia blue blood, but equally fascinated by machinery and the perfection of mechanical concepts. Another self-trained practitioner, Ford had risen by the 1890s to the position of chief engineer for the Detroit Edison Company. His passion was to build a functioning automobile in his backyard workshop. Others preceded Ford in inventing the "horseless carriage," but whereas they were generally unconcerned about the intricacy of their designs, Ford was determined to stress simplicity and reliability in his model. His first car took its maiden trip in 1896; it has been preserved in the Ford Museum in Michigan and even today remains in good operating condition and ready to crank up.

After several false starts, Ford entered the fledgling automobile business permanently in 1901. He tried briefly to attract customers by advertising the high speed of his cars. At one point, Ford himself actually held the land speed record of just under 100 miles per hour—driven over a frozen lake, the best roadbed then available. In the first decade of the century, there were many small automobile companies producing expensive cars for a very narrow market. After a split with his early partners over long-run strategy, which left Ford in control of the firm, he decided to concentrate all efforts on developing a low-priced car for the tail end of the market. Ford calculated that, if he could keep reducing the price of his models, he could tap a huge middle-class market, which had the potential for hundreds of thousands of sales, maybe even millions. Ford had a vision which most of his competitors lacked.

In 1908, Ford came out with his famous Model T, which held the title as the car with the largest and longest production run until finally surpassed by the original Volkswagen Bug sometime in the 1960s. His company quickly became the market leader, and Ford sought new methods of expanding production to meet the burgeoning demand. He embarked on a project to erect the ultimate in assembly line operations. For the revolutionary Highland Park plant, which opened in 1913, industrial architects designed a factory filled with conveyors, rollways, and gravity slides to move the chassis and its parts past workers in a carefully planned sequence of operations. At first, the moving assembly was run at a modest pace, but after a few weeks the speed picked up considerably. The labor time expended in assembling a car dropped from 12 hours and 8 minutes, prior to the Highland Park opening, to only 1 hour and 33 minutes by the spring of 1914, a reduction in time of over 85 percent.

Although Ford's moving assembly line generated a huge amount of favorable publicity, many workers in his plants were not completely enthusiastic. With the exception of die-and-tool making, most of the jobs were diminished in terms of skills. A worker on the assembly line usually performed one or two simple tasks (which often could be learned in only a matter of minutes) throughout the day. Wages in automobile assembly plants were usually on a par with those in other industries, and at Ford were even higher for a number of years, yet workers got little job satisfaction. Performing the same simple task over and over was not merely boring but often physically and mentally taxing; dehumanizing was perhaps the proper word.

Discipline was tight and job security was virtually nonexistent. Workers without many skills or the opportunities to learn new skills were easily replaced. The mechanism for filing grievances, where it existed, was heavily weighted in favor of management. Workers who complained too often or too loudly, or, worst of all, tried to promote the idea of a union among their fellow workers were likely to be fired on the spot. Fear was one of the components of the moving assembly line atmosphere in its early stages. It was one of the main reasons for worker dissatisfaction and resentment. This new type of work environment was far different from the more leisurely, undisciplined, and unregimented style of the artisan. Workers no longer experienced the pride of workmanship, and their dignity as producers and individuals was severely undercut.

## THE UNION MOVEMENT

The altered status of labor in the increasingly industrializing American economy intensified worker interest in the creation of stronger union organizations. Prior to the rise of national business organizations, local unions composed exclusively of skilled labor had accumulated a fairly respectable record of success in bargaining for better wages and working conditions. But the rise of big business upset the existing equilibrium. Before 1875, government rarely became involved in labor-management disputes; local governments were either neutral or slightly pro-union during strikes and other labor confrontations. In the last quarter of the century, however, large firms were able to recruit the federal government as an ally in most of the major disputes with workers.

The state and federal courts, including of course the Supreme Court itself, became very antilabor in their outlook. For example, judges began to issue routinely injunctions outlawing strikes as "threats to the public order," and when workers failed to obey such rulings, the executive branch generally responded by sending in the state militia or federal troops to halt picketing, parading, and mass meetings. The failure of workers to create large and successful unions in the nineteenth century stems in part from the raw financial power of big business but also in part because of the alliance that developed between big business leaders and the national government. Later, in the 1930s after the election of Franklin D. Roosevelt, government shifted its support from business to labor and thereby opened the floodgates for the creation of powerful unions for the masses. We will get to that story in a later chapter.

### Knights of Labor

Among the most notable of the nineteenth-century union organizations to ultimately collapse was the Knights of Labor. Founded in 1869, it reached the height of its membership and influence in the 1880s. Under the leadership of its president, Terence Powderly, the Knights attempted to form a genuinely national organization of all members of the so-called producing classes—excluding only liquor dealers, stockbrokers, lawyers, bankers, and others considered parasites on society. It welcomed both skilled and unskilled labor and maintained a very low dues structure to encourage membership. A consequence of that policy was the absence of financial resources and the lack of strong central leadership.

What appalled Powderly and other supporters of the Knights was the wide social and economic gap which had suddenly emerged between employers and their employees. They found it hard to accept the idea that a division between owners and employees (Marxists would say capitalists versus workers) was destined to become a permanent feature of the American economic system. Union leaders were not anticapitalist as long as the system was defined in terms of small units within industries competitive enough that individuals could reasonably aspire to ownership of their own shop. Their objection was to huge enterprises in which management was remote from workers and treated them in an impersonal manner. They also resented the power of big business to overthrow traditional modes of production and unilaterally introduce new work rules and rigid discipline.

What could be done to reverse the course of events? Powderly opposed the tactic of strikes because he believed they were merely stopgap measures that failed to get at the real root of a problem that was growing in magnitude. A victory over owners in a strike action might bring the workers a few more cents per hour, but no fundamental changes in the status of labor were possible simply through strikes. Powderly's solution to the workers' dilemma was much more far-reaching; he advocated the establishment of "producers cooperatives" in which every man (women were still largely ignored) would be his own employer. Within such an institutional setting, Powderly believed that technology, plus the economies of scale which it dictated, as well as the sense of worker participation in a joint business venture could both be accommodated and be made to function in a complementary manner.

For the industrial sector of the economy, however, producers cooperatives failed to provide a viable alternative to the big firm owned by shareholders and administered by salaried managers. Some skilled workers did cooperate in creating such organizations on a small scale, but the antagonism of competing firms, which vowed to undersell them, plus internal bickering proved their undoing. The producers cooperative was not a workable institution for eliminating the separation between owners and workers in industrial firms, as Powderly and other idealists had hoped. In fairness, however, we should point out that the cooperative idea was not a completely untenable strategy for solving the problems of certain groups. It eventually took hold not in industry but in agriculture; at present, farm cooperatives, composed of thousands of farmers of fairly equal status, buy supplies and equipment at discount prices and market their output jointly at the best prices obtainable at home and abroad.

### Haymarket Affair

Ironically, it was strike-related activity—a tactic Powderly philosophically opposed—that led to an incident which helped undermine the existence of the Knights of Labor. Indeed, the absence of sufficient financial resources and the inability of the titular head of the national organization to control strikes points up just how weak this union was at its core. The Knights of Labor was really an umbrella organization for hundreds of independent local unions that made their own decisions about when to call a strike and how long to stay off the job.

In the spring of 1886 a local union affiliated with the Knights lost a strike in Chicago against the McCormick Harvester Company. To express frustration over their powerlessness in this situation, local union leaders called for a mass meeting of workers to hear speeches and ventilate grievances. A few speakers railed against the capitalist system, but they called for a legal and peaceful settlement of the issues at hand. Late in the evening a group of policemen arrived to break up the crowd and end the meeting. Someone, never identified, threw a bomb in the direction of the police, which exploded. The police then opened fire with their guns and the workers shot back. When the smoke cleared, seven policemen and four workers had received fatal injuries.

Within hours the organizers of the rally were arrested on the charge of murder. Despite the absence of any genuine evidence against them, eight union leaders were found guilty; seven were given the death sentence and one got 15 years in prison. Two of the seven condemned were later granted executive clemency; one committed suicide and four were executed. The trial was political rather than criminal. The goal of the prosecutors was to plant in the minds of the jury members and the public, aided by conservative newspaper owners, the idea that unions were closely linked to European radicalism and the outbreak of violence. The strategy was effective. In the years ahead, riots and civil disturbances were frequently associated with major strikes, and employers often hired spies and provocateurs to make certain that some incident occurred which then could be used to discredit the union.

The Haymarket affair alone did not account for the decline in the membership of the Knights of Labor, but it contributed to a weakening of the organization. By 1888 union membership had fallen from a high point of 700,000 to less than 200,000, and by the end of the century, the Knights had disappeared. Its failure to accept the permanence of the division between owner/managers and workers and its inability to offer a viable alternative to large capitalist enterprises were the root causes of its demise. Powderly and his associates had a vision of a different type of industrial society, in which equality would be the paramount consideration, but they were simply unable to alter significantly the path of American industrial development.

### Showdown at Homestead

Another union group that failed to prosper in the late nineteenth century was the Amalgamated Iron and Steel Workers. Its failure stemmed not from any deficiencies in its outlook or policies but because it had the misfortune to run up against the raw power of big business. Composed exclusively of skilled ironworkers, this union traced its origins back to the pre-Civil War decades. Up until the 1890s, it was generally able to hold its own in negotiations with employers over wages and work rules on the job. Most iron producers were small or medium-sized firms. Iron workers were generally highly skilled workers who were difficult to replace, and thus they were able to use the tactic of strikes to achieve their goals. In a sense, a balance of power existed between owners and workers in this earlier era; the iron firms recognized unions as legitimate bargaining units and negotiated with them.

A change came about, however, when the industry evolved from iron into steel and the size of the successful producers increased dramatically. As a result of his policy of horizontal combination, Andrew Carnegie acquired several steel mills in which the Amalgamated Iron and Steel Workers was already well entrenched. For several years in the 1880s, Carnegie and his partners recognized the union and reached agreements lasting up to three years with their workers. In 1892, Carnegie was persuaded by his associate Henry Frick, who had assumed the position of chief executive officer (CEO is the modern acronym) of the steel business, to try to eliminate the union from the Homestead mill in Pennsylvania. Frick contended that union work rules were so elaborate that they were impeding progress toward greater efficiency, the adoption of new technology, and higher profits.

Ironically, Carnegie was one of the few late nineteenth-century business leaders to go on record publicly as recognizing the right of workers to form unions to negotiate with owners like himself. Much to the horror of some of his wealthy peers, Carnegie had the audacity to publish his views in some of the leading magazines of the time. For years he was extremely proud of his relationship with his work force. By the early 1890s, however, he had begun to reassess his priorities. His ambition to make higher profits and become perhaps the richest man in the world, and one of its most powerful, began to take precedence over other considerations.

When the contract with the union expired in 1892, Carnegie and Frick had already decided not to renew it. Carnegie left for his vacation castle (literally) in Scotland, leaving Frick in charge of the whole matter. In response to the firm's withdrawal of recognition, the union called a strike at the Homestead mill. Frick's plan was to bring in strikebreakers who would take the jobs of the union members. Because the union had vowed not to allow any "scabs" (the slang word for strike-breakers) to enter the plant, Frick had made arrangements with the Pinkerton Detective Agency to supply a private army of several hundred armed men. The Pinkertons planned to seize the plant and then act as escorts for the scabs. Know-ing that they might encounter a mob of hostile strikers, the Pinkertons tried to approach the mill indirectly by a river route early one morning.

But union members had gotten advance warning of the invasion plan, and they were on the banks of the river waiting for the barges to arrive. The workers erected barricades to protect themselves, and when the Pinkertons got within range, the union members opened fire. A pitched battle went on for most of the day. At one point the workers poured oil on the river and set it afire in an effort to engulf their adversaries in flames. They were playing for keeps in this confrontation. After the towboat pulling the barges chugged off, leaving the private army without a line of retreat, they hoisted a white flag and surrendered. Three Pinkertons were already dead and many more were wounded. The Homestead conflict was one of the most spectacular victories for labor in a military-style confrontation with owners.

The victory was a hollow one, however. The next week the Pennsylvania state militia arrived to keep the peace after an appeal from Frick reached the governor. Carnegie vowed to keep the mill shut until the union capitulated. Finally, after months of stalemate, many of the steel workers disaffiliated from the union and accepted the employment terms dictated by the company. Homestead was a major landmark in business/labor relations because it represented a confrontation between big business and a previously very strong union organization. In a show-down, big business, supported by government, won out. The Amalgamated union was completely smashed. In the ensuing years, unions were ousted from their footholds in virtually every large oligopolistic industry. Unions for the masses of workers in big business enterprises were temporarily denied; revival came decades later with the New Deal.

### American Federation of Labor

While most other unions were having serious difficulties, one labor organiza-tion with a different strategy enjoyed a fair amount of success. Organized on a national basis in 1886, the American Federation of Labor was led for over a quarter of a century by Samuel Gompers. Born in London, England, in 1850, Gompers came to New York with his family in the 1860s. He followed in the foot-steps of his father and became a cigar maker. When he was elected president of the American Federation of Labor (AFL), Gompers advocated a conservative strategy, which stressed the immediately achievable rather than the prospect of a major change in the relationship between owners and workers. In other words, he ac-cepted the permanence of the class system, and, most important, the position of his fellow workers within that system. His goal was simply to obtain as much as possible from owners and managers in terms of higher wages, better working conditions, and shorter hours. He did not attempt the impossible or improbable.

The AFL was a national organization composed of hundreds of local craft unions such as carpenters, printers, cigar makers, and other skilled trades. It was elitist and exclusive; not included were blacks, other minorities, women, and the semi-skilled and unskilled. Union members were employed by small or medium-sized firms; they avoided big business. One of the reasons for restricting membership to skilled workers only was that they could afford the payment of substantial dues. The AFL was a high-dues union, and it used the money to build up a formidable strike fund. Strikes or the threat of strikes were the main tactic used to advance the interests of workers.

Gompers believed in hard bargaining, but he also believed in respecting the terms of contracts with owners once agreements had been signed. Local unions might call wildcat strikes of their members at any time and over any alleged grievance, but locals could draw on the national strike fund only if the AFL leadership approved and endorsed the strike action.

Gompers had strict rules about granting support for strike activity. First, the strike could only be called upon the expiration of an existing contract, or if an employer broke an existing agreement, and, second, the chances of winning the concessions in dispute had to be reasonably good. He had no desire to create labor martyrs, participate in lost causes, or pour money into hopeless situations. If the demands of the local union applying for financial aid seemed out of line to the AFL leadership, then assistance was denied. As a rule Gompers did not favor strikes in response to wage cuts during depressions, since he realized that business firms were legitimately suffering and probably had insufficient revenues to maintain wages. Instead, he advocated waiting for improved business conditions, when businesses were making good profits and would not want production disrupted, to make up for lost ground. Moreover, in boom periods, the supply of unemployed skilled labor was very low and owners would have difficulty locating replacements for workers on strike for higher wages.

The Gompers approach to business/labor relations, often labeled "business unionism" or "bread-and-butter unionism," was viable in the late nineteenth and early twentieth centuries. The AFL established a record of many small victories in negotiations with employers in competitive industries. The problem was that, by choice, it aimed to serve only a small percentage of the entire American working class—white, skilled males who worked for small to medium-sized firms that were vulnerable to strike activity. The workers in that category represented only about 15 percent of the total labor force. Skilled workers employed by big business were not union members; nor were millions of semi-skilled and unskilled workers employed by firms, large and small.

The majority of American workers were therefore unrepresented by any union organization; they had neither the financial nor political power to challenge the dominance of the business sector. The old equilibrium which had existed in business/labor relations prior to 1870, with government as a neutral force, had been

**FIGURE 10** Samuel Gompers
(Source: New York Public Library
Picture Collection)

disrupted. The wages of workers continued to climb in real terms over the period from 1870 to 1920, but the political power of the working class and its union representatives was very limited. American society had become very pro-business in its orientation, and it would take a severe depression and an alteration in values before workers and their unions would have a prominent voice in determining the course of the nation.

### SELECTED REFERENCES

BERNSTEIN, IRVING. *The Lean Years: A History of the American Worker, 1920-1933.* Boston: Houghton Mifflin, 1960.

BRODY, DAVID. *Labor in Crisis: The Steel Strike of 1919.* Philadelphia: Lippincott, 1965.

DUBOFSKY, MELVYN. *Industrialism and the American Worker, 1865-1920.* Arlington Heights, Ill.: Harlan Davidson, 1975.

GROB, GERALD. *Workers and Utopia: A Study of the Ideological Conflict in the American Labor Movement, 1865-1900.* New York: Quadrangle Books, 1969.

HABER, SAMUEL. *Efficiency and Uplift: Scientific Management in the Progressive Era, 1890-1920.* Chicago: University of Chicago Press, 1964.

HILL, PETER. "Relative Skill and Income Levels of Native and Foreign-Born Workers in the United States," *Explorations in Economic History* (1975), 47–60.

LIVESAY, HAROLD. *Samuel Gompers and Organized Labor in America*. Boston: Little, Brown & Co., 1978.

NELSON, DANIEL. *Managers and Workers: The Origins of the New Factory System in the United States, 1880-1920*. Madison, Wisconsin: University of Wisconsin Press, 1975.

_____. *Frederick W. Taylor and Scientific Management*. Madison, Wisconsin: University of Wisconsin Press, 1980.

NEVINS, ALLAN, and FRANK HILL. *Ford: The Times, the Men, and the Company*. New York: Scribners, 1954.

# CHAPTER SIXTEEN
# GOVERNMENT
# REGULATION
*Banks, Railroads,*
*and the Environment*

Prior to the creation of a national transportation network and the emergence of large firms selling in the national market, the federal government had played only a limited role in the functioning of the economy. Congress passed laws related to the composition of the money stock and the level of tariffs, but little else. At the state level, governments were usually involved in drafting laws pertaining to their respective banking systems, and each one was somewhat different. From 1792 to 1836, the federal government had also been involved in the creation of two large banks, which had the sole privilege of establishing branch offices across state lines, but President Andrew Jackson's opposition to the perpetuation of the bank ended that phase of federal participation. In general, the United States had an economic system often characterized as laissez faire, a French term meaning that government interfered very little with the operations of the business system.

It was not until the 1880s that the federal government reversed course and began to take a more active role in supervising or regulating certain sectors of the economy. This development occurred gradually, largely on a piecemeal basis, but over the last 100 years the federal government has—for better or worse—progressively extended its reach into almost every facet of the American economy. Today it is commonplace for us to think of government as an overseer of business activities affecting product safety, the environment, energy, communication, financial markets, and a host of other areas of public concern.

In this chapter we make no effort to examine the origins of all federal regulatory agencies and institutions, or even the most important ones. Space simply does not allow such extensive coverage. Instead we have chosen a few critical areas for detailed discussion. We selected banking because it lies at the core of the nation's financial system. The railroad industry was selected because it was the first to come under national supervision, and the methods adopted provided a model for subsequent regulatory legislation. Finally, we picked the environment because of the importance this subject has assumed in recent years.

## BANKING: 1835-1865

As mentioned in reference to the evolution of the United States banking system in Chapter Seven, President Jackson had put an end to the Second Bank of the United States by vetoing in 1832 the congressional bill to renew its charter for another twenty years. For the next three decades, the federal government had no direct involvement in the nation's banking system; it chartered no new banks and set no rules for existing institutions. Banking became strictly a matter for state control and supervision. As a result, there was no uniform system; banking rules and regulations varied from state to state. Most important of all, however, the United States had no single large financial institution with branches throughout the nation which could exert some degree of control over financial markets and provide leadership for smaller banks. As a consequence of the political decision to allow the general economy to function without a central bank to coordinate the activities of other financial institutions, the United States deviated significantly from the pattern established by all of the other industrializing nations around the world. In Europe, for example, the Bank of England and Bank of France were probably the most influential business institutions within their respective economies during the nineteenth century. But the United States had no counterpart. In fact, the federal government almost completely disavowed any responsibility for the operation of the nation's financial system or even the general performance of the overall economy.

### National Banking Act of 1863

During the Civil War the Union government resumed the policy of granting banking charters. But, unlike in the past, it did not attempt to create one very large institution. Rather, it tried to lure existing banks, which numbered over one thousand, to give up their state charters and convert to the status of national banks. The new plan was proposed not because of any allegedly major defects in the state banking systems, but primarily because the Union wanted to obtain the support of commercial banks in the northern states in financing the war. Under the terms of a national charter, a bank was permitted to issue banknotes in amounts up to the value of the United States government bonds it had purchased. Those bonds, in turn, provided secure collateral since, even if the bank subsequently failed because of making too many bad loans to business firms or individuals, noteholders would still receive reimbursement upon the sale of the designated bonds.

The absolute safety of the note issue was the key feature meant to convince existing state banks to join the national system. In the process of converting, they would create a huge market for government bonds and thus perform a valuable service in supporting the war effort. But the attraction of a government-guaranteed currency (not deposits) was a stronger inducement on paper than it was in actual practice. Few state banks converted to national charters in 1863 and 1864. Most of them had been operating successfully for years under state charters, which generally had more lax rules than the regulations outlined in the new national charters.

Since so few state banks were persuaded to shift voluntarily to national status, Congress finally decided to pass punitive legislation which would force most of them to convert. It enacted a 10 percent tax on all notes issued by state banks, thereby eliminating any potential for profit on their issuance. Any bank that hoped to continue issuing notes to borrowers, and thus earn interest on its outstanding loans, had little choice except to apply for a national charter. We must emphasize here a very critical point: most banking leaders and their customers viewed the issuance of currency as the primary method of making business loans. It was possible for banks to make loans simply through the creation of deposits, but this practice was not widely accepted in the 1860s. The enactment of the punitive 10 percent tax on state banknotes had the desired effect; by 1870 institutions holding over 85 percent of the nation's banking assets had converted to national charters. From this point onward, the full value of American currency was de facto guaranteed by the federal government. Many people believed that most of the problems of instability previously associated with the banking system had been permanently solved and without the creation of any large central bank.

However, as in many human affairs, no sooner had one problem been eliminated than another popped up. During the 1880s and 1890s the use of checks rather than currency became the predominant way of conducting much of the nation's business. The number of state-chartered banks, which had declined precipitously in the immediate postwar era, began to rise again. These institutions discovered that they could stay in operation by making loans strictly through the creation of deposits. The privilege of issuing currency was no longer highly valued. Moreover, state charters usually allowed banks more leeway in the types of business in which they could engage and were more lax about the maintenance of reserves. By 1890 the number of state-chartered banks actually outnumbered national banks and their assets were larger. This trend toward a greater expansion of the various state banking systems continued over the next quarter of a century.

By the last decade of the nineteenth century, the American banking system, which included thousands of state and national banks, was revealing signs of increasing instability. The system was becoming increasingly susceptible to panics of minor and major magnitude, the most serious of which were the monetary disturbances of 1893 and 1907. The main problem to arise was linked to the increase in deposits within the banking system. In the pre-Civil War years, noteholders had tried to convert their paper into specie during a panic atmosphere, and there was invariably an insufficient amount available because all banks held only fractional reserves. In the postwar era a similar process occurred, except that depositors now tried to convert their balances into specie *and* currency (which was government-guaranteed and thus as good as specie). Again, reserves proved inadequate, and many banks succumbed in a financial panic, leaving their depositors to absorb tremendous losses.

## PROPOSED SOLUTIONS

To solve the problem of banking instability, three different reform solutions were publicly considered. One idea was for government to guarantee bank deposits, just as it had the currency. A few states tried deposit guarantees within their borders, but these plans implemented on a strictly local level ultimately failed, and thereby discredited the whole approach. Proposals to institute a federal deposit guarantee program were not given very serious consideration by Congress prior to 1915. Most of the leading banking experts and economists of that era argued that all such proposals were inherently unworkable and the pipe dreams of irresponsible crackpots. Later, as we shall see in a subsequent chapter, a federal deposit guarantee plan was revived during the throes of the Great Depression, gained respectability, and actually became law.

The second plan advanced to reform the banking system around the turn of the century was sponsored by the leading bankers in the northeastern states, especially New York. It was the least complicated of the three main proposals. The idea was to permit banks in periods of financial crisis to print *temporarily* more currency than the law normally allowed. For this privilege, they would pay a stiff tax, but they could use the freshly printed currency to pay out to panicky depositors who demanded conversions of their account balances into currency. After the crisis had passed, the temporary currency was to be retired and business was expected to return to normal. The net effect was to permit banks to create additional reserves on their own initiative, but at a high cost, and without having to rely upon the willingness of some other very large institution, such as a central bank, to grant them loans in an emergency.

In the aftermath of the Panic of 1907, the Aldrich-Vreeland Act, based on the principle of permitting the issuance of additional currency in an emergency for short periods of time, was passed by Congress in 1908. It was considered merely a stopgap measure, however, since Congress simultaneously created a National Monetary Commission to make an exhaustive study of the entire banking system and to come up with a more permanent solution. The Aldrich-Vreeland bill was only used once—in November 1914 following the outbreak of World War I in Europe. On that date, the idea proved as good in practice as in theory, for the emergency issue of currency cooled the panic atmosphere and got the banking system back on its feet very quickly. Despite a record of success in its only trial, this approach to solving the problem of financial instability was abandoned in 1915 and superseded by an even more comprehensive reform measure which created the Federal Reserve System.

### Federal Reserve System

The third idea proposed to cleanse the financial system of its tendency to break down periodically was the establishment of a central bank, or some institution similar to a central bank. A central bank would not transact business with the general public but only with other banks—in other words, a bankers' bank. The original First and Second Banks of the United States (1792-1836) were only quasi-central banks; for one thing, they did the bulk of their business with the general public, not other banking institutions.

A central bank could bring stability to the financial system because of its ability to lend reserves to other banks throughout the nation in times of crisis and, thereby, thwart panics. The Bank of England provided the model. The belief was that a properly managed central bank could keep the financial system and indeed the whole economy on an even keel. No one expected a central bank to prevent business recessions, but its proponents argued that the bank could reduce the amplitude of fluctuations in economic activity and keep recessions from degenerating into prolonged depressions.

By 1910 most political leaders had determined that the United States needed a central bank, but there was still debate about its form. One contingent wanted to establish a single large institution owned completely by the government. Some wanted private ownership. Another powerful coalition sought not just one central bank, but several large regional banks to serve the interests of specifically designated states. This last group feared the dominance of eastern financial leaders, especially New York bankers, under any plan which called for a single location.

The final outcome was, not surprisingly, a compromise solution. Twelve regional banks were created, and ownership fell to member banks in the Federal Reserve System (FRS). All banks with national charters (about 7,500 in 1913) were required to become members. State-chartered institutions, if they met certain minimum capital requirements, had the option of joining. By 1920 only about 10 percent of the state banks had become members of the FRS. Nonetheless, by that date, national and state banks holding over 60 percent of the nation's deposits were included in the system.

To coordinate the activities of the twelve reserve banks, Congress created a Federal Reserve Board, with headquarters in Washington. Its seven members were appointed by the President. The political concept applied in this case was that government, rather than private bankers, would have control over the operation of the FRS. Board members were given long terms in office to spare them from appeals to partisanship in making decisions, and the spirit of the agreement was that the number of Republicans and Democrats on the board would be roughly the same.

One question never completely settled, however, was how decision-making authority would be apportioned between the main board in Washington and the respective managements of the twelve regional banks. In an attempt to compromise centralization and regionalism, Congress had constructed an institution without clear lines of authority and responsibility. In theory, the Washington board had ultimate authority, but as events unfolded during the first fifteen years of operation, the regional bank in New York frequently assumed a position of leadership on important matters. The goal of making all the regional banks equal in status was impossible to achieve because New York was undeniably the financial center of the nation and by the 1920s rivaled London as the global leader. This division of influence between New York and Washington caused some difficulties, but they did not seriously undermine the ability of the system to perform effectively throughout the twenties. During the first fifteen years of operation, the FRS verified most of the claims of its supporters; there were no panics, and recessions, while sometimes cutting deeply into business activity, were short-lived.

Serious problems arose only in the early 1930s. The Federal Reserve System, despite its promise, proved incapable of dealing with the Great Depression. We will discuss that catastrophe in the next chapter.

## REGULATING THE RAILROADS

The first major sector of the nonfinancial economy to come under permanent federal regulation was the railroad industry. The railroads were the first American enterprise to grow into large business firms. When the typical citizen in the nineteenth century thought about the one industry most representative of "big business," the railroads invariably came to mind. Moreover, since they had started earlier, the railroads were the first industry to reach an advanced stage of maturation. The legislation creating the Interstate Commerce Commission (ICC) passed the Congress in 1887. Over the years, the powers of the commission were widened and by the end of the first decade of the twentieth century, it had gained the authority to approve or disapprove railroad routes and rates, thereby effectively controlling prices and profits for the industry.

This commission and many others established later were unique institutions. They combined in one body the three main powers of government otherwise separated in the Constitution. The ICC could make rules (legislative), administer them (executive), and hear appeals to its rulings and actions (judicial). The regulatory commission became, in one sense, almost a fourth branch of government. Its powers were delegated by Congress, which retained the authority to expand or curtail the scope of any commission activities.

For almost one hundred years now, regulatory commissions have been a controversial part of our government structure. Critics have attacked them from all sides; some argue that commissions have exerted too much unchallenged power over business, but others counter that they have been too weak. Questions have been raised as well about whose interests are primarily served by regulatory commissions: the public or the industry itself. These matters are difficult to pin down, and nothing illustrates this principle any better than the following discussion about the origins and early history of the ICC.

Even after nearly a century, historians are still not absolutely certain about why the Interstate Commerce Act was enacted in 1887 or whose interests it served. They have advanced at least three major hypotheses about the ICC. For decades what we will call the "traditional hypothesis" held sway. It viewed the coming of the ICC as inspired by public pressure for governmental control over an industry which had allegedly exerted too much economic power over a significant part of the population.

According to this line of argument, farmers and small shippers were incensed about discriminatory railroad rates and vowed to do something to control them. Farmers objected mainly to the different rates for short hauls and long hauls. The cost of transportation *per mile* was invariably higher, often much higher, on short railroad lines serving remote, strictly agricultural markets, than on those lines running between urban areas. The accountants employed by the railroads justified these differing rates because of the seasonal variation in the volume of traffic on the smaller roads, but farmers remained unconvinced. They were absolutely certain that, as a result of some conspiracy between railroads and bankers, the farm sector was, in the modern vernacular, being ripped off.

Small shippers everywhere objected to the volume discounts granted to larger shippers; in the nineteenth century, these discounts were called rebates. Small firms believed that railroads were giving big shippers an "unfair" competitive advantage by granting discounts. The railroads claimed that pressure from volume shippers had forced them to grant rebates; either they granted rebates or lost traffic to competing railroad lines. But that argument fell on deaf ears. Small firms were convinced they were victims of greedy railroads, who took advantage of them because of their weak economic position. In addition, both farmers and small shippers were livid about the tendency of railroads to enter into pooling agreements—in other words, to form cartels (like OPEC today). Through them, the railroads acted jointly to prevent price competition and thus hold up rates. Many pools gave railroads the power to divide up traffic as they saw fit, even when such divisions ran counter to the wishes of shippers about the exact destination of their goods.

Given the absence of economic strength vis-a-vis the railroads, so the traditional argument goes, farmers and small shippers turned to government. They would substitute political power for economic power. They could use their votes to influence legislators. They started at the state level. In 1876 a coalition of protesters persuaded the Illinois legislature to pass a law giving a local commission the authority to control all railroad rates within state borders. The railroads promptly appealed to the courts, arguing that the Illinois law permitted excessive interference in the rights and freedoms of private enterprise. In the famous case of *Munn* v. *Illinois*, the United States Supreme Court ignored the railroads' contentions and surprisingly upheld the Illinois statute. This ruling represented a significant turning point in government-business relations; it signaled the beginning of the erosion of laissez faire.

Astounded at the court's ruling, the railroads' lawyers did not give up the fight. They initiated new cases in an effort to force the Supreme Court to review again its attitude toward local control over transportation rates. Finally, in 1886, they succeeded. On this occasion, the Supreme Court reversed itself. (This happens from time to time, in part because the court personnel changes over the years and because sitting judges alter their views over a period of years.) The justices ruled that local regulation of railroads crossing state lines was unconstitutional. Under the commerce clause, only the federal government was empowered to exercise control over interstate transportation.

With local initiative stymied, reformers focused their attention on the federal government. Separate bills were introduced in the House and Senate. One aimed at outlawing rebates, forbidding pooling, and bringing greater uniformity in rates per mile. The second bill merely called for the establishment of a regulatory commission, with broad powers to investigate matters and recommend solutions. The final act, hammered out in committee, reflected both approaches. The Interstate Commerce Act of 1887 created a five-person commission with the duty of enforcing new federal laws against rebates, pooling, and discriminatory rates. Over the next quarter century, the federal courts often ruled in ways to undermine temporarily the authority of the ICC, but Congress always responded by clearing up ambiguous language and restrengthening the commission.

By the end of the first decade of the twentieth century, the ICC exerted uncontested control over the railroad industry. It determined railroad rates and thereby profits on railroad assets. According to the traditional hypothesis about the origins and effects of this legislation, the establishment of the ICC represented a prime example of the ability of citizens to marshall the power of government to oversee the operations of an entrenched business interest.

## THE CAPTURE HYPOTHESIS

Beginning in the 1960s, a totally new interpretation of the origins and role of the ICC emerged. It stood the old argument on its head. Spearheaded by historian Gabriel Kolko, the capture hypothesis asserted that the railroads themselves, not the general public, were more responsible for the enactment of regulatory legislation in 1887. Unable through cartel arrangements, which invariably broke down after a few years, to keep their house in order, the railroads turned to government to maintain stability and guarantee profits to vulnerable lines periodically threatened with bankruptcy.

In reading through the testimony given by railroad officials before congressional investigating committees in the 1880s, historian Kolko discovered that several witnesses had actually recommended the involvement of government in railroad affairs. The previous assumption had been that business leaders consistently opposed any form of government interference in their operations. But Kolko revealed that this argument was simplistic and overstated.

Witnesses representing some of the most profitable railroad lines as well as the manager of the most successful cartel arrangement were not opposed to government supervision on principle. Regulation might be beneficial to all parties, they conceded, as long as it was the right kind of legislation. Problems existed which government might be able to resolve. Railroads were not necessarily opposed to laws against rebates; they granted such volume discounts mainly because of the competitive pressure exerted by large shippers. Rebates represented lost revenues, and if individual rail lines believed they could deny discounts without risking the loss of traffic, they would be more than willing to offer identical prices to shippers of all sizes. Other railroads were concerned about labor disruptions. They hoped govern-

*PEOPLE WHO MATTERED — Ralph Nader*

He became nationally famous in the 1960s as a spokesman for consumers following his attack on the poor safety record of American automobiles. The publication of his book, *Unsafe at Any Speed,* was instrumental in persuading Congress to investigate standards of automobile safety. During congressional hearings, it was revealed that General Motors had hired private investigators to spy on Nader's personal life and harass him generally; the aim was to "get something on him" and to use the embarrassing information to "shut him up." The investigators came up empty-handed, however, and the public disclosure of GM's unsavory tactics against its foremost critic discredited the firm and the entire business community. In 1966 Congress passed a vehicle safety act, which called for seat belts and other improvements in design.

Born in Connecticut in 1934 to Lebanese immigrants who operated a restaurant and bakery, Nader attended Princeton University on a scholarship and later graduated from Harvard Law School. During his law school years, he studied auto injury cases and became convinced that existing law placed too much blame on driver negligence and not enough on faulty vehicle design. Thereafter he wrote magazine articles and made speeches calling for tougher safety standards. After the publicity generated by his confrontation with General Motors, Nader created an organization, funded on a shoestring budget, to discover other areas where consumers needed greater government protection from the power of vested business interests. Viewed as a crusader by the press, Nader gave an enormous impetus to consumer protection groups all across the nation. Later, in the 1970s, Nader and his associates turned their attention to the functioning of many government regulatory agencies. In reports and books, "Nader's raiders" alleged that too many agencies created, in theory, to serve the public had been captured by business interests. In several instances he even suggested that the public might be better served by the deregulation of certain industries and the disbanding of government agencies that protected firms from vigorous price competition.

Nader is considered a hero in many quarters because he demonstrated how much one dedicated man with a small organization could accomplish in battling entrenched economic interests, whether in business or government.

ment might declare strikes illegal on the grounds that they disrupted the public's right to reliable transportation.

The primary reason several prominent railroad leaders favored government intervention, according to the new capture hypothesis, was the hope that a regulatory commission with broad powers would be able to sanction pooling and other forms of cartel behavior. Government supervision held out the possibility of stability. It had the potential of ending rate wars, which had so often brought railroads to the brink of bankruptcy. The prospect of ending "excessive competition," granting every rail line a "fair share" of the existing traffic, and guaranteeing a "reasonable" profit in combination had much appeal. As a result, some railroad leaders gave support to the bill introduced into Congress which called for the creation of a commission with unspecified duties and no prohibitions on policy formulation. Conceivably such a commission could have authorized and enforced a government-sponsored cartel.

Moreover, the new hypothesis pointed to the performance of the ICC as further evidence of its industry orientation. The members of the commission were not citizens drawn from the ranks of farmers and small shippers; rather, they were ex-railroad executives, business leaders, or politicians who usually came around to view matters mainly from the perspective of the railroads. In the bulk of the cases adjudicated by the ICC, the railroad won out over protesting citizens. Eventually, the commission gained sufficient power to set rates at levels high enough to guarantee most railroads a profitable return on assets. After 1910 the commission treated the industry very much like a public utility, such as the telephone or electric power companies.

Contrary to the traditional hypothesis, the new version emphasized the contribution of railroad leaders to the formation and functioning of the ICC. The commission was not, according to Kolko and others, foisted upon the industry by public-spirited citizens. On the contrary, the ICC had much industry support and over the years the commissioners who served were captured by the railroads and failed to act consistently in the public interest.

## MERCANTILE HYPOTHESIS

Largely in response to the vigorous ideological thrust of the new capture hypothesis, a third interpretation explaining the origins of the ICC emerged in the late 1960s. Advanced by historian Albro Martin, it focused on the activities of a well-organized group of wholesalers and merchants in New York City. This group was opposed primarily to the traffic pools operated by the railroads between midwestern and eastern port cities at various times in the 1870s and 1880s. Such pooling agreements normally called for a division of the existing freight business among railroads serving Boston, Philadelphia, Baltimore, and New York.

To encourage a more even distribution of traffic, freight rates were usually lower to cities other than New York. Its merchants resented these differential rates because their application cut the flow of business through their city and thus reduced mercantile commissions and profits. In the absence of the "artificial" pools, New York merchants were convinced their business would be much improved. A coalition of mercantile firms, acting primarily through the chamber of commerce, lobbied Congress to pass the Interstate Commerce Act with the expressed goal of forbidding pooling once and for all and thereby price discrimination against New York.

In a further attack on the new perspective, Martin asked why, if the railroads had captured the ICC, so many lines were on the verge of bankruptcy by the middle of the twentieth century. His answer was that while the railroads had admittedly won most of the minor skirmishes in battles with complaining citizens, in the most important fight over the general level of rates and profits, the public had been victorious. True, the ICC had brought stability and guaranteed earnings to the railroad industry, but the profit rate allowed was in the range of only 6 to 10 percent. Other types of successful business ventures invariably earned higher rates of profit. Over the years the railroads were unable to compete in the capital markets for funds to maintain and upgrade their service. When trucks, private autos, and airplanes began to cut into their freight and passenger revenues, the ICC refused to permit the railroads to *lower* their rates and diversify their transportation services to meet the new competition. The commission applied a slowly tightening stranglehold to the railroads, according to Martin; it was a case of "enterprise denied" by misguided government interference, with both the railroads and the public losers in the long run.

Who is right about the reasons for the formation of the Interstate Commerce Commission? Which is the most valid hypothesis: traditional, capture, or mercantile? Unfortunately, we do not know for sure! There is probably an element of truth in all three approaches. Events in the past can, and usually do, have multiple causes. The value of studying history is not that the discipline can provide explanations for human events: rather, the greatest virtue is the process of analysis itself. The means, as in most educational efforts, are more important than the ends. The ability to study a subject from several different angles is an invaluable tool which we hope you will permanently retain.

One statement we can make with a fair amount of certainty. Much government regulation and the functions of regulatory agencies will remain for the foreseeable future among the most controversial features of American public life. As our foregoing discussion reveals, this issue is among the most difficult for the average  citizen to assess properly. Business leaders often rail against government regulation and often blame such interference for their poor performance, yet behind the scenes these same leaders are often lobbying legislatures for new rules which will help their industry. When President Carter sponsored a bill to deregulate the airline industry in the late 1970s, every major airline except one—United—testified against making the industry more competitive. The trucking industry and the powerful Teamsters Union have likewise fought deregulation. Whose interests are served by governmental regulatory agencies? It depends on which one you are discussing and at what point in time. One warning is merited: snap judgments about these matters should be avoided.

## ENVIRONMENT

Until the late nineteenth century, few Americans were much concerned about the quality of the environment. No doubt some individuals did become alarmed about the deteriorating quality of air and water in industrial regions, but most simply accepted these changes as the price of economic growth. Some types of pollution did require immediate attention, however. Cities usually took steps to improve the cleanliness of drinking water as a public health measure. Sewer systems were also installed to stall the spread of communicable diseases, but the waste water—treated or untreated—was simply emptied into nearby rivers and streams. Virtually nothing was done about the quantities of wood and coal smoke pouring into the atmosphere in factory areas.

The first movement at the national level was for the preservation of certain areas of undeniable beauty for recreational enjoyment. In 1872 the federal government created Yellowstone National Park in northwestern Wyoming with the intention that the scenery would be preserved in unspoiled condition for future generations. Over the years more parkland was incorporated into the national system. Indeed, the American national parkland program became a model for other nations throughout the world. Beginning in the 1960s there was a renewed interest in preserving wilderness areas, and rivers were added to the list of protected assets. With few exceptions, the parkland movement has not conflicted seriously with economic interests since most of the land in question was remote from markets and labor supplies and thus not very attractive for industrial development.

## FOREST CONSERVATION

The earliest efforts to protect natural resources rather than scenery was in the forestry industry. Concern about the maintenance of adequate supplies of timber prompted Congress to provide for the establishment of forest reserves in 1891. Ten years later under the administration of President Theodore Roosevelt, a Bureau of Forestry was set up. A program of "scientific forestry" was inaugurated; trees were to be harvested periodically and then replanted to sustain timber supplies in perpetuity. One of the prime reasons such laws breezed through the legislature was that they normally had the support of the large timber companies. The large firms sought ways of raising lumber prices, and the denial of easy access to federal lands by smaller cutters reduced supplies in the short run and boosted timber prices. By the end of Roosevelt's presidency in 1908, the national forests constituted over 150 million acres.

He was the first prominent American to call public attention to the importance of scientific management of the nation's forest resources. Serving as head of the Forestry Service, which he urged Congress to establish in 1905, Pinchot received unqualified support from President Theodore Roosevelt in his efforts to develop a rational policy for the protection and use of national forests. A conservationist, Pinchot advocated a balance between the goals of naturalists, who opposed all commercial development, and timber firms, which wanted inexpensive access to forests irrespective of future costs. He summed up his philosophy as follows: "to make the forest produce the largest amount of whatever crop or service will be most useful, and keep on producing it for generation after generation of men and trees."

Born in 1865 to a wealthy New York mercantile family, Pinchot traveled extensively overseas during his youth, and he was greatly impressed by the European tradition of forest management. His life's goal became to transfer those ideas to his native country. After receiving a degree from Yale in 1889, he did postgraduate work at the French National Forestry School. His first employment was as manager of the woodlands of a huge private estate in North Carolina. Later Pinchot set up a forestry consulting office in New York. He entered government service in 1898 as chief of the fledgling Division of Forestry. His tenure as the government's leading forestry official ended during the administration of President William Taft, after he clashed with Richard Ballinger, a commissioner in the land office of the Interior Department. Taft supported Ballinger, and Pinchot was fired in 1910 after alleging that this rival was involved in an effort to fraudulently obtain claims to coal fields in Alaska. None of the charges were ever proved, but the Pinchot-Ballinger controversy helped to split the Taft administration, which was defeated in the presidential election of 1912.

Pinchot subsequently was elected governor of Pennsylvania for two terms —in 1922 and 1930. A grant from his father was used to establish the Yale Forestry School in 1900, and Pinchot served thereafter as nonresident lecturer and professor. He died in 1946 at the age of eighty-one, having led an extremely active life.

## RESERVING NATURAL RESOURCES

The movement which began with forests quickly spread to other natural resources. The idea was accepted that government had the right and obligation to control river flows in an effort to prevent flooding and to aid in irrigation. In 1902 a program designed to reclaim arid lands through the construction of reservoirs and irrigation works was launched. The Withdrawal Act of 1910 reserved all the coal, gas, and phosphate lands still in the public domain and protected them from private development.

One of the greatest public scandals in our history involved land originally set aside in Wyoming as a naval oil reserve in 1915. The reserve was named Teapot Dome after a nearby geographical formation. Soon after the election of President Warren Harding in 1920, this land was illegally transferred from the administration of the Navy Department to Secretary of the Interior Albert Fall. An avowed enemy of conservation, Fall permitted private oil companies to draw down most of the petroleum in the supposed reserve. When the Teapot Dome fraud was finally uncovered, Secretary Fall was forced to resign and the record of the Harding administration was seriously blemished. By the 1920s the concept was firmly implanted in public opinion that certain lands, primarily in the western states, should be held back from private development and saved for the benefit of future generations.

## NEW DEAL CONSERVATION PROGRAMS

During the Depression years of the 1930s, conservation received another boost. The Civilian Conservation Corps was organized in part to provide public jobs for thousands of unemployed workers. The corps replanted millions of acres of trees in overcut and barren lands. Another new initiative taken by the Franklin D. Roosevelt (a distant cousin of the earlier Roosevelt) administration was the establishment of a federal agency to fight soil erosion on private lands.

The most ambitious project in the 1930s was an effort to link economic development with conservation. The Tennessee Valley Authority (TVA) had a major impact on several southeastern states. Numerous dams were built to prevent flooding and soil erosion. The water generated electricity which was sold locally at low rates in an effort to stimulate the regional economy. At its inception, the TVA project was highly controversial and political conservatives attacked it years later because of its allegedly "socialist" thrust. There was some truth in that criticism; the best proof being that Third World countries, often with avowedly socialist governments, sent representatives to this country to study the success of the TVA project with the goal of imitating its program in their own nations. On the other hand, the fear that regional development at government initiative would lead to the spread of the "disease" of socialism throughout the United States was farfetched and is now largely forgotten. TVA stimulated private initiative and never aimed at replacing it.

## ENVIRONMENTAL MOVEMENT

In the 1960s public concern moved beyond mere conservation to include the repair of previous and continuing damage to the environment. Too many industrial cities had air which was unhealthful to breathe. Too many rivers, streams, and lakes were dying; industrial and agricultural pollutants made the water inhospitable to fish and humans. Lake Erie was at one point declared virtually dead.

Efforts to improve conditions ran up against formidable opposition because they threatened the vested interests of powerful corporations and unions. How were the costs of repairing environmental damage to be apportioned? If a single firm took voluntary action to cease polluting the environment, then its costs would rise relative to competitors and its profits would disappear. Likewise, if firms were forced to pass the costs of pollution control on to consumers in the form of higher prices, then demand fell and jobs were lost. The only practical solution was the implementation of federal laws which would enforce all firms within an industry to meet the same standards.

The breakthrough legislation in this field was the congressional bill to control automobile emissions, passed in 1965. Over the years the standards have risen; new cars were required to use engines that burned fuel without lead additives, for example. Subsequently, new rules were applied to industrial plants as well. Cities like New York, Pittsburgh, and Los Angeles, just to name a few, which had poor air quality for decades, witnessed significant improvements in the 1970s and 1980s. Congress also moved to upgrade water quality beginning with legislation in 1966. Fish began returning to waters where they had been absent for over a century. Humans were able to swim again in rivers and lakes previously hazardous to their health. Lake Erie was even put on the recovery list; previous damage had been serious but not irreversible. Given a fair opportunity, nature revealed the capacity to heal itself.

To reinforce its commitment to improving the quality of life, Congress created the Environmental Protection Agency (EPA) in 1969. The EPA was charged with coordinating government activities in cleaning up and monitoring the environment. Although most Americans conceded that the goals of a better environment were worth pursuing, conflicts arose about how fast the rate of progress should be. The EPA conducted a balancing act between demands for an immediate end to pollution and concerns about the impact on individual firms and industries and their employees. Invariably, environmentalists protested delays in the implementation of rules and regulations, while business leaders emphasized the impracticalities of change that was too swift and uncompromising.

## DEVELOPMENT VERSUS ENVIRONMENT

History is replete with examples of revolution and counterrevolution. The environmental movement had its reaction too. Opponents claimed that environmentalists went too far in constraining economic growth. The argument was particularly strong after the oil supply crisis in 1974 revealed the extent to which the United States relied on foreign sources of energy. The fear that shortages of other raw materials might one day cripple the economy was expressed by many political and business leaders. The slowdown in the growth of the overall economy in the early

1980s was also blamed in part on the overly strict application of environmental regulations.

President Ronald Reagan, elected in 1980, appointed as his Secretary of the Interior, James Watt, a Colorado lawyer who had previously represented powerful clients in cases challenging environmental legislation and regulation. Watt quickly became a controversial figure because of his flamboyant style and because he attempted to shift the direction of public policy and open up more government land to private development. Continued objections to his administrative style eventually persuaded Secretary Watt to resign in the fall of 1983. Nonetheless, the issue of preserving the environment versus economic growth remained in the public eye.

The problem arose in large part because the federal government has assumed several different and conflicting responsibilities in the twentieth century. On the one hand, government has become the protector of the environment. On the other hand, government also has taken responsibility for stimulating the economy and for insuring that the nation does not become overly dependent on overseas supplies of energy and raw materials. The tendency has been for government to stress the strengthening of environmental regulations during boom years and then to relax their application in recessionary periods.

### SELECTED REFERENCES

HAYS, SAMUEL P. *Conservation and the Gospel of Efficiency: The Progressive Conservation Movement, 1890-1920.* Cambridge: Harvard University Press, 1959.

HUGHES, JONATHAN. *The Governmental Habit: Economic Controls from Colonial Times to the Present.* New York: Basic Books, 1977.

KOLKO, GABRIEL. *Railroads and Regulation, 1877-1916.* Princeton: Princeton University Press, 1965.

MARTIN, ALBRO. *Enterprise Denied: Origins of the Decline of American Railroads, 1897-1917.* New York: Columbia University Press, 1971.

PETULLA, JOSEPH M. *American Environmental History: The Exploitation and Conservation of Natural Resources.* San Francisco: Boyd & Fraser, 1977.

TIMBERLAKE, RICHARD. *The Origins of Central Banking in the United States.* Cambridge: Harvard University Press, 1978.

WHITE, EUGENE. *The Regulation and Reform of the American Banking System, 1900-1929.* Princeton: Princeton University Press, 1983.

WICKER, ELMUS. "Federal Reserve Monetary Policy, 1922-33: A Reinterpretation," *Journal of Political Economy* (1965), 325-43.

WIEBE, ROBERT. *Businessmen and Reform: A Study of the Progressive Movement.* Cambridge: Harvard University Press, 1962.

# CHAPTER SEVENTEEN
# THE GREAT DEPRESSION

The Great Depression, which lasted throughout the 1930s, was the biggest catastrophe in American economic history. It cut deeper and lasted longer than all previous depressions. This downturn in business activity was not restricted merely to the United States but afflicted Europe and the rest of the world as well. Many observers viewed the events in this decade as a crisis for the whole capitalist economic system. Some feared, as Marxist critics had predicted, that capitalism might collapse of its own weight and never recover. People were frightened.

Now, half a century later, historians have generally expressed surprise at the resiliency of the United States economic, social, and political systems. Despite desperate times, the population remained patient; the nation did not resort to any genuinely revolutionary programs. Some reforms were instituted, especially in financial markets. The government took a more active role in the economy, but the basic structure of American society was not significantly altered. The so-called New Deal, when it was initiated in the administration of President Franklin Roosevelt in 1933, was criticized in some quarters as a radical departure from traditional American values, but the historical view now stresses mainly its mildly reformist thrust.

## BUSINESS CYCLES: 1865-1925

Periods of expanding business activities followed by mild recessions or occasionally full-blown depressions, which had begun in the pre-Civil War era with the Panic of 1819, were a normal feature of the American economy in the period from 1865 to 1925. Business cycles emerged as a permanent feature of an advancing industrial society. Although the process of growth was uneven, the peaks of economic activity rose higher and higher. A graph depicting the movement of the economy would reveal an upward sloping line having the appearance of the jagged teeth of a wood saw. The downturns and temporary suffering borne by bankrupt firms and unemployed workers were considered unfortunate side effects of economic prog- ress. Recessions were viewed as unavoidable, although some nineteenth-century opinion makers believed that a more effective banking system might be able to prevent panics and halt the deterioration of short-lived recessions into depressions. That issue was discussed in the previous chapter and we noted how such concerns led to the creation of the Federal Reserve System.

The first major contraction in the economy after the Civil War occurred in 1873. Banks and businesses failed in droves and hundreds of thousands were thrown out of work. Because statistics to measure accurately economic activity were not refined in this period, we are not certain exactly how deep this depression cut into business volume or even exactly how long it lasted. Nonetheless most accounts list the depression in the 1870s as one of the three most serious in United States history. Other long periods of business stagnation were recorded beginning in 1882, 1893, and 1907.

Although recessions and depressions plagued the economy, recovery had al- ways begun within a few years. Moreover, improvement came without any positive action on the part of government. Few people believed that government had either the power or responsibility for stimulating business activity. The general belief was that little could be done to speed recovery; patience was the only known prescrip- tion. The theory was that recessions wrung the "excesses" out of the economy and eventually established a base for renewed opportunities.

Cycles of boom and bust were accepted as inevitable. The goal of policy makers in the early twentieth century was merely to discover a means of moderat- ing the fluctuations in economic activities. Many believed that the creation of the Federal Reserve System in 1913 would be the device for eliminating much of that unevenness. For the first fifteen years of its operations, the FRS did a reasonably commendable job. The post-World War I recession in 1920-21 cut sharply into business activity, but recovery followed quickly and the economy moved ahead at a rapid pace for the next few years.

Through the actions of the FRS, the government had discovered a tool for influencing the course of the economy. It is called monetary policy. The implemen- tation of monetary policy was indirect, since it was initiated not by the executive or legislative branch but by a separate, independent agency of the federal govern- ment. Among the techniques used by the FRS—or the "Fed" as it was popularly called—was the power to influence interest rates. During periods of slow business activities, the Fed tried to hold down interest rates in an effort to stimulate production, consumption, and investment. On other occasions, when the economy appeared to be overheating, the Fed pushed up rates in an effort to slow down business activities and thus prevent a sharper contraction later.

Another technique of monetary policy used even more frequently during the 1920s came to be known as "open-market operations." The governors of the FRS discovered, almost by accident, that they could influence the level of reserves in the entire banking system and the level of money in the economy by buying or selling government bonds in the so-called open market. This is how it all worked: When the FRS bought bonds from other banks, it paid for them by increasing their reserves. With their reserves higher, these banks were normally prone to make more business loans and thus boost the economy. On the other hand, when the FRS sold bonds to the same banks, it absorbed and reduced their reserves. Consequently, banks tended to reduce their business loans, and economic activity slowed. The net result was that the Fed could exert an influence on the general performance of the economy *both* through changes in interest rates and open-market operations. To reiterate, these techniques are part of what is called "monetary policy."

By the late twenties, the Fed was becoming more and more confident about its ability to manage the economy. There was even talk about "fine tuning" the business system to keep it on an even keel indefinitely. Optimism prevailed.


## THE ROARING TWENTIES

The twenties are usually depicted in history books as a roaring time because of the excitement and flamboyance of speakeasies, jazz, flappers (daring young women), sleek automobiles, and other cultural excesses. And the economy roared too. The gross national product went up nearly 50 percent between 1922 and 1929, while individual incomes rose on the order of one third. Inflation was low, under 2 percent annually. Unemployment was likewise negligible, averaging about 4 percent (even in boom times a fraction of workers are always between jobs). Corporate profits were growing, and stock prices kept climbing. With only a few weak spots such as coal mining, the economy seemed to be in wonderful shape. Many people believed an era of permanent prosperity had dawned; capitalism reigned supreme.


## THE DOWNTURN: 1929–1930

Suddenly, the direction of events shifted course. Usually cited as a harbinger of subsequent events was the stock market crash of October 1929. After rising steadily for almost a decade, stock prices plummeted. Many speculators who had borrowed

FIGURE 11   Standard Oil Gas Station in New Jersey, 1927 (Source: Culver
Pictures)

heavily to finance their stock purchases were wiped out in a matter of days or even
hours. A few of the distraught leaped to their deaths from tall buildings in the New
York financial district. The losers were not only financial professionals, but also
millions of middle class Americans who had been drawn into the stock market by
the lure of high returns.

Without in any way diminishing the excitement or importance of this dramatic episode, the stock market crash alone did not dictate the onset of the Depression. Prices in the stock market, whether high or low, do not have a very close
connection to the performance of the economy in terms of the production of goods
and services. Sometimes the economy and the stock market are in harmony, but
more often they are not. Moreover, soon after the crash in October, stock prices
actually rebounded for several months in late 1929 and early 1930. The long,
steady, less spectacular, but uninterrupted, decline in stock market prices began in
the spring of 1930. From their high point in 1929 to their low point in mid-1932,
stock prices fell in value by 80 percent. Many certificates became virtually worth-
less. Charges of fraud and irresponsible financial practices were common, with the
presidents of some of the leading New York banks implicated in unsavory transactions. The image of Wall Street at home and abroad suffered immensely.

By 1930 experts acknowledged that the nation was headed into a recession.
But few people were unduly alarmed, since they assumed that the downturn would
be short-lived.

## DEPTH OF THE DEPRESSION: 1930–1933

This was a recession, however, that turned into the most serious depression in United States history. Over a four-year period, GNP declined by nearly one third in real dollars. New investment in factories virtually halted. Unemployment climbed from about 6 percent of the labor force in 1929 to over 20 percent in 1931 and stayed that high for three years. Unemployment above 50 percent prevailed in many regions and sectors of the economy. Many people began to lose hope that recovery would ever take place. Some predicted the end of American capitalism; others the collapse of western civilization.

The cold statistics do little to convey how the Depression affected personal lives. Many individuals suffered hunger and physical deprivation for months or years; the self-esteem of many workers was also seriously undermined because of their inability to find employment. The lives of millions were permanently scarred by the psychological trauma of prolonged depression.

Oddly and ironically, a substantial part of the population actually saw their living standards rise during the Depression years. Salaries and wages tended to fall less steeply than prices so that those individuals who managed to hold on to their jobs in the 1930s often enjoyed higher real income. Yet even they feared that unless the economy improved, their jobs might also be threatened.

FIGURE 12    An Apple Seller on the West Side of New York, 1932 (Source: New York Public Library Picture Collection)

## HOOVER'S POLICIES

Herbert Hoover, who had been a very successful business leader, engineer, and later Secretary of Commerce in the 1920s, had the misfortune to become elected President just before the start of the Depression. Although Hoover has been the target of unending criticism for his failure to bring about recovery, the policies he pursued corresponded to the traditional wisdom of the era. For the first two years he did very little, except to express confidence in the economic system to regenerate— as it had always done in the past. Some even believed that the deeper the cutback in business activity, the stronger would be the rebound in the months ahead. Hoover repeatedly issued optimistic press releases citing evidence that the end of the Depression was just around the corner.

Finally, even Hoover began to despair. He started to take a more activist role in considering new programs designed to stimulate the economy. Usually described by contemporaries and critics as a rigid reactionary, Hoover actually became reasonably flexible in his approach to possible solutions to the nation's plight. No previous incumbent of the presidency had ever done as much.

Hoover's main accomplishment was the Reconstruction Finance Corporation (RFC), created by Congress in 1932 to help businesses avoid bankruptcy and get back on their feet. This government agency loaned millions of dollars to business organizations in serious trouble. A large share of the funds went, however, to large banks on the verge of insolvency. The justification was that the banks were the life support system for thousands of retail and manufacturing firms, and therefore by aiding financial institutions, the government was indirectly acting to prop up the whole economic system. Moreover, a few big loans to a few large banks were easy to arrange and administer quickly. Nonetheless, critics charged that such a policy was just another example of Republican favoritism towards big business while ignoring the needs of medium-sized and small firms.

## ELECTION OF FRANKLIN D. ROOSEVELT

In the fall of 1932, the American electorate overwhelmingly voted for a new administration with the hope that it could bring the nation out of the Depression. Surprisingly, Franklin D. Roosevelt differed very little from Hoover in his campaign speeches. He too advocated conservative policies and a balanced budget. But once in office, he behaved in a very bold and vigorous manner. In a dramatic address to the nation in the spring of 1933, he told his fellow citizens that the only thing they "had to fear was fear itself." Roosevelt held no firm ideas about economic principles or strategies, thus he was willing to experiment with a series of different programs.

FIGURE 13   Franklin D.
Roosevelt (Source: Culver
Pictures)

## NEW DEAL

The various reform policies pursued by the Roosevelt administration in the 1930s are known collectively as the New Deal. Some were designed to pull the country out of the Depression; others were put forward as reforms required to insure the future stability of the economic system. In the latter category was new legislation affecting the financial markets, a bill to provide federal government financing for unemployment and retirement programs, and laws fostering the union movement within the big business sector. The Wagner Act in 1935 recognized the legitimacy of unions and provided a mechanism to promote their formation and viability. We shall discuss the implications of the Wagner Act in Chapter Nineteen.

## FINANCIAL REFORMS

Congress passed new laws in the 1930s affecting both banking and the stock market. Although most financial experts believed that the creation of the Federal Reserve System in 1913 would prevent massive bank failures, that faith proved misplaced. Thousands of banks failed from 1930 to 1932. Many were small state banks which had never joined the FRS, but there were failures too among banks which had become members of the system. Individuals with money deposited in these banks often lost thousands of dollars of their savings. For the nation as a whole, it added up to millions of dollars.

An old idea, which had been largely discredited in the first decade of the century, was revived and became law. Congress created the Federal Deposit Insurance Corporation (FDIC) in the summer of 1933. The FDIC guaranteed deposits up to a stated maximum for individual depositors—initially the figure was $1,000, then $2,000, and now it is $100,000 or more. The object was to prevent panics by promising citizens that their deposits were safe even if a given bank ultimately failed. If a troubled bank did not have sufficient resources to return cash to depositors, then the FDIC would independently come up with the money. The FDIC obtained its funds by collecting insurance premiums from participating banks based on the size of their total deposits. The agency also played a role in regulating these banks.

Previous deposit guarantee plans had not worked at the state level because participating banks were too vulnerable to regional economic fluctuations. The national plan was successful in part because it included a diversity of financial institutions from all across the nation. The greatest reason for its success, however, was that the public knowledge of a comprehensive insurance program served to promote confidence in the banking system. Since citizens were convinced that their funds were safe, they were not prompted to descend on a given bank in a panic at the mere rumor of financial difficulties. The FDIC program was a highly effective insurance program not only because it compensated potential victims for their losses, but also because it actually reduced the risk of bank failures. Indeed, the FDIC is one of the least controversial government agencies, and it has won praise from politicians, bankers, and academics of all political persuasions.

### Securities and Exchange Commission

Until the 1930s, the federal government had never passed any legislation related to the bond and stock markets. When the American capital market emerged in the nineteenth century, first in response to the demands of the railroads and later industrial firms, only a small percentage of the total American population had any involvement in buying and selling corporate securities. Investments were made only by the wealthy and upper-middle classes.

Beginning in the 1920s, however, millions of middle class investors, hoping to profit from the unprecedented prosperity, were lured into the market. While most of the stocks and bonds sold to the general public by investment companies were legitimate, the absence of laws to protect buyers opened the gates for dishonest operators as well. Moreover, the mood was so optimistic even respected institutions that had acted prudently in the past became lax in their standards.

When the stock market crash exposed the weakness of many of these questionable practices, the public demanded stronger government involvement in the securities field. Congress created the Securities Exchange Commission (SEC) in 1934 to regulate the issuance of new stocks and bonds. President Roosevelt, in an adept political move, appointed a businessman and Wall Street confidant, Joseph P. Kennedy (father of President John F. Kennedy), as the first head of the SEC. The business sector accepted Kennedy as one of their own. The SEC stipulated that every potential investor in a new security issue had to receive a formal prospectus, which provided up-to-date and accurate information about the issuing company. Other rules were likewise designed to give investors more information so that they could make sounder judgments about their investments. Perhaps most important, the law made the dissemination of inadequate or fraudulent investment information not merely a civil but a criminal offense. The criminal statutes invariably called for prison sentences, not just fines. This crackdown on fraudulent and irresponsible investment practices has had a profound effect on the securities field. The new laws could not, of course, guarantee to the public that all their investments would turn out favorably, but it did give them the assurance that they would normally have access to current and accurate data. Public confidence in the honesty and integrity of individuals involved in the investment field has risen dramatically since the creation of the SEC.

*PEOPLE WHO MATTERED — Charles Merrill*

He was a founding partner in the stock brokerage firm which became in the 1950s the largest in the United States—Merrill Lynch & Co. During the revival of the investment banking and brokerage field in the post-World War II era, Merrill introduced a number of new competitive practices which eventually became standards for the securities industry. First, he advocated the cultivation of accounts from unsophisticated middle class investors, who were given generally reliable and conservative financial advice. The firm's sales people were put through an extensive training program, and they were supported by a large number of qualified security analysts. Investment opinions were passed on to any customer free of charge. In an effort to demystify Wall Street operations, Merrill Lynch took out full-page advertisements in leading newspapers explaining to the uninitiated investor the mechanics of security transactions. The firm opened up more of its own financial records for public inspection. Eventually these policies were imitated by virtually every other firm on Wall Street, and the net effect was to reduce the degree of secrecy within the investment field.

The son of a Florida physician and drugstore owner, Merrill was born in 1885. A good athlete, he once played minor league baseball. He started his career in the investment field in 1913. His reputation as a good judge of values was enhanced after investors recalled in the 1930s that Merrill had advised his clients that stocks were inflated prior to the great crash in October 1929. On the basis of the innovations he promoted, Merrill Lynch attracted so many customers in the 1950s that the firm handled anywhere from 10 to 20 percent of all transactions on the New York stock exchange.

Merrill died in 1956 and much of his estate of $25 million was used to establish a trust fund to make grants for educational, medical, religious, and other charitable purposes.

### Social Security Act

Certainly one of the most important pieces of New Deal legislation—in terms of its long-run impact on American society—was the Social Security Act of 1935. Other industrial societies in Europe had created financial support systems for unemployed and retired persons in the late nineteenth and early twentieth centuries, but the United States had not responded in a similar fashion. Most Americans had considered the provision of such support a private matter and the responsibility of individuals and their families. The Great Depression revealed, however, the extent to which private resources were inadequate in catastrophic times. The new legislation called for the establishment of permanently funded programs, with the premiums for unemployment insurance paid solely by employers and the taxes for old-age benefits shared equally by employees and employers. Over the last half century social security programs have grown enormously and have become an integral part of the services routinely provided by government.

### National Recovery Act

One new program advanced by the Roosevelt administration intended to pull the country out of the Depression was the National Recovery Act (NRA) of 1933. The idea was to bring together business and government, with the assistance of labor, to develop a program to stabilize the economy and to create conditions favorable for recovery. Business firms within industries were encouraged to cooperate with each other in maintaining prices, wages, and employment levels. The antitrust laws were suspended to permit competitors to join together in solving common problems. Eventually voluntary codes of "fair practices" were drawn up for over 500 separate industries.

The NRA was established as an emergency measure and thus it generally received the support of a wide spectrum of Americans in 1933. As months passed, however, a number of citizens, especially those holding conservative political opinions, began to express serious reservations about the wisdom of permitting so much government control over the private business sector. Some feared that the NRA set a bad precedent—one that might eventually lead the way to radical changes in the American political and economic systems. To their delight, therefore, the United States Supreme Court declared the whole act unconstitutional in 1935, ruling that Congress had illegally granted legislative powers to the executive branch. Since the effectiveness of the act had proven questionable—with industrial production only slightly improved two years after passage—the Roosevelt administration accepted the end of NRA with little protest.

### Pump Priming

The most effective government programs in the 1930s were those that put money directly in the hands of the destitute and unemployed. People with inadequate financial resources invariably took the money given them by government and spent it immediately on needed goods and services. In so doing, they raised the aggregate level of demand and gave an incentive to others to boost their output. The funds they spent "primed the pump" and helped stimulate the economy.

The methods of distributing and allocating public funds varied. In several instances, the federal government raised its contributions to relief programs that provided food, clothing, and shelter for the unfortunate. Other programs gave public employment to individuals seeking jobs. The Works Progress Administration (WPA) and the Civilian Conservation Corps (CCC) were two new government agencies which hired millions of eager workers. As we discussed in the previous chapter, members of the CCC planted trees on barren land all across the nation. WPA projects included roads, hospitals, bridges, schools, and other types of public construction. Such programs not only provided income for workers (although wages were modest), but they also boosted the spirit of millions of citizens who felt useless and unproductive.

## RECOVERY: 1933-1940

The economy stopped contracting in the second half of 1933 and began to recover. The rate of growth in GNP was rapid over the next three years. By the spring of 1937 aggregate output had climbed back to the level reached in 1929. But that statistic is misleading; despite the rebound in production, about 15 percent of the workforce remained unemployed. The work force had expanded steadily over the eight-year period from 1929 to 1937, yet the number of jobs had not increased at a similar pace. Conditions were improved, but the Depression was not over.

In 1937 the economy suffered another setback. Production declined and unemployment rose from 14 to 19 percent of the work force. Doubts that the American capitalist system would make a full recovery were intensified in many quarters. In seeking explanations for the pause in business expansion, economic analysts noted two policy changes which seemed to have had negative results. First, the Roosevelt administration, believing that the economy was already headed in the right direction, decided to curtail many public works projects previously planned for 1937. Second, the Federal Reserve Board in Washington, worried about the possibility of inflation, had raised reserve requirements of member banks and thereby reduced the bank funds available for business loans.

During 1938 both of those policies were reversed. For the first time, the administration submitted a budget to Congress with a planned deficit. Since 1930, federal government spending had exceeded revenues every year, but these deficits were viewed as necessary evils—necessary to meet the pressing needs of desperate citizens. Now there was a growing realization that the unintended deficits had probably been good public policy and were perhaps responsible in part for the advancement of the economy from 1934 to 1936.

## KEYNESIAN ECONOMICS

This reversal in attitude toward deficit spending represented the initial acceptance of a new set of economic principles conceived by the British economist John Maynard Keynes. Because those ideas are so important to the operation of our modern economy, we need to examine them briefly here. Previously, economists had generally agreed that an economy going through a depression contained within itself all the elements required for eventual regeneration. Keynes disputed that idea. He held that a depressed economy could undergo perpetual stagnation. The problem was the absence of sufficient demand for goods and services to prompt renewed production. If the private sector was unable to generate that demand, then, according to Keynes, only government through deficit spending had the ability and power to create sufficient demand and stimulate recovery. The use of deficits, and also surpluses, to affect the level of economic activity is called "fiscal policy."

Keynes had been urging capitalist governments both in Europe and the United States to assume a more activist role since the early 1930s, but his ideas were still considered too heretical. President Roosevelt and his main economic advisors had been exposed to Keynes's thoughts since taking office in 1933, yet they felt his new economic concepts were too radical and unproven. After the economic downturn in 1937, however, they reassessed their thinking about the merits of fiscal policy. Deficit spending in previous years did not appear to have had any harmful effects, and they were now prepared to consider the possibility that, just as Keynes had claimed, the deficits had had a very positive influence. One of Roosevelt's main characteristics was his willingness first to experiment and then to endorse policies which appeared to be working no matter what their origins or guiding principles.

## WORLD WAR II: END OF THE DEPRESSION

Spurred on in part by a modest program of deficit spending, the economy improved somewhat between 1938 and 1939, but only the massive government outlays on war materials beginning in the summer of 1940 pulled the nation out of the Depression. Plants, equipment, and individuals, idle for most of the last decade, were rushed back into productive activities. The rate of unemployment dropped to under 2 percent. With millions of men in uniform, women were recruited into the labor force to perform a whole host of new jobs. Women proved time and time again that they could perform tasks traditionally performed solely by men. Women drove heavy equipment, welded steel rivets, and learned hundreds of new job skills. They helped build tanks, warships, and airplanes. (After the war, the vast majority of women in such nontraditional occupations were laid off and their jobs given to returning soldiers.)

Between 1940 and 1944, the nation's production of industrial goods nearly doubled. After adjusting for wartime inflation, gross national product went up by nearly one half, rising at an annual rate of nearly 10 percent. During these years government deficits were astronomical: in 1941 the figure was $19 billion; in 1942, $54 million; in 1943, $46 billion; and in 1944, $45 billion. Indeed, over this four-year period funds borrowed by the federal government, mostly through the sale of bonds to commercial banks, accounted for over one fifth of the nation's total output. In other words, the war provided the opportunity to pursue Keynesian economics on a grand scale. The result was a cure for the Great Depression.

## WORLD WAR II TO THE PRESENT:
## MONETARY VERSUS FISCAL POLICY

In the post-World War II era few challenged the principle that the federal government had responsibility for maintaining a strong economy. Congress passed the Employment Act of 1946 committing the government to the pursuit of policies (unspecified) which would hold down the level of unemployment. But disagreement existed over the most advantageous method of exercising control. From 1945 until 1980, Republicans generally favored monetary policies to keep the economy on an even keel. They looked to the Federal Reserve Board as the primary institution for fine tuning the business cycle.

The Democrats, in contrast, tended to look more toward fiscal policy. President John Kennedy sponsored in 1961 a program designed to get the economy moving ahead at a faster pace through planned deficits.

In response to criticisms that New Deal fiscal policy was flawed because it had failed to bring the nation out of the Great Depression in the 1930s, Democrats pointed to the research findings of economist Cary Brown. In an important article authored in 1956, Brown argued that the main reason deficit spending at the federal level had been so ineffective was because state and local governments in the aggregate had run substantial budget surpluses after 1932. These state and local surpluses offset much of the federal deficit, and therefore the economy as a whole experienced little actual stimulation. Brown claimed that the New Deal did not represent a fair test of Keynesian economics, since, in actuality, it had not been vigorously applied.

By the early 1980s, the positions of the two major political parties on the merits of fiscal versus monetary policy as the prime tool of government had become more alike. President Ronald Reagan, for example, proposed a budget with a deficit of almost $200 billion in 1983, with the aim of bringing the nation out of the most serious economic downturn since the 1930s. At present, there seems to be a consensus among leading American politicians that combinations of both monetary and fiscal policies are necessary to manage properly the modern American economy.

## EPILOGUE: WHAT CAUSED THE GREAT DEPRESSION?

For the last two decades, one of the most hotly pursued topics in scholarly circles has been the effort to identify the causes of the Great Depression. Over a half century after its occurrence, economic historians are still divided about the origins. One camp, led by economist Milton Friedman, puts the blame primarily on the failure of the Federal Reserve Board to act decisively in 1930 and 1931. Allegedly, the board's policies were halting and passive. By increasing the reserves of commercial banks at critical points through open market operations, the Fed, it is claimed, had the power to increase the nation's money supplies and thereby set the stage for recovery. But at a time when prices and wages were falling dramatically, the Fed was diverted by irrelevant fears about such matters as the revival of inflationary pressures. The performance of the central bank in this crisis was disastrous, according to its critics; the board managed to convert a mild recession into a major depression because of inept leadership and misguided actions.

Another group of economic historians is unwilling to place so much blame on the Federal Reserve Board. They agree that the central bank's policies were uninspired, but they are convinced that the real causes of the Depression lie elsewhere. This group points mainly to the slowing of private demand in the 1920s, both for consumer goods and new investment in plant and equipment. They believe too that the stock market crash contributed somewhat to the depth of the economic downturn since potential consumers curtailed purchases of goods and services after their financial assets had diminished in value. Yet even this group of experts has been unable to ferret out sufficient data to account for much more than about one fourth of the observed decline in total demand. Rejecting the theories about monetary causes yet able themselves to generate only enough information to offer a partial explanation for the origins of the Depression, this group of historians has simply conceded that the subject remains a mystery—a puzzle yet to be solved.

Perhaps the realization that decades of hindsight have not provided clear analyses of past events will lead us to have greater tolerance for the difficulties faced by our current leaders in trying to cope with the problems of today's economy.

### SELECTED REFERENCES

BROWN, CARY E. " Fiscal Policy in the Thirties: A Reappraisal," *American Economic Review* (1956), 857–79.

CHANDLER, LESTER. *America's Greatest Depression, 1929-1941.* New York: Harper & Row, 1970.

FRIEDMAN, MILTON, and ANNA J. SCHWARTZ. *A Monetary History of the United States, 1867-1960.* Princeton: Princeton University Press, 1963.

LEUCHTENBURG, WILLIAM. *Franklin D. Roosevelt and the New Deal, 1932-1940.* New York: Harper & Row, 1963.

STEIN, HERBERT. *The Fiscal Revolution in America.* Chicago: University of Chicago Press, 1969.

TEMIN, PETER. *Did Monetary Forces Cause the Great Depression?* New York: W. W. Norton, 1976.

WALTON, GARY M., ed. *Regulatory Change in an Atmosphere of Crisis: The Current-Day Implications of the Roosevelt Years.* New York: Academic Press, 1979.

# CHAPTER EIGHTEEN
# BUSINESS
# IN THE TWENTIETH
# CENTURY

The nineteenth century witnessed the origin of the large industrial firm, while the twentieth century saw its maturation, diversification, and continued expansion overseas. New industries also rose to prominence which had never existed in the previous era, including aviation, motion pictures, television, computers, and home appliances. They were based on the development of new technologies. Indeed, by mid-century many leading firms had created research and development divisions with the assigned task of discovering new products and finding other uses for exist: ing products. Meanwhile, in an effort to cut costs, manufacturing firms often turned to automation, substituting machines for workers. Another trend was the growth of service industries—firms which did not manufacture tangible products but provided services, especially in the fields of finance, transportation, information gathering and processing, and entertainment.

The business world took on a more international flavor over the course of the century. American manufacturing firms, which had already begun to push overseas in the nineteenth century, expanded rapidly in Canada and western Europe during the 1920s and then again after World War II. In the 1960s, Japanese and European firms began to penetrate the American market for such products as automobiles, cameras, television sets, textiles, shoes, and others. American technology, which had led the world for most of the twentieth century, was faced with a serious challenge from overseas.

Another major change during the twentieth century was the shift to new sources of energy and new methods of transmitting energy on the job and in the home. At the beginning of the century, coal was the primary fuel both for operating factories and running the nation's railroads. Machines were powered by steam engines located on the factory site. After the turn of the century, however, electric motors became increasingly common, and they could draw their power from generating stations long distances away. Over the decades petroleum and natural gas constantly undercut the position of coal. Both were cheaper to extract and transport overland than coal; moreover, they burned with cleaner flames and caused less pollution. By the 1970s these two modern fuels provided over 70 percent of the energy used in the United States, while coal accounted for less than one quarter of the energy market.

## NEW ORGANIZATIONAL STRUCTURES

Based on new technologies and economies of scale, many industries became dominated by a few large firms in the late nineteenth and early twentieth centuries. The emergence of an oligopolistic industry structure initially brought stability to existing firms, both in terms of sales volumes and profits. However, as time passed, many of these large firms, which had originally concentrated on the manufacture or distribution of a single line of products, began to diversify their operations in an effort to expand their markets and income. In most cases, such firms simply moved into new fields in which the technology was compatible with their main areas of strength. The Du Pont Co. provides an excellent example of this type of development.

In the nineteenth century, the Du Pont Co. was largely a manufacturer of a single product—black powder for explosives and guns. (Dynamite was added in the late nineteenth century.) Soon after the turn of the century, the firm came under the control of two younger Du Pont brothers, Coleman and Pierre, who had earned engineering degrees from the Massachusetts Institute of Technology. They set out to rationalize the firm's operations and administrative structure. They consolidated manufacturing into the most efficient plants, thereby realizing economies of scale. The brothers also established an effective centralized administrative structure based on the performance of functions such as purchasing, manufacturing, selling, and other duties. Following the strategy of concentrating on a single line of closely related products in the explosives field and employing a centralized administrative structure organized around functions, Du Pont was an extraordinarily successful firm from 1902 until the end of World War I. During the war years the company's research and development division—one of the very first established in the nation—came up with a host of new products derivative of the chemistry and technology of explosives and gunpowder.

After the war ended in 1918, the Du Pont Co. aggressively began the production and marketing of these new products. The company sold dyestuffs, paints, film, fibers, and a host of other recently developed items. Virtually all of them were distributed through marketing channels with which the firm had no previous experience. Corporate executives predicted huge profits from these new fields of endeavor.

Rather than profits, however, the firm began to experience huge losses after 1919 in these new product areas. Something had gone awry. A special committee was appointed to study the problem. After careful analysis, the committee concluded that the old organizational structure was not well suited to the firm's new strategy of product diversification. Therefore the existing administrative structure, organized according to function, was scrapped. In its place, Du Pont established a series of separate divisions organized around individual products or small groups of products. Each division had its own purchasing, manufacturing, selling, and other functional departments. The role of the central office was reduced in terms of its involvement in day-to-day operations. Instead, the executives in the central office, supported by an ample staff, focused their attention on coordinating and appraising the operations of the various divisions and on planning for the future growth of the company. This multidivisional administrative structure proved a salvation for the Du Pont Co., and profits soon reappeared and rose to higher and higher levels.

What happened at Du Pont occurred in most other large American business firms in varying degrees over the course of the century. As companies pursued the strategy of diversification, they discovered that excessive centralization hindered operations. Eventually the large business enterprise adopted the multidivisional structure with a small central office to supervise operations and allocate capital and personnel between the various product divisions. This type of administrative structure was an American innovation. Large firms in other nations, primarily in Western Europe and Japan, did not begin to imitate American administrative techniques until the 1960s and 1970s.

### Conglomerates

Prior to the 1950s American firms tended to diversify their product lines by adding items closely related to their main line of expertise. Thereafter, however, several fledgling entrepreneurs began to assemble companies with separate divisions which were almost totally unrelated to each other. We call such enterprises conglomerates—another American innovation. They emerged for three principal reasons. After 1910, the Supreme Court's interpretation of the antitrust laws ruled out mergers between large firms in similar fields, but no legal impediments arose to prevent the consolidation of separate companies in unrelated industries. Second, the multidivisional administrative structure proved highly adaptable to the corporate strategy of offering a host of different products and services. Since each division functioned fairly autonomously, it did not seem especially important that their technology had little in common. Third, the stock market rose to record heights in the 1960s, and investors were willing to pay very high prices for these novel enterprises, which naturally encouraged their formation.

Initially many conglomerates established excellent performance records in terms of sales growth and profits. By the 1970s, however, many were facing difficult times, and the creation of new conglomerates slowed markedly. The test of time revealed that firms which diversified around a core technology or a certain expertise—like Du Pont—were generally more successful over the long run.

### New Industries

Two flourishing industries in which United States firms continued to exert world leadership well into the 1980s were aircraft construction and computers. For 30 years following the first powered flight by the Wright brothers at Kitty Hawk, North Carolina in 1907, airplane construction remained a small industry. After a brief surge during World War I, when several of the combatant governments—including the United States—built planes largely for reconnaissance flights and strafing troops, the industry languished. A few commercial airlines were formed in the twenties and thirties but they relied extensively on air mail contracts with the Post Office to maintain solvency.

The next boost in aircraft construction and technology came again from the stimulus of war. By the end of World War II, building military planes had become the nation's largest industry in terms of employment and sales. At the end of the war, aircraft companies concentrated on developing a dual market—commercial airliners and military aircraft. The so-called Cold War—a continuing rivalry between the United States and the Soviet Union—guaranteed that the major firms would receive production contracts as well as new funds for research and development on more advanced war planes. Although commercial air traffic did not take off spectacularly as some firms had hoped, it nonetheless climbed steadily in the immediate postwar years.

A significant change in the fortunes of the aircraft industry came with the adaptation of jet propulsion to commercial planes. First developed for use in military fighter planes, the jet engine doubled the cruising speed of airliners to over 500 miles per hour and soon made the airplane the preferred choice of long distance travelers. The Boeing 707 was introduced in 1958 and the Douglas DC-8 the following year. Airlines placed orders for hundreds of new planes. During the period from 1948 to 1966, the air transport sector of the economy recorded productivity gains of 14 percent annually—the highest for any American industry and over three times the average rate for manufacturing in general.

American aircraft builders have maintained their leadership position not only at home but in foreign markets as well. When the price of fuel escalated in the early 1970s, they developed new planes that were not only more efficient but could take off and land on shorter runways, thus making more cities accessible to service by jets with large carrying capacities. The only serious threat to United States dominance has come from the Eurobus plane, a jumbo jet introduced in the 1970s by a consortium sponsored by several Western European governments to compete with the Boeing 747 and the McDonnell-Douglas DC-10.

### Computers and High-Tech Industries

Another general area where American leadership has prevailed has been computers and other so-called "high-tech" industries. Prior to World War II, several companies manufactured business machines to aid in processing accounting data, but complex computers were still in the developmental stage. During the war years the government's interest in cryptology—creating and deciphering secret codes— led to increased research into building electronic machines that could process information at superhuman speeds. Scientists made substantial progress, but when the war ended in 1945, their work was not yet complete. Three men important in the development of ideas within this field were John von Neumann, John Mauchly, and Prosper Eckert.

The return to a peacetime economy created uncertainty about the wisdom of continued research on computers because of reservations about their commercial value. The technical principles were already fairly well understood, but the cost of construction was projected as being very high and applications to everyday business transactions remained questionable. The prospect of at least a limited market within government—the military and perhaps the Census Bureau—and the hope that commercial uses might arise at a later date were factors that encouraged some entrepreneurs to proceed with their work. In 1946 Mauchly and Eckert, working under an army contract at the University of Pennsylvania, introduced the first electronic computer; equipped with a maze of vacuum tubes, the Electronic Numerical Integrator and Calculator (ENIAC) could perform 4,500 additions in a second. Later they became employees of Sperry-Rand Corporation, and Mauchly and Eckert were instrumental in designing and constructing UNIVAC, the first giant computer on the commercial market.

Another firm, which got a later start but eventually came to dominate the industry, was International Business Machines (IBM). The outbreak of the Korean War in 1950 was the event that pushed IBM to put more resources into computer development. In 1952 the firm produced its 701 Defense Calculator, an electronic data processing machine equipped with a punch card entry system, magnetic drums, and tape storage of information. More advanced models of this basic machine offered software packages and other programming aids.

IBM did not necessarily have superior technology, but it swamped competitors with an effective sales organization and a service department to assist customers in obtaining the maximum use of their equipment. The firm discovered a myriad of applications for its computers in the commercial market. Its growth in terms of sales and profits was phenomenal in the 1960s. Investors drove up the price of its shares to such heights that IBM became the firm with the single highest aggregate market value for its stock in the entire capitalist world. During this period the company claimed from 75 to 90 percent of the computer market, and IBM and the computer became almost synonomous.

During the 1970s and early 1980s, other firms began to make inroads on IBM's share of the computer market. The range of equipment and software became wider and much more varied. Several companies cultivated the household market, as the use of transistors and microchips lowered drastically production costs. Another new term, high-tech, entered the general vocabulary to encompass all the firms in these advanced fields.

Two regions specializing in high-tech industries were the so-called Silicon Valley in northern California and the Boston, Massachusetts, area. In a strange twist of fate, many of the old stone-walled textile mills built in the early nineteenth century, and long ago abandoned, were refurbished and outfitted for high-tech firms. Lawrence, Massachusetts, once the home of the most up-to-date textile technology—in the 1820s—became a new mecca for state-of-the-art firms in a radically different field where American leadership was once again in evidence.

### Mechanization and Automation

One of the methods American firms followed to improve their competitive position both at home and abroad was to increase the use of better machinery on the job. Mechanization tended to speed up the work process and permit smoother and more continuous operations. The uninterrupted rolling of sheet metal provides an example of the advances in this area. Introduced in the twenties, it allowed molten iron to be converted into steel beams, sheets, and plates without passing through several stages of cooling and reheating. In the shipping industry, the acceptance of prepacked containers from manufacturers, which could be loaded by cranes directly on board vessels, eliminated hours of unnecessary packing and unpacking of cargoes by dock hands.

Whereas in most instances new machinery merely aided workers in increasing productivity, in other situations machines actually took over whole parts of the work process. The labor force was frequently divided about the impact of automation. Displaced workers complained about their fate, but remaining workers normally were rewarded with less strenuous assignments and higher wages.

The latest concept in automation has been the development of robots with many of the versatile capabilities of human beings. With a computer for a brain and a television camera for vision, robots not only have the capacity to perform routine tasks but also to react to new situations in a changing working environment. Already several factories in Japan, relying heavily on the use of robots, function smoothly with few humans on the premises. It is conceivable that sometime during the next few decades, robots will perform hundreds of industrial tasks.

### Multinationals

American business enterprises did not restrict their operations to their native soil but moved overseas to seek growth and profits. This trend had already emerged in the nineteenth century and it continued thereafter. Two types of foreign operations were common. In one category, firms extracted natural resources or foodstuffs for shipment out of the host country. In the second category, they manufactured products for local sale. With few exceptions—Canada was one—these

FIGURE 14  Chrysler Using Robots on the Assembly Line (Source: Chrysler Corporation)

two types of operations were performed in different parts of the globe and in nations with very different levels of economic development.

Companies interested in extraction for export invested mainly in the Western Hemisphere. In the Caribbean and Central America, numerous firms produced tropical foodstuffs for shipment back to the United States. Bananas were the most important crop. Firms such as United Fruit and Standard Fruit invested heavily in Nicaragua and Honduras just after the turn of the century. They built new towns, ports, and railroads where none had previously existed; they planted thousands of acres in banana trees. Although these banana growers contributed significantly to the economic development of the host countries, eventually local citizens began to resent the enormous economic power, and sometimes political influence, of the Americans. To thwart local criticism and demands for greater local control, these firms surrendered ownership of a vast majority of their land holdings to resident Latin American growers in the post-World War II era.

The other extractive industries were in mining and oil. Mines containing valuable minerals such as lead, nickel, copper, and nitrates were opened in Mexico, Chile, and Canada. Early in the twentieth century, oil was discovered in Mexico, and that nation became for a few years the third largest producer after the United States and Russia. Deteriorating relations between the government and foreign oil companies in the 1920s and 1930s, however, led to the Mexican seizure of much United States oil property, and compensation was at a figure far below the estimated value.

In the 1920s Venezuela surpassed Mexico as a producer of petroleum, and the development of its fields was largely the work of American oil firms. Since the

United States was a net exporter of petroleum until the 1950s, most Latin American oil in the first half of the century went to Europe, where American firms had extensive distribution systems.

The exploration and development of oil fields was the primary factor leading to American investment in the Middle East, Africa, and Southeast Asia. United States oil companies were instrumental in developing producing wells in Saudi Arabia, Kuwait, Nigeria, Angola, Libya, Indonesia, and Iran (where the British were active first). American involvement began in the 1930s and expanded greatly after World War II. The bulk of the petroleum produced in these areas was sold in Western Europe and Japan. Initially, United States oil companies controlled the foreign oil fields. That position quickly eroded in the 1970s as the nations that organized OPEC (Organization of Petroleum Exporting Countries) assumed more power over prices and the rate of production. By 1980 most of the oil-exporting countries had earned sufficient funds from the accelerating price of crude petroleum to purchase, at fair prices, most of the producing properties of the American firms operating within their borders.

### Overseas Manufacturing

American manufacturers exhibited a completely different pattern of investment. Their plants were built primarily in Western Europe and Canada, areas where incomes were high and labor skills were highly developed. The products manufactured overseas were mostly uniquely American inventions. In the nineteenth century, sewing machines and agricultural machinery were two of the first products to be manufactured in a foreign country. In the twentieth century automobiles, home appliances, and machinery led the way.

American firms decided to build plants overseas only after their exports to a specific country had reached a substantial volume. They knew beforehand that the demand for their product was sufficient to support a local manufacturing facility. The ability to cut transportation costs was usually a major factor in deciding to invest overseas. Another motivation was to avoid the payment of tariffs (taxes) imposed by foreign countries on American imports. By manufacturing in the host country for the local markets, American firms discovered that their overall costs were lower and their profits much higher.

## INVASION OF THE U. S. MARKET

For decades American manufacturers had the domestic market largely to themselves. Foreign goods were generally inferior in quality and higher in price. Starting in the 1950s and accelerating thereafter, foreign firms discovered that they were able to penetrate the United States market. Among the foreign products widely accepted by American buyers were automobiles, steel, textiles, cameras, stereos, and television sets. The German Volkswagen, commonly called the Bug, was the first clearly identified foreign product to earn a significant foothold in the United

States. Stressing economy and reliability, as did Ford's original Model T, Volks-wagen opened a door through which other automakers in Europe and Japan later entered. By the 1980s imports accounted for 20-25 percent of American car sales; on the West Coast the figure was nearly 50 percent. In the assembly of television sets, foreign manufacturers, largely based in Japan, likewise made huge inroads on the United States markets. Sony became the standard for high quality. The steel in-dustry, once the symbol of American technological superiority, felt the competi-tion of overseas producers who operated more efficient furnaces using lower paid workers.

### Imports: Beneficial or Threatening?

During the last decades or so, much public discussion has focused on the merits versus the disadvantages of allowing imports into the United States so freely. Some critics have proposed the imposition of higher tariffs, which would raise the price of foreign goods and make them less competitive. Nearly all economists do not favor building a tariff barrier. First, they argue that consumers benefit enor-mously from free trade, since they have a wider range of selection in terms of quality and prices. Lower prices for imports also tend to hold down the prices of domestic goods. Moreover, economists assert that pressure from imports forces American firms to adopt more efficient production methods, which will make them more competitive in the long run.

To counter that argument, certain industries and unions advocated the use of higher tariffs to reduce imports and protect their jobs. Hundreds of thousands of

**FIGURE 15  U.S. Arrival of Foreign-Made Cars (Source: Toyota Motor Sales, U.S.A., Inc.)**

American workers have lost their former livelihoods. These laborers have suffered financially and psychologically from long periods of idleness. Many possessed few skills transferable to other jobs.

Union organizations concerned primarily about the welfare of members have frequently joined corporate executives in lobbying Congress for greater protection from foreign competition. In response to pleas for relief, the United States government negotiated an agreement with Japan in the early 1980s to limit the number of imported cars sold in the American market. The aim was to stabilize the market for American automakers and to preserve as many existing jobs as possible for United States auto workers.

Whether the United States allows relatively easy access to its vast market or restricts imports in order to preserve domestic markets for United States firms and workers may be one of the major political issues debated in the years ahead.

## ENERGY SOURCES AND USES

At the beginning of the twentieth century, the nation's manufacturing plants were overwhelmingly powered by coal. In 1900, coal fueled the railroads and heated the vast majority of America's homes and offices, especially in urban areas. A petroleum industry had existed since the 1860s, but the main product refined from crude oil remained kerosene, which was used primarily as an illuminant in lamps. Oil and natural gas combined accounted for under 10 percent of the commercial energy market. (The commercial market excludes wood and vegetable matter.)

Over the course of the century, however, coal gave ground to these new liquid and gaseous fuels. The growth of the automobile industry after 1910 was responsible for a greater emphasis on the refining of gasoline from petroleum. Meanwhile, superior furnaces and better delivery systems encouraged more factories and homes to convert to fuel oil for power and heat. From the mid-twenties onward, the fastest growing fuel in terms of attracting new markets was natural gas. An extensive pipeline system across the nation made delivery of the fuel very convenient to both home and factory. By 1975 the three leading fossil fuels divided up the commercial energy market as follows: oil—44 percent; natural gas—31 percent; coal—22 percent. Hydro/nuclear energy claimed the other 3 percent of the market.

Overall, Americans have consumed energy at very high rates. They used over 11,000 kilograms per capita in the 1970s, double the usage in other advanced countries in Europe and Japan. On the other hand, in terms of the rate of annual increase in energy consumption since 1925, the United States ranks very low among the nations of the world—which means that it started the period with a very high base, nearly 6,000 kilograms per capita. Indeed, the American economy has been becoming much more efficient (meaning that aggregate output has risen faster than energy usage) for over half a century. The increase in energy prices in the early 1970s gave an added impetus to this movement, but the trend toward greater fuel efficiency was already well established.

For most of the twentieth century, the United States was self-sufficient in energy sources. From 1920 to 1950 the nation produced nearly one half of the world's commercial energy and exported roughly 5 percent of its net output. In fact, oil production was so great during this period relative to consumption that business and government cooperated in various programs designed to slow down the rate of expansion. Nonetheless, the real price of energy actually fell over the first six decades of this century.

The situation began to change in the early 1960s. Domestic oil production lagged behind demand, and, for the first time, petroleum was regularly imported. Since large quantities of United States coal were also routinely exported to Europe and Japan, the net energy balance remained fairly close to equilibrium. But during the 1970s, self-sufficiency was lost. Up to 35 percent of oil consumption came from imports, and that figure represented about 15 percent of all commercial energy. By the 1980s, however, the dependency on foreign energy sources had diminished. Imports of OPEC oil fell from a high of 6.2 million barrels daily in 1977 to only 2.1 million barrels in 1982. Prices rose dramatically for all fuels, which spurred higher domestic production of coal, natural gas, and petroleum. Meanwhile, conservation measures—for example, automobiles delivering more miles per gallon—aided in slowing the growth in the demand for energy. The so-called energy crisis, which had appeared so serious in the 1970s, no longer seems so threatening.

## SELECTED REFERENCES

CHANDLER, ALFRED D. *The Visible Hand: The Managerial Revolution in American Business.* Cambridge: Harvard University Press, 1977.

DARMSTADLER, JOEL et al. *Energy in the World Economy: A Statistical Review of Trends in Output, Trade, and Consumption since 1925.* Baltimore: Johns Hopkins University Press, 1971.

GALBRAITH, JOHN KENNETH. *The New Industrial State.* Boston: Houghton Mifflin, 1967.

PERKINS, EDWIN J., ed. *Men and Organizations: The American Economy in the Twentieth Century.* New York: Putnam's, 1977.

ROSENBERG, NATHAN. *Technology and American Economic Growth.* New York: Harper & Row, 1972.

SCHURR, SAM H., and BRUCE NETSCHERT. *Energy in the American Economy, 1850–1975.* Baltimore: Johns Hopkins University Press, 1960.

SOBEL, ROBERT. *IBM: Colossus in Transition.* New York: Truman Talley Books, 1981.

WILKINS, MIRA. *The Maturing of Multinational Enterprise: American Business Abroad from 1914 to 1970.* Cambridge: Harvard University Press, 1974.

# CHAPTER NINETEEN
# BIG LABOR
# AND A CHANGING
# WORK FORCE

In the United States today, it is frequently said that power is exercised by a trium-
virate of big business, big government, and big labor. While this statement is an
oversimplification about how our society functions, there is still much truth in this
observation. The 1930s were the decade when labor unions began their rise to a
position of power and influence. For the first time, the federal government gave its
support to union efforts to organize workers employed in big business firms. Union
membership climbed from 3.5 million to over 20 million between 1930 and 1970.
Although the decline in the percentage of workers in blue-collar occupations over
the last quarter century has contributed to a decline in membership rolls, the AFL-
CIO remains a powerful force in the economy and in public affairs generally.

In addition to the emergence of labor as a power center in the political arena,
other changes also affected the labor force. As a result of increases in productivity,
wages continued to move upward. Many skilled workers, in particular, realized a
rise not only in their incomes, but also in their status within society. They increasingly became members of the American middle class, especially in those homes with
two steady incomes. The two-income family was one consequence of another
change in the composition of the working population: more women, and particularly married women, had entered the work force.

The pattern of employment shifted over the course of the century as well.
More workers performed so-called service jobs as opposed to the direct production

of foodstuffs, raw materials, and manufactured goods. People in this category are found in a wide range of occupations: teachers, professionals, clerical workers, salespersons, technicians, managers, and a host of others. In 1900 such workers accounted for about 25 percent of the work force, but by 1980 the figure had risen to over 60 percent.

## LABOR IN THE 1920s

The twenties were a mixed period for American workers. Wages rose during the business boom. Many families were able to afford such luxuries as an automobile, a radio, and new household appliances such as refrigerators. Unemployment was low; people who wanted jobs could usually find them without too much difficulty.

On the other hand, labor unions lost strength. Their membership declined from over 5 million in 1920 to 3.6 million in 1930. Employers mounted an offensive against independent unions. Union supporters were often fired or threatened with transfers to lower paying jobs. In many areas labor organizers were attacked verbally as "communist sympathizers" and sometimes even attacked physically by thugs hired by fearful employers. Newspapers, which were invariably owned by political conservatives, constantly linked labor activity with the outbreak of violence in their news reports and editorials. The idea that unions were subversive and "un-American" was becoming more widespread. The federal government, and especially the Supreme Court, remained probusiness and antiunion.

## LABOR AND THE GREAT DEPRESSION

The decline in economic activity beginning in 1930 had a profound impact on American labor. With industrial production down by one third, millions of factory workers lost their jobs. Some remained unemployed for years. Unemployment rates were between 15 and 20 percent for most of the decade. Many workers who had been optimistic in the twenties now were discouraged about future prospects. Factory laborers became increasingly aware of their powerlessness because of the absence of effective organizations to look out for their interests. The sentiment in favor of creating strong unions for the mass of workers grew rapidly.

### Government Support for Unions

Soon after the election of President Franklin D. Roosevelt in 1932, the federal government shifted from its traditional probusiness stance to a position which supported the efforts of union organizers. Ironically, the first evidence of this alteration in government policy was revealed in emergency legislation designed primarily to assist business in coping with the Depression. The National Recovery Act (NRA), discussed in Chapter Seventeen, encouraged firms within industries to cooperate in solving common problems by suspending, in part, the antitrust laws. In order to compensate workers for granting this favor to the business community, labor was permitted to insert a section in the bill (section 7a), which recognized the workers' right to form their own independent unions. Section 7a was little more than a statement of principles, since it created no enforcement mechanism, but nonetheless its insertion in the National Recovery Act was a major turning point in business/labor relations.

### Wagner Act (1935)

After the Supreme Court ruled the NRA unconstitutional in 1935, that part of the bill dealing with unions was revived and strengthened in a new piece of separate legislation. Section 7a evolved into the Wagner Act. The Democratic Party finally realized how important the labor vote had been in recent national elections, and party leaders took steps to solidify that support. Indeed, the coalition between Democrats and unions was one of the key reasons why this party superseded the Republicans as the majority party in the United States for most of the next half century. The alliance between labor and the Democrats weakened in the 1970s, but by the early 1980s it showed signs of renewal after the main labor organization in the nation endorsed formally, for the first time in its history, a Democratic candidate for the Presidency in the fall of 1983.

The Wagner Act, named after the Senator from New York who was its main sponsor, contained much more than a mere statement endorsing the goal of workers to form independent unions in all business firms irrespective of size. The act created the National Labor Relations Board (NLRB) to serve as an enforcement agency. It issued rulings designed to prohibit employers from intimidating organizers or existing members of a union. Upon receipt of a petition signed by 30 percent of a given work force, the NLRB was empowered to call and supervise an election in which workers had the option of voting for representation by the union or the continuance of their nonunion status. If the union won the election by a simple majority, the business firm was directed to recognize it as the official bargaining agent for all employees. The NLRB was also granted the authority to take to federal court any business that failed to "bargain in good faith" with a duly elected union organization. This government agency has served as an influential force in business/labor relations since its creation in 1935.

### Creation of the CIO

Despite increasing evidence that government was shifting its allegiance from business to labor, the American Federation of Labor (AFL) was slow in responding to new opportunities for expansion. The AFL was mainly a collection of independent craft unions composed largely of skilled workers who were employed by small or medium-sized firms. Only one affiliated organization, the United Mine Workers (UMW), was a genuine industrial union—meaning that everyone who worked in the mines, irrespective of skill level, was a member of the same union. The president of the UMW, John L. Lewis, urged other AFL leaders to press on with attempts to organize other industrial unions, but they ignored his pleas. Past efforts to create new industrial unions had failed and ended up costing substantial sums of money. Moreover, many members of the AFL were not enthusiastic about the prospect of bringing hordes of unskilled and semi-skilled workers into the existing organization. A substantial portion of these workers were recent immigrants, minorities, and women, and the AFL had a long history of racism and sexism.

The issue finally came to a head at the annual convention of the AFL in November 1935. The delegates voted against a motion to fund an organizing effort directed at the big business sector. Utterly frustrated, Lewis and other UMW officials walked out and joined with several other dissatisfied independent unions to form a completely new labor organization, the Congress for Industrial Organizations, commonly known by its acronym—CIO.

### Sit-Down Strike at General Motors

The CIO adopted a different strategy in its efforts to establish a permanent labor organization. The AFL had proceeded cautiously in its formative years under Samuel Gompers. But the CIO leadership decided on a bolder plan. The decision was to challenge a few of the very largest business firms, with the anticipation that victories in these confrontations, if they came, would quickly establish the legitimacy and strength of the CIO.

General Motors, which was among the largest employers of assembly line workers, was targeted for an organizing drive. The goal was first to obtain the firm's recognition of the union as the official bargaining agent for all workers in its plants and then to negotiate an improved contract. General Motors, as well as the other major automobile manufacturers, had been successful in fighting unionization for years. The CIO decided to try a new tactic which had only recently been used against recalcitrant employers: the sit-down strike. Instead of leaving their jobs and staying at home, the workers remained at their work stations all day and all night. Their wives and friends periodically brought in food and supplies. The key advantage of this tactic was that it prevented the company from bringing in newly hired workers (scabs) to break the strike.

The location selected for a showdown was a General Motors plant in Flint, Michigan. The time was late December 1936. The firm responded like big firms in similar situations in the past; it appealed to the courts to declare the actions of the strikers illegal. The courts complied, ruling that the seizure of the plant by the workers breached laws relating to the sanctity of private property. The company then asked Michigan Governor Frank Murphy to call out the state militia to enforce the court order.

For the previous half century, government had invariably responded positively to such requests for military assistance. On this occasion, however, Governor Murphy refused to act. General Motors next turned to the federal government for support, but President Roosevelt merely endorsed Governor Murphy's proposal that the two sides meet and work out their differences over the conference table. Finally, the executives at General Motors decided in mid-February 1937 to give up the fight and recognize the United Automobile Workers, which was affiliated with the CIO.

The victory over General Motors was a major event in business/labor relations. The next month U.S. Steel signed an agreement recognizing a CIO union as the bargaining unit for its workers. The tide had turned. The legislative and executive branches of government were now mainly allies of labor, and the courts later came around to a more neutral position—upholding, for example, the constitutionality of the Wagner Act. The aggressive stance of the CIO was instrumental in bringing strong representation to the working masses in oligopolistic industries which had resisted unionization for so long. The rise of industrial unions brought representation to large numbers of women and minorities for the first time. Competition from the CIO stimulated the AFL to reverse its policies and launch new efforts to establish industrial unions of its own.

The American worker benefited substantially. Wages and working conditions were improved because of union activities, but the main alteration was in the balance of power between managers and workers. Previously, individual workers had felt powerless in their work environment. Their grievances could be easily ignored and they were often subject to dismissal without explanation. The union was now there to act as an advocate for worker rights and to serve as an intermediary in solving disputes. The union helped give back to the worker a measure of the dignity and self-esteem which had been undermined by mechanization and the decline of job skills.

Between 1930 and 1940 the number of workers represented by recognized unions more than doubled from 3.6 to 8.9 million. During World War II most of the big employers who had continued to resist unionization in the late 1930s finally acceded to the demands of workers. It was partly in response to governmental pressure to promote business/labor harmony and boost production for the war effort. But probably the main incentive was the desire to avoid disruptions due to strikes during a period when the economy was moving ahead rapidly after a decade of drift. By the end of the war, union membership had climbed to nearly 15 million workers. They accounted for about one quarter of the civilian labor force.

## MERGER OF THE AFL-CIO

In 1955 the AFL and CIO called a truce in their competition to draw workers into their separate organizations. By this date, the AFL had 10 million members and the CIO claimed the allegiance of 6 million workers. The unified organization elected George Meany from the AFL as its president and Walter Reuther from the CIO as first vice-president. There were several reasons for the merger. One belief was that unification would increase labor's political clout in elections and in influencing the policies of state and federal governments. Consolidating the power of big

He was among the founders of the United Auto Workers (UAW), which affiliated with the Congress of Industrial Workers in the mid-1930s. He later became president of the CIO and first vice-president of the merged AFL/CIO in 1955. In a dispute with President George Meany of the AFL/CIO, largely over American policy in Vietnam (which Reuther opposed), he pulled the UAW out of the parent organization in 1968 and created his own independent union. Reuther differed from most other American labor leaders because of his commitment to partisan political action and social reform.

Born to an immigrant family in Wheeling, West Virginia in 1907, Reuther espoused the radical ideas of his European father as a youth. During his twenties, he went to the Soviet Union for over a year, where he worked as a die maker in a primitive automobile plant. Reuther was drawn to the ideals of socialism and communism but he was repulsed by the absence of democracy and political freedom in the Soviet Union. As a leader of the UAW back in the United States, he helped remove known communists from the organization in the 1940s. But Reuther was not so staunchly antisocialist in his attitude toward American foreign policy.

Reuther negotiated a series of excellent wage contracts for auto workers in the 1950s and 1960s. He obtained agreements with cost-of-living escalators. He added pension plans, medical insurance, and other fringe benefits. He was generally successful in playing one of the big three auto makers off against the others—using the strike when necessary to obtain his goals. Reuther died unexpectedly in the crash of a small airplane in 1970.

labor was thus one aim. Both organizations were also concerned about a slowing in the growth of membership. The announcement of the merger corresponded with a renewed emphasis on attempts to increase the size of the labor movement. But expansion proved elusive. Union membership did not keep pace with the growth of population over the next quarter century, and the percentage of workers enrolled in unions fell from one quarter to one fifth of the work force. The decline corresponded to the general shift of labor away from blue-collar and assembly line jobs because of mechanization at home and the competition of foreign goods in the United States market. The union has had some success in organizing workers in the public sector such as teachers, police, fire fighters, bus drivers, and the like. In general, however, the size and influence of the organized labor movement seemed to have stabilized by the 1970s.

## NEW PATTERNS OF EMPLOYMENT: THE SERVICE SECTOR

Occupations can be grouped into three major categories. The primary sector includes workers in agriculture and mining; the secondary sector contains construction and manufacturing; and the tertiary, or service, sector is a broad grouping for all other occupations. From the colonial era until the 1880s, the primary sector, mostly farmers, accounted for over half of the work force. As technological improvements in agriculture reduced the need for so many farm laborers, workers shifted into other occupations. The secondary sector grew rapidly. The percentage of laborers in manufacturing, for example, rose sharply between 1800 and 1870, climbing from around 3 to 19 percent.

Over the last one hundred years, however, the service sector has shown the greatest expansion. In 1870 it accounted for 21 percent of the work force; by 1920 its share had jumped to 42 percent; and by 1980 the service sector claimed the majority of workers, over 60 percent. Although this sector has extremely diverse components, a substantial share of employment is in fields such as transportation, wholesale and retail trade, finance and insurance, government, and health services.

The service sector also includes a wide spectrum of workers in terms of skills and income. The range extends from medical doctors to parking lot attendants. Within the sector several classifications are identifiable. Professional, technical, and managerial personnel are the high income groups, and their share of total employment climbed from 10 to over 20 percent between the turn of the century and the 1970s. Among the common characteristics of this classification was a high level of educational achievement. This demand for more educational opportunities stimulated a large expansion in the number and size of colleges and universities in the post-World War II era.

A second broad classification of workers, typically with lower incomes, included such occupations as office clerks, sales people, household workers, and the like. Between 1900 and 1970 these workers increased their share of total employment from 17 to 36 percent. Clerical workers had among the most rapid rates of increase, multiplying thirteenfold over this time period.

## WOMEN IN THE SERVICE SECTOR

During this century the number of women participating in the work force has risen dramatically. Most of the growth has occurred in the service sector. By 1980 four fifths of employed women were service workers of some variety. An examination of patterns of female employment in two separate markets—manufacturing and clerical—is instructive. In 1900 one third of employed women worked in factories, where they accounted for one fifth of the total manufacturing work force. Although the absolute number of women entering factory work continued to climb and had more than doubled by mid-century, women made up only about 11 percent of the manufacturing work force in 1980.

In the twentieth century clerical work became the main occupation of women. This had not been true in the past. Prior to 1880, the vast majority of clerical work was performed by males. For young men, secretarial and bookkeeping jobs were entry-level positions with the prospect of promotion in a few years to increased responsibilities and salaries. Andrew Carnegie, for example, started his career as personal secretary to the president of the Pennsylvania Railroad Co. in the 1850s, and within a decade, he had assumed important managerial duties. The beginning of the mass substitution of women for men coincided with the introduction of the typewriter into many offices in the late nineteenth century. By the turn of the century one quarter of all clerical jobs were already held by women.

Between 1900 and 1980 the number of clerical jobs expanded very rapidly and women became the primary source of additional labor. By mid-century women held over 60 percent of all clerical positions and the figure rose to over 80 percent in the 1970s. An occupation which had previously held out the possibility of advancement became instead mainly a dead-end job. Sexist traditions in American business and society prevailed, and few women were given an opportunity to move into positions of increased responsibility and power. Those women who were promoted usually became supervisors of other female employees. The thought of working under the direct supervision of a woman holding a management position was abhorrent to most males, irrespective of her qualifications and abilities.

This negative attitude toward women in a business environment began to change in the post-World War II era. Slowly in the 1950s and then fairly rapidly in the 1970s, women made their presence felt in professional, technical, and managerial positions. An increasing number of jobs in our advanced economy required a strong educational background, and millions of women were college graduates. Initially, many educated women became public school teachers, but as demographic forces led to a decline in the number of available positions, women looked for new opportunities in other fields. Among the fields they entered in substantial numbers were medicine, law, and business; professional schools in these disciplines increased substantially the number of women in their entering classes in the 1970s. The new role of women in these fields was reflected in employment patterns. By 1980 over 40 percent of professional and technical workers were women, and they comprised 25 percent of managers and administrators. The growth of the service sector coincided with the rising aspirations of millions of American women for equal opportunities in our economic system.

### Married Women in the Work Force

Another trend in twentieth-century employment patterns was the increased entry of married women into the work force. In urban areas during the nineteenth century, the image of an ideal household included a male who was employed and earned sufficient income to maintain his wife and children. Some married women held jobs outside of the home but it was invariably justified as a financial necessity, not a voluntary choice. In 1900 less than 15 percent of employed women were married.

Since that date the number of married women seeking employment outside of the home has climbed steadily. By the 1920s over one fifth of married women were employed; by the 1940s the figure was over two fifths; and in the 1980s more than one half of all married women held jobs. Social and economic historians have pointed to several factors to explain this change in employment patterns. The growth of the service sector offered more opportunities for women. A decline in the birth rate eased the burden of child care; meanwhile, it became more socially acceptable to place young children in day-care facilities. The decision on the part of husbands and wives to increase their standard of living and acquire more luxuries through the addition of a second steady income was important as well. And finally the desire of women to seek new challenges outside of the home and participate in both the social and monetary benefits of outside employment has had an enormous impact.

Indeed, the unwillingness of the current generation of young professional and managerial women to allow marriage and especially childbearing to interrupt their careers has had a major impact on their progress within the business world. Prior to the 1960s, millions of young women with administrative potential routinely dropped out of the labor market between their mid-twenties and mid-forties to devote their time completely to rearing children. These are the years when individuals usually acquire the managerial skills required to move them into the top administrative positions later in their careers. In the 1980s many young women have

*PEOPLE WHO MATTERED — Helena Rubinstein*

By the middle of the twentieth century, she was generally acknowledged as the world's most successful businesswoman. Her profits came from the sale of creams, lotions, perfumes, and cosmetics at high prices to women seeking beauty and a more youthful appearance. Rubinstein opened a series of salons in major cities around the world, which reinforced her firm's image as a leader in the high glamour field. Her products were sold in first-class department stores and specialty shops, and they were supported by extensive advertising budgets.

Rubinstein's route to the United States was circuitous. She was born in Poland in 1882, one of eight daughters of a middle-class Jewish merchant. At the age of twenty, she traveled to Australia to visit relatives. Importing skin creams from her native Poland, Rubinstein opened a small shop in Melbourne in 1903. Hugely profitable, she soon sought out larger markets in Europe, opening her first salon in London in 1908. After marrying an American chemist, she moved to New York in 1914. Four years later she had salons in New York, Chicago, Boston, Los Angeles, and other metropolitan cities. She promoted not only her products but her persona as the ultimate in international glamour. By purchasing the Rubinstein line of beauty aids, American women were encouraged to participate vicariously in the lifestyle of the rich and famous.

Rubinstein was perhaps the prime example of the successful woman entrepreneur. A workaholic, she was once quoted as follows: "You must be very smart, very clever; in this business you must work twenty-four hours a day and 300 years in a lifetime." She died in 1965.

discovered ways—in cooperation with employers—to combine marriage and mother-hood with a career outside of the home. This major shift in attitudes and prefer-ences is certain to continue to have an impact on our economy and society in future decades.

## BLACKS AND OTHER MINORITY WORKERS

The service sector also attracted large numbers of black and other minority workers, especially over the last three decades. At the beginning of the century, most minority workers were engaged in agriculture. Most still resided in the south-ern states. Spurred on by labor shortages during World War I and almost simulta-neously by the rise of mass production automobile factories, thousands of black families began to move into northern urban areas after 1915. The tightening of immigration laws in the 1920s also cut down the flow of cheap foreign labor into northern markets and gave minorities encouragement to migrate northward. In-deed, the movement of blacks out of the South continued unabated until the dramatic revival of economic conditions in the so-called Sunbelt states during the 1960s and 1970s.

Initially, migrating blacks usually went into factory and other blue-collar work. Since mid-century, however, an increasing percentage of blacks and other minorities have found employment in the service sector. This sector employed over 60 percent of all such workers by 1980—a percentage virtually the same as for the population as a whole. Within the service sector, however, minorities still tend to be concentrated in the lowest paying jobs. In response to better educational opportunities and lessened racial prejudice, substantial numbers of minority women have shifted out of household employment within private homes into clerical posi-tions. Furthermore, because of affirmative action laws and greater upward mobility generally, more minorities of both sexes are currently entering the professional, technical, and managerial fields.

Despite progress in opening up a wider range of occupations to minorities, their income levels and employment patterns still differ significantly from the white majority. Unemployment rates are significantly higher for minority workers. In many large urban areas, for example, the unemployment rate for black teenagers often exceeded 50 percent in the early 1980s. These differences in economic oppor-tunities for the white majority and minorities is partly a reflection of differences in skills and education and partly the heritage of prolonged racial discrimination. The general tendency has been for the gap between whites and minorities to shrink during good economic times and then widen again during recession years.

Certain groups of minority workers made gains more rapidly than others. For example, black women employed full-time all year received only slightly more than one half of the earnings of their white counterparts in 1955. By 1980, however, black women in this category received over 90 percent of the earnings of white women. Younger heads of households of both sexes made significant gains too. For

*PEOPLE WHO MATTERED—Berry Gordy, Jr.*

He founded Motown Records, which became the most successful black enterprise in the nation with sales exceeding $50 million annually in the 1970s. The firm's first gold record was "Shop Around," by Smokey Robinson and the Miracles in 1960. Over the next two decades Gordy placed under contract and developed a host of black singers, including Stevie Wonder, Gladys Knight, Marvin Gaye, and the Temptations. Motown's hottest artists in the 1960s were Diana Ross and the Supremes, with record sales totaling over $12 million, second only to the Beatles. In the 1970s, the Jackson Five became Gordy's most valuable performers; Michael Jackson was the youngest member of that group. In the 1980s Lionel Ritchie became a superstar.

Gordy was born in Detroit in 1929. His father was a plasterer and his mother an insurance agent. They lived in the city's black ghetto. Gordy dropped out of high school to become a prize fighter, but after only three bouts, he was inducted into the army in 1951 at the height of the Korean War. After his discharge he opened a record store in Detroit and went bankrupt two years later. While employed as an assembly-line worker at a Ford factory, Gordy wrote songs as a sideline and recruited local singers to record them. Some of his compositions became hits under the Decca label. Dissatisfied with the way white-owned recording companies were producing his material, Gordy borrowed $700 from his family to establish Motown Records in 1959. Elvis Presley and Bill Haley were acquainting white audiences with "rock-and-roll" music, which had its origins in black culture. Gordy thought he saw an opportunity for entrepreneurship in the recording industry promoting black singers and helping them to gain broader acceptance.

In 1972 Gordy moved the headquarters of Motown from Detroit to Los Angeles and began producing motion pictures. His first film was *Lady Sings the Blues* starring Diana Ross; it was based on the life of Billie Holiday, one of the greatest black singers of jazz music in the 1920s and 1930s. The film won five Academy Award nominations in 1972. Gordy is one of the nation's most financially successful minority business leaders.

family units headed by persons aged 18 to 24, black and white income levels in the late 1970s were nearly identical. But substantial differences in income levels remained for older individuals. From 1950 to 1980 the family income for all minorities rose from around one half to over two thirds of the income of the white majority. Parity was not achieved, but the trend since mid-century was toward a narrowing of the income gap between racial and ethnic groups.

## SELECTED REFERENCES

BARNARD, JOHN. *Walter Reuther and the Rise of the Auto Workers.* Boston: Little, Brown & Co., 1983.
BRODY, DAVID. "The Emergence of Mass-Production Unionism," in J. Braeman

et al. *Change and Continuity in Twentieth-Century America.* New York: Harper & Row, 1964.

DUBOFSKY, MELVYN, and WARREN R. VAN TINE. *John L. Lewis: A Biography.* New York: Quadrangle, 1977.

FILIPPELLI, RONALD. *Labor in the USA: A History.* New York: Knopf, 1984.

FINE, SIDNEY. *Sitdown: The General Motors Strike of 1936–1937.* Ann Arbor: University of Michigan Press, 1969.

FREEMAN, RICHARD. "The Evolution of the American Labor Market, 1948–80," in M. Feldstein. *The American Economy in Transition.* Chicago: University of Chicago Press, 1980.

GREEN, JAMES R. *The World of the Worker: Labor in Twentieth-Century America.* New York: Hill and Wang, 1980.

KESSLER-HARRIS, ALICE. *Out to Work: A History of Wage-Earning Women in the United States.* New York: Oxford University Press, 1982.

ROTELLA, ELYCE. "The Transformation of the American Office: Changes in Employment and Technology," *Journal of Economic History* (1981), 51–58.

# CHAPTER TWENTY
# THE RISE OF BIG GOVERNMENT

For three centuries after the first English settlement at Jamestown in 1607, this country had a tradition of small and limited government. In the twentieth century that tradition was significantly altered. Government revenues and expenditures rose rapidly. At the federal level, defense and social welfare accounted for most of the spending increase. Meanwhile, state and local governments funded a steady expansion in the educational and highway systems. By 1980 total government expenditures were responsible for over one third of gross national product (GNP). Big government had become the nation's largest economic enterprise.

## STATE AND LOCAL SPENDING

When most people talk about the growth of government in recent decades, they usually have in mind the federal level. But state and local governments were important too, and their role in the economy has expanded as well. Between 1900 and 1975, state and local governments increased their share of GNP from 5 percent to 14 percent.

The main area for increased expenditures at the local and state level was education. Government spending on education climbed from just over 1 percent of GNP in 1900 to about 6 percent in the 1970s; over 90 percent of the funds were provided by state and local units. Over this century the average length of schooling for the general population has risen from six to twelve years. Expenditures for education climbed from one fifth to over one third of state and local budgets. Much of the additional money went for the support of vast systems of community colleges and state universities, which expanded rapidly in the post-World War II period.

Another area of increased spending was for highways and roads. The popularity of the automobile after 1910 led to public demand for improved roadways. By the 1920s, up to one quarter of state and local budgets were devoted to building new roads and upgrading old ones. The federal government assumed the financial responsibility for building a system of interstate highways beginning in the 1950s. Although the absolute amount of dollars spent on streets and highways continued to rise after mid-century, this category of expenditures took a declining share of total revenues. By the 1970s such costs accounted for less than 10 percent of state and local budgets.

A third spending category which increased over the course of the twentieth century was public welfare. The expenditure of tax funds for charitable purposes can be traced back to American colonial cities. Nonetheless, programs to provide regular financial resources on a large scale to individuals without jobs or steady incomes have their origins in the Great Depression. Between the late 1920s and mid-1930s, public welfare jumped from a mere 2 percent of state and local budgets to 13 percent. Since that date public welfare has accounted for 8 to 15 percent of total expenditures. The divorce rate accelerated after mid-century, and the number of unmarried, teenage mothers deciding to keep their children also rose. The bulk of welfare funds went to unmarried women and their children at home.

The burden of financing welfare costs did not fall completely on state and local taxpayers since the federal government has provided grants-in-aid for such purposes since the 1930s. Indeed, by the 1950s federal grants in the aggregate were great enough to cover the entire cost of public welfare. This arrangement is one example of cooperation between different levels of government; in this case the federal level provided the funds while state and local governments performed the administrative services.

The ratio of state and local versus federal government spending has changed considerably during the twentieth century. In 1900 state and local expenditures were more than three times greater, which reflects the limited role of the national government in the economy at that time. With the exception of 1918 and 1919, when the cost of equipping the American army during World War I caused federal expenditures to jump ninefold in a period of two years, state and local governments had budgets up to two times greater than their federal counterpart until the 1930s. During World War II, national expenditures for military purposes again skyrocketed. The outbreak of the Cold War between the United States and the Soviet Union in the late 1940s dictated the continuance of high defense expenditures. In 1950 the federal budget was double the size of state and local governments. Between mid-century and 1975, state and local budgets rose slightly faster and climbed to 80 percent of the federal total. Big government was not centered merely in Washington, D.C., but could be found in state capitals, courthouses, and city halls across the nation.

## STATE AND LOCAL REVENUES

The sources of state and local revenues have undergone several changes during this century. In 1900 the property tax was the primary source of funds, providing 90 percent of revenues for city and county units and about half of the revenues for state governments. The importance of property taxes decreased somewhat over the decades, but they continued to generate over 80 percent of the funds for local governments in the 1970s. In a few metropolitan areas where many people worked in a core city but resided in outlying suburbs—New York, for example—income taxes were sometimes imposed on all persons employed within city limits in order to assist in the provision of essential services.

At the state level the shift has been away from property taxes toward sales and income taxes. Since these two sources tend to increase and decrease in unison with movements in the general level of economic activity, state revenues have become subject to more fluctuation than in past decades. To lessen the degree of unpredictability, the federal government increased substantially its contributions to state budgets. During the presidency of Richard Nixon in the early 1970s, Congress passed a comprehensive revenue sharing bill, which provided for large block grants to the states. Ironically, when the national government was running modest deficits during the subsequent administration of President Jimmy Carter, the states had surpluses which offset up to three quarters of the federal red ink. By the 1980s funds allocated by the federal government rivaled sales taxes as the major source of revenue in many states.

## FEDERAL SPENDING

During the twentieth century the budget of the federal government has grown from under 3 percent of GNP to over 20 percent. Government purchases of goods and services, including defense costs, have accounted for less than one half of the percentage growth. The largest expansion has come in what are called transfer payments, which were a relatively small item in 1900 but had climbed to approximately 12 percent of GNP by the 1980s.

What are transfer payments? They represent a redistribution of current income from certain groups of citizens to other groups of citizens. The government acts as an intermediary, collecting funds from some taxpayers and then *transferring* the money to other recipients. Social security and Medicare are prime examples of programs involving transfer payments. These social welfare programs were designed to help provide income security for the retired and disabled and to offer protection to senior citizens for the high cost of health care.

The social security program was instituted in 1935. At first benefits were modest. In 1940 payments to individuals accounted for a mere 4 percent of the federal budget. In the post-World War II era the social security program continued to grow—steadily through the 1960s and then spectacularly in the 1970s. Five factors were important in the expansion of social security costs. First, the system expanded to cover new groups of workers—farmers, teachers, the self-employed, and others. Second, over the years more individuals became eligible for benefits simply as a result of meeting the minimum annual requirement for participation in the program. Third, the life span of Americans continued to lengthen because of improvements in medical science and health care so that participants collected benefits over a longer period of time. Fourth, the minimum age to begin the collection of cash benefits was lowered from 65 to 62—although the recipient choosing early retirement had to accept reduced monthly payments. Finally, during the 1970s Congress agreed to increase benefits on a fixed schedule which exceeded the inflation rate. Between 1970 and 1980 social security funding rose from $43 to $180 billion, increasing at an annual rate of 15 percent. Its share of the overall federal budget rose from 23 percent in 1970 to 34 percent in 1980. In the mid-1970s social security alone actually exceeded (temporarily) defense as the most costly item on the list of federal expenditures.

A second social welfare program which had a major impact on the federal budget was Medicare. It provided funds for paying medical bills incurred by senior citizens. Typically a large percentage of a given individual's lifetime medical expenses are incurred in the last year of life. Previously, the high cost of modern medical care had fallen on individuals and their families and had often depleted their savings. Congress enacted the Medicare bill in 1965 during the administration of President Lyndon Johnson. Between 1965 and 1970 funds allocated for health programs climbed from $2 to $13 billion. In 1984 the figure passed $90 billion, and expenditures on health programs had become in only fifteen years the third largest item in the federal budget.

In 1975 transfer payments combined exceeded for the first time in American history expenditures for goods and services. A sweeping revolution has occurred since 1930 in terms of the role of the federal government in the economy and in society generally. One of its key functions had become to serve as financial protector for the retired, elderly, and disadvantaged. What has accounted for this change in the role of government? Ultimately government is very responsive to the demands of citizens for services when those demands are articulated by a large and forceful block of voters. As a result of a declining birth rate and greater longevity, the percentage of the United States population aged 50 and above has risen sharply since mid-century. This group has traditionally had a high rate of voter participation in Congressional elections. Moreover, the expansion in social welfare has occurred with the acquiescence at least, if not the whole-hearted support, of younger voters. Many of them were relieved to know that government had assumed a major share of the financial burden, actual or potential, of caring for aging relatives. They knew too that, in time, their own generation would have the opportunity to benefit from similar services, and this knowledge made them feel more secure about the future.

## DEFENSE EXPENDITURES

Until the middle of the twentieth century, the United States had a long tradition of maintaining a small peacetime army. Military costs accelerated during wars, but then fell back sharply in postwar eras. This sequence prevailed after the Civil War, the Spanish-American War, and World War I. For a few years at the end of World War II, it appeared that there would be no deviation from past experience. A realization about the implications of the atomic bomb and United States-Soviet rivalry in the world arena, however, soon changed the strategy for national defense. Following a heating up of the Cold War with the Soviet Union in the late 1940s, the United States adopted the policy of spending substantial sums for defense on an annual basis.

Except for the war years 1916 to 1919, the United States rarely expended as much as one percent of GNP on defense over the first four decades of this century. During many peacetime years the navy, which had ships deployed in both the Atlantic and Pacific Oceans, received more funds than the army. Indeed, the width of the oceans was for the United States its first line of defense, for the country had no threatening neighbors along its borders. The United States itself was considered safe from invasion, and only its overseas possessions and territories in the Caribbean Sea and Pacific Ocean were thought vulnerable to possible military attack. Indeed, when the Japanese initiated hostilities in 1941, the attack came in Hawaii—then still a territory, not a state—rather than against the mainland. None of the nation's adversaries in World Wars I and II ever made any serious plans to invade the continental United States.

## THE ATOM BOMB AND THE COLD WAR

Beginning with a steady build-up of the military following the German invasion of Poland and the outbreak of World War II, defense expenditures rose from just over one percent of GNP in 1939 to about two fifths of GNP in 1943, 1944, and 1945. By the late 1940s, military spending had fallen to 4 to 5 percent of GNP, but it dropped no further. Disputes with the Russians about the fate of Eastern Europe kept American troops stationed in the western sector of Germany and in other parts of Western Europe. A complete withdrawal of troops, which had occurred soon after the end of the First World War, never took place in the post-World War II era.

A second factor which held up military spending was associated with the development of the atomic bomb (and later the hydrogen bomb). The existence of such awesome power for destruction meant that any further war might conceivably last only a few days and lead to the total annihilation of the vanquished nation. The only sure protection seemed to be constant preparedness. National security came to rest on the maintenance of extensive systems to deliver quickly these lethal bombs to targets in the Soviet Union. Initially, the reliance was on manned bombers, but subsequently the emphasis shifted to missiles launched from land bases or submarines. After the Russians exploded an atomic bomb in 1949, the two superpowers quickly entered an unending competition for the development and deployment of the most advanced and sophisticated weapons systems.

The outbreak of the Korean War caused defense expenditures to rise to 13 percent of GNP in the early 1950s. After the end of the fighting in 1953, defense spending remained high. For the ten-year period spanning 1955 to 1965, defense spending ranged from 8 to 10 percent of GNP—an unprecedented figure for this nation during peacetime. It was during this period that President Dwight Eisenhower, who had formerly been the supreme commander of allied forces in Europe during World War II, warned in his farewell television address about the potential danger of allowing citizens to be controlled and manipulated by an avaricious "military-industrial complex."

The Vietnam War, which engaged United States troops from 1965 to 1973, was unique because it was fought without increasing defense spending as a percentage of GNP. Indeed, the winding down of American involvement in Vietnam coincided with the beginning of a ten-year decline in the real cost of defense. By 1976 national security took only 5 percent of GNP, the lowest share since mid-century. The election of President Ronald Reagan in 1980, based in part on a platform to boost defense expenditures, brought about an increase in military spending of approximately 35 percent in real terms by 1984. These sharp increases pushed defense expenditures up to around 7 percent of GNP, a figure higher than those prevailing in the late 1970s but lower than those in the 1950s and 1960s.

## LEVEL OF FEDERAL SPENDING

One of the nation's greatest literary figures, Mark Twain, once remarked, "Everyone complains about the weather; but no one does anything about it." An analogy can be drawn about the growth of the federal budget. Politicians have spoken repeatedly about the importance of efficiency in government and the need to limit the role of government in the lives of citizens, yet that role has increased for decades. Aggregate spending has risen irrespective of whether Congress or the Presidency was in the hands of Democrats or Republicans, liberals or conservatives. By the mid-1980s federal government spending accounted for approximately 25 percent of GNP, an increase of around 10 percent over the level prevailing two decades earlier.

Why do government budgets keep growing, and is such growth unusual for a technologically advanced society? The answer to the latter part of this question is no; other nations with comparable income levels typically channel even higher

percentages of their annual output into governmental services. In the leading economies in Western Europe, government expenditures on goods and services or transfer
payments are on the order of 40 to 60 percent of GNP. Thus, by shifting a larger
share of its economic life out of the private sector and into the government, the
United States has followed a pattern well established by other countries with similar living standards and political values.

Now to return to the first part of our question—what has caused the federal
budget to grow in size year after year. The key words are a search for security. The
search for military security in an era of hydrogen bombs and missiles that can reach
their targets in a matter of minutes has led to a strategy of constant preparedness.
Substantial defense budgets have been a constant fact of life since the entry of the
United States into World War II in 1941.

The second search has been to provide security for senior citizens: income security and the security of knowing that up-to-date medical facilities were available
without overriding considerations of cost. An aging population profile and demands
for more generous benefits have dictated an expanding role of government in this
sphere of American society. Some critics of social security and Medicare have
argued that private insurance and retirement programs could provide the same (or
a higher) level of benefits to citizens and thereby lessen the role of government.
While such alternative proposals appear technically feasible, their advocacy has
proven politically unpopular.

A third form of security has been public assistance to the unemployed and
households with dependent children and no steady sources of income.

## FEDERAL REVENUES

The rise in spending at the national level was accompanied by a large increase in tax
revenues. Federal tax receipts rose from 3 percent of GNP in 1900 to 18 percent in
the mid-1980s. The sources of revenue changed substantially, too. The shift was
away from a heavy reliance on customs duties (taxes on imports) and excise taxes—
on tobacco, alcohol, and a few other products—to an emphasis on income taxes and
payroll taxes. Although revenues rose dramatically, they still failed to climb as
swiftly as expenditures; additional funds came from borrowing, especially during
wartime and in recessionary years after 1930.

## TARIFFS AND EXCISE TAXES

The federal government relied primarily on revenues from tariffs and excise taxes
from the time of the adoption of the Constitution in 1789 until the American entry
into World War I in 1917, a period of over 125 years. Both were indirect taxes in
the sense that consumers paid them in the process of buying imported goods or
designated items such as tobacco or liquor. The tax was disguised, or hidden, in the

price of the goods. With defense costs generally low and few social programs to support, Americans paid very low taxes relative to income in comparison to citizens of European countries. Mild taxation by the central government was a heritage of the colonial era.

## BACKGROUND FOR THE INCOME TAX

Income taxes were first imposed by the federal government during the Civil War. They were enacted as one of a series of temporary measures, necessary because of the wartime emergency. The rate structure was progressive, meaning that the rate was not uniform but rose in stages as income increased. The initial rate in 1862 was 3 percent on income over $600 and 5 percent on income above $10,000. In 1865, the last year of the war, the income tax accounted for 18 percent of total federal revenues. About 450,000 returns were filed in 1866, which represented about one out of every 15 persons gainfully employed. The tax remained on the books for a few years after the war but at reduced rates. In 1872, the last year the tax was applied, the rate was no longer progressive, but a flat 2.5 percent on all income over $2,000.

In the early 1870s, some political leaders tried to retain the levy on income as a permanent feature of the tax system. They argued that it was the only federal tax based on the "ability to pay." But conservative critics asserted that the tax was "socialistic" and thus inappropriate for the United States.

The income tax expired in the early 1870s, but the debate over its legitimacy raged on. Agrarian interests in the southern and western states continued to push for reinstatement. They claimed that the existing system of tariffs and excise taxes imposed too large a burden on farmers and that income taxes would force urban residents, especially in the big northeastern cities, to assume a fairer share of the cost of government. They also wanted to apply the tax to corporations as well as individuals. As in the colonial era, the debate was as much about the principles of fair taxation as about the actual economic impact on specific groups. Federal budgets were very modest from 1865 to the end of the century, with pensions to Civil War veterans the largest single item over the last fifteen years.

## INCOME TAX OF 1894

The idea of an income tax was revived in 1894. Congress had under consideration a bill for reform of the tariff—a legislative perennial—and the income levy was attached as a rider. In addition to arguments about the equity of taxing incomes, especially high incomes, proponents asserted that the government needed more funds to make up for the loss of revenues from lower tariffs. The new tax applied to both individuals and corporations; the rate was a flat 2 percent on all incomes over $4,000. It was expected to boost federal revenues by roughly 20 percent.

The income tax of 1894 was never collected, however, because the Supreme Court ruled it unconstitutional the following year. Lawyers attacked the new law on two fronts. First, they raised the old bugaboo that the income tax was inherently socialistic, meaning that it discriminated against the wealthy. The second major argument was more technical. The Constitution of 1789 stated that Congress could not impose direct taxes (generally understood in the eighteenth century as head taxes) unless they were apportioned to the states according to population. Since the distribution of income across the nation failed to coincide with the distribution of population, the Supreme Court, in a 5 to 4 vote, decided that the income tax was a direct levy and hence unconstitutional. This ruling merely stirred the ire of advocates of tax reform who thereafter vowed that subsequent efforts would be focused on the legalization not merely of an income tax, but of one with a progressive rate structure.

## SIXTEENTH AMENDMENT

The pressure for an income tax never subsided. Finally, financial conservatives, among them President William Howard Taft, concluded that acceptance of the measure was necessary in order to thwart demands for even more radical changes in American society. The Socialist Party was growing; its presidential candidate, Eugene Debs, attracted 6 percent of the vote in the national election of 1912— a high point for the party. A new round of tariff reduction in 1909 provided the opportunity for new initiatives. Congress approved a constitutional amendment, the sixteenth, for submission to the states for ratification. It was designed to counter the Supreme Court's ruling of 1895 by making the collection of income taxes unrelated to the distribution of population in the states. Meanwhile, an income tax on corporations was passed—but called deceptively an excise tax, imposed for the privilege of conducting business in order to circumvent the court. The rate was a flat 1 percent on all corporate income over $5,000. Taxing corporations was one of the main goals of all the splinter parties challenging the Democrats and Republicans.

By 1913 three fourths of the states had ratified the Sixteenth Amendment, and Congress acted immediately to pass new legislation. The tax structure was progressive, beginning with 1 percent on personal income over $3,000 (at least $25,000 in 1984 prices), 2 percent on amounts above $20,000, rising to a height of 7 percent on all income over $500,000. No exemptions or deductions were allowed; the tax was on gross income. Married couples were given a slight break since the threshold figure for the application of the tax was raised to $4,000 for them. The law required employers to withhold taxes from the salaries of employees and remit the funds periodically to the newly created Bureau of Internal Revenue; the rules on withholding were strengthened in the 1940s.

In its first full year of application in 1914, income taxes provided about 10 percent of total federal revenues. Out of a population of around 95 million, only

350,000 individual returns were filed. Forty-four individuals reported an income higher than one million dollars; taxed at the maximum rate of 7 percent, they paid on average $77,000 to the tax service. But the typical taxpayer paid less than $100.

## IMPACT OF WORLD WARS I AND II

The largest source of revenue during World War I was the income tax. In 1918 income taxes brought in $2.8 billion, or 68 percent of total government revenues. Rates were raised drastically. The minimum rate rose from 1 to 6 percent for individuals and up to 10 percent for corporations; the maximum rate was set at 77 percent for individuals and 65 percent for corporations. The wartime experience revealed the extent to which the income tax was capable of producing substantial revenues for the federal government. After the war rates declined, but income taxes still provided one half of the government's funds during the 1920s.

The income tax was equally important in financing World War II. At the height of the fighting from 1943 to 1945, the levy on income provided three fourths of total revenues. The collection of funds from individuals and corporations were roughly equal. Taxes from all sources paid for about 45 percent of wartime expenses, with the remaining financed by borrowing. The rates on incomes soared. Unmarried persons with incomes above a mere $500 were liable for payment. The minimum rate was 3 percent and it rose in progressive stages up to 91 percent on income above $200,000. Corporate taxes were likewise raised; the minimum rate was 15 percent, but income in certain categories was assessed at rates as high as 60 to 95 percent. Despite the increased rate of taxation, the economy improved so much during the war years that wages rose sufficiently to cover the tax burden and still leave workers with higher real income.

## POSTWAR TO THE PRESENT

The importance of the income tax continued after the end of World War II. Rates dropped somewhat but not as much as in the twenties. The maximum rate on personal income did not fall from 70 to 50 percent until the early 1980s. Meanwhile, rapid inflation during the 1970s pushed more citizens up into higher and higher tax brackets. Revenues from income taxes climbed steadily, rising from $28 billion in 1950 to $315 billion in 1980. They accounted for over 70 percent of federal revenues in the 1950s and over 60 percent in the 1960s and 1970s.

Debates about the equity of the income tax system have persisted over the decades. Virtually every income group—low, middle, and high—has complained about having to assume too large a tax burden. Nonetheless, it seems safe to conclude that the distribution of payments in the 1980s would likely warm the hearts of those nineteenth-century protesters who had argued that ability to pay was an important criterion for the assessment of taxes. Despite a proliferation of tax shelters and other questionable deductions, the progressive rate structure had a tremendous impact. In 1981, for example, just 10 percent of all taxpayers, about 9.5 million individuals and couples with incomes above $38,700, paid 48 percent of all personal income taxes. Their average tax bill was $14,500. In the nineteenth century, the federal tax burden was slight and fell largely on the middle and lower class, but in the twentieth century the cost of government rose substantially and the wealthy classes were forced to shoulder an increasing share of those expenses.

One of the shifts in the distribution of the tax burden in the post-World War II era has occurred in the relationship between individual and corporate income taxes. Corporate taxes continued to rise in an absolute sense, but relative to individual payments they did not keep pace. In the late 1940s the corporate contribution was about 35 percent of total federal revenues; by the 1960s the figure had fallen below 25 percent. In the 1970s corporate taxes contributed only about 15 percent of federal revenues, and in the mid-1980s the share dropped under 10 percent.

Why had the corporate income tax declined in importance so rapidly over the last quarter century? First, the corporate rate structure was not very progressive. Although business leaders frequently claimed that tax rates were too steep, the rates at least did not accelerate as profits increased, nor did the typical firm move into higher brackets because of inflation. For most of the period, profits were taxed at a flat 50 percent or thereabouts. The rate drifted down to 46 percent in the early 1980s. Second, corporations persuaded Congress to authorize a series of deductions and credits designed to lower their tax liabilities—for example, the investment tax credit allowed firms to reduce their taxes by up to 10 percent of the cost of new plant and equipment. As a result, the average corporation incurred an effective tax rate of only 16 percent on its earnings in 1982.

In light of the declining contribution of corporate income taxes to federal revenues, some critics of the present system have proposed the complete elimination of income taxes on corporations. They suggest two potential benefits. First, corporations treat taxes simply as one cost of doing business and their elimination should lead (in theory) to lower prices for consumers generally. Second, the incentives to reducing tax levels have produced a host of accountants and lawyers who devote their careers to seeking methods of tax avoidance. Such work is unproductive in the sense that it contributes nothing to the output of useful goods and services. Moreover, critics allege that business decisions are influenced too much by short-run tax considerations rather than long-term strategies. Although such arguments have considerable merit, it seems unlikely that citizens will soon agree to allow giant enterprises to escape taxation completely, because it contradicts their sense of fairness and equity.

A more promising approach advocated by some reformers would link the curtailment of deductions and credits to a sharp decrease in rates. The same principle could also be applied to individual returns. Reduced rates on gross income (rather than net income) could be established to yield the same amount of revenue as under existing regulations. Among the opponents of such a simplified system are professional tax specialists who have a vested interest in the perpetuation of a complex and complicated system.

## SOCIAL SECURITY TAXES

The fastest growing source of revenue since 1935 has been social security taxes. They are imposed on both employees and employers. The rates were set at 3 percent on gross wages up to $3,000 per individual in 1937. By the late 1930s social security taxes accounted for about 5 percent of total federal revenue. Benefits were consistently lower than collections so that the social security administration was able to accumulate a sizable trust fund over the years. For decades these funds were used to help in financing the national debt.

Since the implementation of the program, the retirement benefits have been periodically liberalized, and in the 1960s Medicare and Medicaid were added. To cover increased costs, the rates were raised, and the wages on which taxes were applied climbed too. By the early 1980s the rate had passed 6.5 percent, or 13 percent for employee and employer combined, on wages and salaries up to $32,000. For a married couple earning less than $16,500 in 1982, social security taxes associated with their employment were a greater sum than they typically paid in income taxes. The contribution of social security taxes to the federal budget has likewise continued to climb. Its share rose to 16 percent in the 1950s, 24 percent in the 1960s, and 33 percent in the 1970s.

The social security program faced a financial crisis in the late 1970s and early 1980s because revenues failed to keep pace with benefit payments. Moreover, since the number of retirees was growing relative to the number of employed persons as a result of demographic forces, projections of trends indicated that the gap would widen by the late twentieth century. The first year revenue proved inadequate was 1976. To make up for the $3 billion deficit, the social security administration began to draw down the trust fund which had accumulated since the 1930s and had reached $48 billion in 1975. Persistent deficits had reduced the trust fund balance to under $20 billion by the early 1980s. President Reagan appointed a special commission to develop a plan to rescue the program. Its recommendations to slow the rise in benefits and to increase social security taxes in stages over the next half century were adopted by Congress in 1983.

Another important change in the mid-1970s was that social security taxes paid by corporations exceeded, for the first time, their income tax liabilities. Indeed, by 1982 corporate social security contributions accounted for 17 percent of federal revenues versus only 8 percent from taxes on business profits. Viewed from this perspective, corporations were responsible for about one quarter of federal revenues in the 1980s compared to roughly one third in the 1950s. Their relative role as a source of government income has diminished, but not by as much as reference merely to the income tax component alone indicates.

## NATIONAL DEBT

A portion of the rise of big government in this century was financed by an increase in the national debt. During the nineteenth century, the nation experienced long periods when the nation's debt was very small relative to the size of the economy. Indeed, in the 1830s the federal government actually paid off completely its outstanding debt—an unprecedented accomplishment for a developing modern economy. Large increases in the size of the debt were associated almost exclusively with wars until the 1970s and 1980s. For example, the debt rose from a mere $90 million in 1861 up to $2.2 billion in 1865. Borrowing during the Civil War years provided three fourths of the funds required for financing military and other government expenses.

The same reliance on borrowing occurred during World Wars I and II. On the eve of World War I, the national debt stood at just under one billion dollars; by 1919 the sum totalled over $25 billion. Again, increases in the national debt had provided the funding for about 75 percent of the government's expenditures from 1916 to 1919. At the end of the war, the aggregate debt stood at about one quarter of GNP. The scale of borrowing during World War II was even greater. Borrowing accounted for around 55 percent of federal funding during the war years. The debt rose from $40 to $280 billion between 1940 and 1945. It was actually a sum one third greater than GNP in 1946.

From the end of World War II until the 1970s, the size of the national debt remained relatively stable. The government ran deficits in more years than surpluses, but the net addition to the debt was quite modest. The Korean and Vietnam Wars were funded largely by tax revenues and did not require massive debt financing. The national debt as a percentage of GNP fell steadily; by 1974 it had dropped to barely over one third of GNP, a percentage lower than on the eve of World War II.

Since the mid-1970s, however, the downward trend has been reversed. For the first time in the nation's history, the government faced massive peacetime deficits year after year, some unanticipated and others deliberately planned. The deficit rose by nearly one trillion dollars between 1974 and 1984, rising from $486 billion to over $1.4 trillion. By 1982 the national debt had climbed to 37 percent of GNP and by 1984 to over 40 percent of that figure. Huge deficits were incurred in this period, in part because of President Reagan's pledge to cut taxes and raise defense expenditures and in part to stimulate the lagging United States economy. Planned deficits on the order of nearly $200 billion annually in the mid-1980s signified at least the tacit acceptance of the principles of Keynesian economics by both major American political parties. Policy makers expected to get the economy moving ahead again at a rapid pace so that deficits would decline and the national debt would grow at a slower pace than future increases in GNP.

Is the size of the national debt in the mid-1980s too great? Would its further growth threaten the viability of the United States economic system? The historical evidence suggests no. From World War II until 1970 the national debt was always more than 40 percent of GNP. At the beginning of the 1960s, a decade of outstanding gains in output, the debt was still above 60 percent of GNP. How high the debt might be allowed to rise before undermining the economy we cannot determine with any degree of certainty, but we can point out that the heights reached during World War II, one third greater than GNP, did not stifle the performance of the economy in the postwar decades.

## SELECTED REFERENCES

*Economic Report of the President.*    Annual reports to the Congress. Washington, D.C.: Government Printing Office, 1977–1984.

RANSOM, ROGER.    "In Search of Security: The Growth of Government Spending in the United States, 1902–1970," in R. Ransom, R. Sutch, and G. Walton, eds. *Explorations in the New Economic History.* New York: Academic Press, 1982.

RATNER, SIDNEY.    *Taxation and Democracy in America.* New York: John Wiley, 1967.

STUDENSKI, PAUL, and HERMAN KROOSS.    *Financial History of the United States.* New York: McGraw-Hill, 1963.

# CHAPTER TWENTY-ONE
# THE AMERICAN ECONOMY
## *A Historical Overview*

This book has traced the American economy from its origins nearly four centuries ago up until the 1980s. For the most part, it has been an account of the successes of American workers, entrepreneurs, and political leaders in forging a strong economy, which provided an advancing standard of living for citizens. Along the way, there have been some shortcomings too; the most dire was the treatment of black slaves, who had strict limitations placed on their ability to enjoy the benefits of an improving economy. Even today minorities and women still suffer from racism and sexism in many work environments. No one can state that American capitalism has performed perfectly in creating free and open markets in which all participants have had equal opportunities. Yet in comparison with the course of economic development in other parts of the globe, the United States can point to an outstanding record of accomplishment in most areas.

There are two general methods of measuring economic progress in a society. In the aggregate we measure the performance of the nation as a whole; the most common measurement is gross national product. At the individual level, on the other hand, we measure income per capita and try to translate that figure into living standards for individuals. On both scores, the American economy has performed admirably.

## GROSS NATIONAL PRODUCT

During the seventeenth century (the first century of English settlement in North America), the size of the economy remained very small. The total population of Europeans and Africans did not exceed 250,000 until 1700. At that time these sparsely settled colonies had a gross output that was little more than 4 percent of England's. By the time of its separation from England in the 1770s, however, the population had grown to around 2.5 million, and the United States had a GNP approaching nearly 40 percent of the English total. This new nation was already rising rapidly as a force in the world economy.

Population continued to expand and so too did the productivity of capital investments and labor. New technologies affected agriculture, transportation, and industry. Somewhere around 1860 the United States bypassed Great Britain to become the world's largest national economy. It is a lead this nation has never relinquished. By the end of the nineteenth century, the United States alone accounted for around one quarter of gross economic activity around the world.

The United States' role in the global economy continued to expand during the first half of the twentieth century. Heavy immigration from eastern and southern Europe augmented what was already rapid natural population growth between 1890 and 1910. New technologies based increasingly on the application of scientific discoveries boosted productivity in the factory and on the farm. Meanwhile, other industrializing nations in Europe, plus Japan in Asia, experienced temporary setbacks in their economic development because of the devastation of two world wars. The United States suffered no serious physical damage during these two major military conflicts, and indeed their occurrence actually stimulated the American economy. By 1950 the United States was generating over one third of the world's output of goods and services. The immediate post-World War II era was the high point for the United States in terms of its dominant position in the global economy.

In the decades after mid-century, the United States economy performed reasonably well by historical standards, but many other nations moved ahead at an even faster pace. Japan is a case in point. In 1950 the Japanese economy generated a mere 8 percent of the American GNP, but by 1975 it was 30 percent of our GNP and gaining ground year after year. The nations in capitalist Western Europe which had suffered during the war produced, in combination, about three quarters as much as the United States in 1950. After reconstruction, however, most of the countries in Western Europe (Britain was one exception) enjoyed vigorous economic growth. By the mid-1970s this region had reached par with the United States in terms of aggregate output.

The Soviet Union, under a communist government, also improved its position relative to the United States in the postwar decades. In 1950 the Soviet economy was about one third as large as the United States economy. By the 1980s, however, Soviet output was slightly more than one half of the United States figure. By devoting up to 15 percent of its total resources to the military sector, the Soviet Union was able to match or even exceed defense spending in the United States. Countries in other parts of the world gained vis-à-vis the United States in the period from 1950 to 1980. Numerous Latin American, Middle Eastern, and African nations claimed larger shares of the global economy.

The net result was that the United States witnessed relative economic decline in the third quarter of the twentieth century. By 1980 this nation accounted for around one fourth of global output—about the same relative position as at the beginning of the century. For a period of 350 years the United States had constantly improved its position vis-à-vis other nations. As a result Americans developed attitudes of superiority in virtually all matters related to business and economics. Thus the realization and acceptance of the sudden reversal of that trend over the past three decades has been a difficult adjustment for many Americans to make. No longer on the upswing, many American industries, long considered the most advanced anywhere, found themselves on the defensive in meeting foreign competition overseas and at home. Steel and automobiles were among the most visible in this category.

Despite the end of an era of American economic omnipotence, there are good reasons for citizens not to despair about the future. American firms have assumed leadership in the high-tech fields. The growth rates of rival nations slowed markedly after the energy crisis in the early 1970s, which affected Japan and Western Europe much more than the United States. The communist nations in Eastern Europe, including the Soviet Union, were no longer advancing at the same rate as before. Moreover, the United States still retained a wide lead in gross output over any other single nation, including the Soviet Union and Japan. Indeed, in the absence of some completely unforeseeable event—such as nuclear war—the American position of leadership in the global economy appears safe for the next quarter century.

## LIVING STANDARDS

Americans have enjoyed very high living standards relative to other citizens of the globe throughout their history. That fact explains in large part why we call this book *A Prosperous People*. The only exception to this generalization came during the earliest years of settlement before farmland was cleared and put into steady production. The first generation of settlers sometimes had difficulty adjusting to the unfamiliar climate, and death rates were high. But after the initial two or three decades, the living conditions of our colonial ancestors improved substantially. Eventually they laid claim to probably the highest level of material and physical welfare any human beings ever had experienced within the constraints of an agricultural-commercial economy.

The main reason for such affluence in a preindustrial setting was the large amount of land available for individual farmers. Most farms in North America were over 100 acres and much of the land was extremely fertile. American farmers easily grew enough food to feed their families, and they had surpluses to fatten livestock and sell in the marketplace. Moreover, the majority of white settlers owned their farms, whereas in most other societies around the world, farmers were generally tenants. Because colonial Americans were well fed and lived mainly in rural areas, devastating diseases did not sweep across the landscape periodically and wipe out a large fraction of the population. The air was clean; the rivers and streams were generally pure; and cheap energy, in the form of abundant firewood, was readily available in most places. Death rates for adults and children were low compared to the rest of the world. In fact, the quality of life in colonial America was superior to that in most nations on the Asian mainland and in Africa in the 1980s.

The single most important indicator of colonial well-being was the American diet. Food was plentiful and there was a wide variety of grains, vegetables, and fruits available. Meat consumption, mainly pork because it could be preserved more easily than beef in the absence of refrigeration, was already high; some historians of United States nutrition put personal meat consumption at 200 lbs. annually—a level hardly different from today.

From the colonial era to the present, American food production and consumption have remained the envy of the world. Preferences for foodstuffs have changed over the last two centuries, but the typical American diet has always been nutritious. Food production was invariably adequate not only to provide fulsome meals for the domestic population but also to provide substantial surpluses for export overseas. The cost of food has taken a declining share of family income over this period—at present the figure is around 15 percent. Moreover, American agriculture has become so efficient that under 4 percent of the work force is currently engaged in farming compared to up to 85 percent in the colonial era. Agriculture has been one of the great American success stories.

Housing was another area in which colonial Americans ranked high on a comparative scale. The chief building material was wood, and it was plentiful and inexpensive. Wood was simultaneously the main source of energy within the home, and its availability kept American living quarters fairly well heated in the winter months. Over the last several centuries, the quality of housing has continued to improve. The number of people in households declined while the square footage of homes increased. The living space occupied by each person has risen enormously; millions of people inhabit single-person households—something rare until the twentieth century. The typical American remains a homeowner, or (increasingly in the 1980s) a condominium owner, whereas in most other societies, including others with high income levels, most citizens are renters rather than owners. Meanwhile, new forms of energy have provided even better heating plus electricity to power light bulbs, a myriad of labor-saving home appliances, and air conditioning for hot summer months.

In the colonial era the horse and wagon provided local transportation, and ships were the only effective mode of transport over long distances. News traveled no faster than goods. The nineteenth century witnessed numerous improvements in these sectors of the economy. Roads were much improved; turnpikes were built in some states. The railroad provided year-round transportation both for persons and products. The telegraph, operational in the 1840s, divorced the transmission of news (and prices) from the slow movement of tangible goods.

The twentieth century saw the coming of the automobile and airplane. Americans enjoyed the convenience of driving wherever they wanted to go whenever they wanted to, and until the oil crisis of the 1970s, they rode in comfortable cars with high-powered, gas-guzzling engines. Meanwhile, telephones became common in American homes, and individuals could converse with businesses and friends quickly and cheaply across town, in other states, and increasingly over the oceans. No other country could boast such widespread ownership of automobiles and access to telephones.

Our colonial ancestors, it turns out, were a fairly hearty and healthy people. Many lived into their sixties and seventies. Probably the worst aspect of the primitive system of medical care was that so many women feared pregnancy because the death rate associated with childbirth, both for mother and infant, was very high. Mild infections in both men and women could also develop into fatal illnesses. Medical progress in the nineteenth and twentieth centuries was substantial, and health care was increasingly accessible to the whole population. Childbirth ceased to be so dangerous; antibiotic drugs and vaccines became effective in fighting infectious diseases. The medical care enjoyed by Americans in the 1980s was, according to several measures, not the best in the world, since some other advanced countries ranked higher in overall quality, but the facilities available were nonetheless very effective in maintaining good health.

How much have American living standards improved over the last two centuries? The price data is not perfect and the measurement systems do not fully take into account improvements in the quality of certain products, but generally speaking, living standards in the United States in the 1980s are probably about eight to ten times higher than in the colonial era.

American world leadership in per capita income, which probably began in the eighteenth century, was sustained up until very recent times. As recently as 1950, personal incomes were about 2½ times greater than in Western Europe, then the nearest competitor in the race for economic affluence. In the 1950s and 1960s, however, the gap narrowed significantly. Some countries in Europe experienced booming economies. In the mid-1970s both Sweden and Switzerland passed the United States in per capita income. When the price for crude oil skyrocketed after 1973, several small states in the Middle East, among them Kuwait and the United Emirates, reported per capita incomes 2 or 3 times higher than in any other nation. The United States was no longer the world leader that it had been for almost 250 years, but Americans still enjoyed one of the highest living standards around the globe.

Despite the problems of meeting foreign competition and overcoming persistent recessionary periods, Americans in the 1980s were still a prosperous people with a long tradition of economic successes.

## SELECTED REFERENCES

PERKINS, EDWIN J. *The World Economy in the Twentieth Century.* Cambridge, Mass.: Schenckman Publishing, 1983.

ROSTOW, W.W. *The World Economy: History and Prospect.* Austin, Texas: University of Texas Press, 1978.

SCHEIBER, HARRY. "America in the World Economy," in G. Lyons, ed. *America: Purpose and Power.* Chicago: University of Chicago Press, 1965.

WOODRUFF, WILLIAM. *America's Impact on the World: A Study of the Role of the United States in the World Economy, 1750–1970.* New York: John Wiley, 1975.

# GLOSSARY

**Aggregate demand:** Total dollar amount spent on goods and services in a given period of time, usually a year or less, by individuals, business firms, and governments.

**Balance of trade:** Offset of imports versus exports in dollars over a period of time. An excess of exports over imports translates into a *favorable* balance of trade; the reverse is *unfavorable.*

**Bank, central:** Official institution of government which influences the size of the money supply and coordinates the activities of the commercial banks in the economy. It is often called a banker's bank.

**Bank, commercial:** Financial intermediary which deals extensively with the general public and businesses. It accepts deposits and makes short-term and intermediate term loans, among them funds to finance business inventories and automobiles for individuals.

**Business cycle:** Fluctuations over time in the level of economic activity. Periods of robust growth followed by recessions or depressions.

**Cartel:** Voluntary agreement among sellers to take actions designed to boost profits. The most common act is to restrict supplies and thereby force up prices. The best modern example is OPEC (Organization of Petroleum Exporting Countries).

**Conglomerate:** Combination of firms operating in many different industries under one corporate management structure. Conglomerates emerged in part because antitrust laws would not allow mergers between large firms in the same industry but permitted mergers between large firms in different industries.

**Consumer Price Index (CPI):**   Weighted average (mean) of prices paid by consumers for a predetermined group of goods and services. The CPI is typically cited to measure the rate of inflation experienced by the public.

**Corporation:**   Form of business organization which allows numerous individuals to pool their capital and to limit their liability, in the event of bankruptcy, to the sum invested in the enterprise. The law recognizes the corporation as a person.

**Craft union:**   Association of workers possessing a common skill, for example, carpenters, printers, truck drivers, etc. The American Federation of Labor was originally formed by craft unions in the 1880s.

**Deficit spending:**   Occurs when government expenditures exceed tax revenues. One of the tools of fiscal policy designed to stimulate demand and revive a weak economy.

**Deflation:**   Decline in the general level of prices. The opposite of inflation.

**Depression:**   Sharp decline in the level of economic activity which persists over a long period of time, usually several years. The Great Depression lasted from 1930 until the American entry into World War II.

**Deregulation:**   Reduction in the degree of regulation or supervision by government. In the 1980s the airline and trucking industries experienced a decrease in government regulation.

**Economic growth:**   Increase in the aggregate amount of economic activity. It normally results from an increase in inputs and/or the productivity of inputs.

**Economic growth per capita:**   An increase in the output of goods and services by individuals within a society. This measurement is often used as a close approximate of increases in living standards.

**Economies of scale:**   Term used to describe instances whereby increases in the size of a business firm lead to decreases in the cost of production.

**Entrepreneur:**   Risk taker in a business venture who invests time or capital, or both, in the hope of earning a profit.

**Export:**   Sale of goods and services to foreign buyers. Foreign sales increase employment levels in the domestic market.

**Fiscal policy:**   Use of government deficits and surpluses to influence the aggregate level of demand and thereby to stimulate or moderate economic growth. Sometimes called Keynesian economics, it is often used as an alternative to "monetary policy."

**Greenbacks:**   Money issued by the Union government during the Civil War to assist in paying for military expenses. It was money generated neither from taxation nor borrowing but simply by running the printing presses. Greenbacks were not convertible at par for gold and silver until 1879.

**Gross national product (GNP):**   Value in market prices of the total output of goods and services in a given time, usually one year.

**Inflation:**   Increase in the general level of prices. It is often measured by the Consumer Price Index (CPI).

**Industrial union:**   Association of workers employed within a single industry, irrespective of skills. The Congress of Industrial Organizations (CIO) was formed by such unions in the 1930s.

**Innovation:**   Creation of new goods or services or improved methods of producing existing goods and services. The newness may range from technological change to alterations in organizational areas.

**Investment banker:**   Individual or firm which assists corporations in raising large amounts of capital funds through the sale of stocks and bonds.

**Labor force:**   Includes all persons over 16 years of age employed or actively seeking employment. The word is used interchangeably with the term *work force*.

**Laissez faire:**  Economic system characterized by little or no government intervention.

**Macroeconomics:**  Part of the discipline of economics that studies aggregates of data—for example, gross national product. The prefix "macro" comes from the Greek word for large.

**Mercantilism:**  Economic policy pursued by most European governments in the seventeenth and eighteenth centuries that stressed the importance of maintaining a favorable balance of trade and the accumulation of gold and silver.

**Monetary policy:**  Power of the monetary authorities to influence the amount of money in the economy with the aim of stimulating or moderating the rate of economic growth. It is often used as an alternative to "fiscal policy."

**Money:**  This term, unfortunately and often confusingly, can be defined in several different ways. The government has formulated various alternative categories and labeled them by using the letter "M" plus a series of numbers ($M_1$, $M_2$, $M_3$, $M_4$). The basic $M_1$ category includes currency in the hands of the public plus deposits against which checks may be drawn. Other categories typically include savings accounts, certificates of deposit, and other items.

**Monopoly:**  Market with only a single seller of a good or service—for example (in the current economy), public utilities such as natural gas and electric companies.

**Oligopoly:**  Market in which just a few firms (3–12) normally control a high percentage of total sales—for example, oil and automobiles.

**Open market policy:**  Tool of monetary policy, it is used by the Federal Reserve System (Fed) to influence the amount of bank reserves and thereby the total supply of money. By purchasing government bonds from commercial banks on the open market, the Fed increases the level of reserves. On the other hand by selling government bonds to commercial banks, the Fed reduces the level of reserves.

**Open shop:**  Working place where employees are not required to join a union.

**Parity:**  Index comparing the ratio of prices that farmers receive for crops to the prices paid by farmers to purchase goods and services in the nonagricultural sector. The base period often used to determine parity is 1910–1914, when farm prices were high relative to other prices.

**Personal income:**  Aggregate income of individuals divided by the total population. It is often used as an approximation of living standards.

**Pool:**  A synonym for cartel, used frequently in the United States during the nineteenth century, especially in reference to railroads. See also **Cartel**.

**Primary sector:**  Part of the economy involved in the production of basic resources—food, raw materials, and energy.

**Productivity of labor:**  Rate of output per worker, usually measured on an hourly basis. Increases in productivity usually translate into higher living standards.

**Proprietorship:**  Business firm owned and managed by one person. In bankruptcy proceedings the law normally does not distinguish between a proprietor's business and personal assets in the payments of debts outstanding.

**Quota:**  Limit on the volume of imports or exports. For example, in the early 1980s the Japanese agreed to restrict the number of automobiles exported to the United States, irrespective of the level of demand. As a rule, quotas limit the degree of competition in a market and increase prices. They are sometimes used as an alternative to higher tariff rates.

**Real:**  Term used to denote that the effects of inflation or deflation have been eliminated in making comparisons between data gathered during different time periods. For example, if GNP rose 8 percent during a year the inflation rate was 6 percent, then the "real" GNP increase would be only 2 percent.

**Recession:**  Decline in the level of economic activity over a short or intermediate period of time, usually accompanied by rising unemployment. A recession which persists is called a depression.

**Rediscount rate:**  Rate of interest charged by the Federal Reserve System to member banks. High rates tend to discourage member banks from making new loans and thereby increasing the money supply, while low rates have the opposite effect. Control over the rediscount rate represents a tool of "monetary policy."

**Reserve requirement:**  Amount of money a commercial bank must keep on deposit at the Federal Reserve Bank. It is calculated as a fraction of the commercial banks' outstanding liabilities (mostly deposits) to the general public.

**Secondary sector:**  Part of the economy involved in processing food, raw materials, and energy resources. It produces largely manufactured goods.

**Service sector:**  Part of the economy involved in the provision of services rather than goods. It is sometimes called the tertiary sector.

**Specie:**  Gold or silver used for monetary purposes.

**Strike:**  Action of a group of workers who withhold labor from an employer in an effort to obtain certain goals, normally higher pay, shorter hours, and/or improved working conditions.

**Subsidy:**  Grant of money or of goods and services from the government to firms or individuals. Some examples are payments to farmers for taking land out of production, food stamps, and welfare payments.

**Surplus:**  Occurs when government tax revenues exceed expenditures. This tool of fiscal policy is designed to curb demand and slow down the rate of economic growth.

**Tariff:**  Tax on imported goods. In the nineteenth century tariffs were the major source of revenue for the federal government. The Constitution prohibited the imposition of tariffs on goods merely crossing state borders, which contributed to the rise of a national market without trade barriers.

**Transfer payments:**  Monies collected by government in the form of taxes and then paid out to individuals eligible for the receipt of funds. These persons perform no labor services for them; thus the sums received do not represent earnings. Examples are social security and welfare payments.

**Trust:**  Form of business organization that existed briefly in the 1880s and 1890s. Owners of stock in several firms "entrusted" their holdings to a single trustee who issued trust certificates in return and normally paid dividends on those certificates. The device was used to create large business firms during a period when laws did not permit companies chartered in one state to own the stock of companies in other states. The term soon became a synonym for big business.

**Unemployment:**  Occurs when persons are actively seeking work for pay and cannot locate a position. Individuals who may hope for a job but are not actively seeking one are not included in unemployment statistics.

**Vertical integration:**  Occurs when a firm which traditionally performed only a single function, such as manufacturing, adopts the strategy of performing additional functions, such as the acquisition of raw materials and marketing.

# NAME INDEX

# SUBJECT INDEX